DISCIPLED LEADERSHIP

The Nuts and Bolts of Being Successful Parish Leaders

REV. BENJAMIN A. VIMA

Print information available on the last page.

ISBN: 978-1-4907-9269-9 (sc)
ISBN: 978-1-4907-9275-0 (e)

Library of Congress Control Number: 2018967571

Trafford rev. 12/15/2018

 www.trafford.com
North America & international
toll-free: 1 888 232 4444 (USA & Canada)
fax: 812 355 4082

To the "discipled leaders" who had been my mentors, role models, confessors, professors, counselors, and "Good Samaritans" in my pursuit of becoming a genuine "discipled leader" of Christ.

Rev. Benjamin A. Vima

CONTENTS

ACKNOWLEDGMENT

Thanks to ZENIT, *Commonweal* magazine, National Catholic Reporter, and Vatican Blog from where all the quotes of the Popes had been taken and used in this book.

I gratefully acknowledge all the scriptural verses used here are from the NABRE and NAB Bible translation.

Also, sincere recognition of biblical words that I have used a few times from the Jerusalem Bible translation or liturgical version.

INTRODUCTION

"Church leadership has questions but has answers."

STARTING TROUBLES

Actually, when I began writing this book a few years ago, I titled it as *The Guru-Sishya Tensions* and added a subtitle to it: *Disciples' Struggles to Deal with the Hard Sayings of Master Jesus.* I also set off the book with an introduction explaining the core of its content: Like any other disciples, my initial response to Jesus's sayings is "I should, but I can't!" But later on, as my writing progressed, and as Jesus's Spirit and his workers in his vineyard moved me to concentrate more on the challenges the parish leaders face in adhering to Jesus's hard demands in their leadership ministries, I changed the title, which you see now on my cover page: *Discipled Leadership: The Nuts and Bolts of Being Successful Church Leaders.*

Titles might have been altered; however, the nucleus of their content has unchanged. It is all about the Master's hard-core requirements demanded from those who would wish to follow him as well as to share his leadership in his church. Matthew Dallek may be partly right when he writes about Jesus's historical identity: "Human history is a flow rather than a pattern or a cycle" (*Politico Magazine* 8/13/17). As he explains, if we try to seek the seeds that blossomed into Jesus's Gospel, the age-old Judaic uncompromised an active faith in a God whom the humanity esteemed as their Creator, as their Redeemer, and as their Provider and Rewarder. In addition, besides the Judaic die-hard faith, there were some other seeds that fell into the heart of Jesus, namely, those that were very ancient precepts, practices of "pagan" cultures of his time. However, we like to go further with the light of our faith in the breathtaking factor of "incarnation." The Jewish Jesus was the eternal Word of God, who took the human flesh to reveal and explicate fully and clearly through his life and sayings the mysteries hidden for centuries.

WIDESPREAD PROBLEMS IN CHURCH LEADERSHIP

Any leadership in this world is not certainly a bed of roses. For some, every day seems to be an occasion to redefining what it means to be a leader. Some others see their winning the crown of leadership in this competitive society as a prize they must fight to protect every waking moment. For many other leaders, every day is a test of how to lead a community, not just a faction, balancing competing interests. I tell you, for good many of us, every day is an hour-by-hour battle for self-preservation.

I too acknowledge that one out of hundred leaders within our church campus feels they have nothing to do as Jesus's discipled leader except lisping daily certain prayers a number of times, attending or organizing and implementing certain religious rituals, and as I read in a book titled the *Diary of a Country Priest*, sitting there in the front porch of their beautiful rectory, smoking or reading of some sort, waiting for someone who passes by gets near to them and discusses about something that the world cannot contain or solve. Besides, if our eyes and ears cooperate with us well, then we love to kill our time by accessing all social media, especially browsing all possible TV channels coming from our tower or roof.

There are some timid leaders like me, believing passionately that either our hierarchy or the hardheaded opinion leaders in the community or the progressive youth in our area are out to destroy us. Hence, as any animals like snakes who bite anyone who comes near them out of fear, we, the frightened freaks, conspire within ourselves and for our support, summoning certain leaders of our "one heart, one mind, and one race or one caste" begin to fight back unreasonably and very maliciously sometimes. We can label such trend among leaders as "the way to fighting back and counterpunching."

There are some of us who behave erratically like the street dogs—I am sorry to say this—who never permit other dogs from other streets coming into their territory (jurisdiction?) because they are afraid and feel insecure for losing their puffed-up self. There may be many leaders in our midst who find it hard to adjust to the pastorate situation with its demands and odds. This may be rooted in an unrealistic expectation of our parochial powers, which had been overdone in the Middle Ages. They have assumed to be more akin to the popular image of imperial (aristocratic) command than the sloppy and funny blending of theocratic and democratic reality of having to coexist with too many authorities in and out of their pastorate.

Many times, newly ordained priests encounter such premature ordeals to govern their parish or institution. They, for many years, behave as novices who are gradually learning that the pastoral leadership does not work as they learned both at their homes and seminaries. They come to a point to realize the need to woo, not whack, the leaders they face in their parishes as opinion leaders, voluntary leaders, association leaders, and other parish-oriented councils to get things done.

ANSWER YES OR NO

To introduce this book to my readers, I spent many hours in browsing Jesus's sayings recorded in the New Testament (NT) books, especially the Gospels. The first one among them that captured my attention was the statement Jesus delivered in his Sermon on the Mount: "No one can serve two masters" (Matt. 6:24; Luke 16:13). Certainly, as scriptural scholars are convinced, Jesus was referring to two powers that are attempting to subdue the humans in this world: the Mastership of the Good (God) and that of the evil (mammon). Many preachers interpreting this Gospel verse indicate that Jesus expects us to make a life choice between the true God and not just money or material property but more the "gods" we the intelligent and free humans create during his seemingly absence as the Israelites did in the desert, making and worshipping the "golden calf" (Exod. 32).

On one of those reflective days, during which I was trying to verbalize correctly my thoughts and findings to illustrate my input in this book, I wanted to take some rest in front of my satellite TV and began watching my favorite channel, getTV, where the 1955 classic comedy and musical movie *Three for the Show* was playing. Surprisingly, as soon as I opened it, I got into the scene where Betty Grable was singing a melodious song, which starts somewhat this way: "Among the two, I must decide who is for me!" That speeded up my spirit. I rushed to my desk and began formulating my introduction to this book.

What I first perceived was my Master Jesus asking all his disciples, "Who do you serve? Me or other masters?" He had been firm in this first query as he recruited his disciples. He categorically placed to them this condition to be answered: yes or no. Every disciple has the requirement to fill in the blank, saying, "Yes, Lord, I make you as my one and only Master and not any other masters in the world." They should also add to it Peter's historical response: "Master, to whom shall we go? You have the words of eternal life. We have come to believe and are convinced that you are the Holy One of God" (John 6:68–69).

However, we, the disciples, are only human beings with all sorts of frailties and limitations. While we fervently follow our Master or when we are blessed with being leaders/masters who will be followed by some humans, we would indeed find it hard to walk the walk of our Master or to talk the talk of the "same." At times, we are corned in tension and some other times, in frustration. We would have listened and reread his lifestyle, especially his amazing leadership and his preaching and teaching, so many times. There are too many among his life's events and his sayings that do not correspond to our taste, to our style, and even to our "most reasonable" reason. In this situation, our usual answer to Jesus's question "Are you ready?" is "Yes, Lord . . . but not yet."

I personally esteem our Christian life is nothing but a program, being initiated through baptism and joining in the Master-disciple relationship with the risen Christ. The disciples who are sincerely aiming at following our Master Jesus despite confronting with some struggles to cope with his unique directions to achieve the ultimate goal of life are expected by Jesus to sing each moment of earthly life as the country music star Clint Black sings, "When I said I do, I meant that I will 'til the end of all time be faithful and true, devoted to you."

That is the spirit of commitment all Christian disciples should possess in their relationship with the Master. These disciples firmly believe that the church they belong to is not just some social or physical milieu but also much more a "habitation" or a "shelter" or a "hideaway" where they take theoretical, spiritual, and practical lessons at the feet of their "guru," Jesus, and in all possible ways try to follow in his footsteps of truth, justice, and love to enter one day into his heavenly abode, which he has prepared and reserved for them, telling them, "Come you who are blessed by my Father. Inherit the kingdom prepared for you from the foundation of the world" (Matt. 25:34).

MIND-BOGGLING CONUNDRUMS OF THE MASTER

For centuries, the disciples of Jesus have been dealing with many hard sayings of their Master, especially those directly addressed to them. They have been experiencing something like long-term implications for United Nations-Patience in dealing with the so many never-ending conundrums existing among different nations of the world. Or it may be a sort of poser that postmodern world's mind cannot fathom and answer to how in the world an ancient people were able to build such massive structures such as the pyramids and other world wonders without the benefit of today's knowledge and technology. Usually, I call the demands of Jesus in Christian discipled leadership as conundrums. It is because his every demand seems to me as a puzzle, riddle, enigma, challenge, and surely the mystery to be cracked, broken, swallowed, and digested.

Christian discipleship can never be a product achieved in a stipulated time. It is indeed a lifelong process of both understanding and applying in day-to-day life. In that process, the Spirit promised by our Master accompanies us. "I have told you this while I am with you. The Advocate, the holy Spirit that the Father will send in my name—he will teach you everything and remind you of all that [I] told you" (John 14:25–26).

IMPENDING THREATS TO GOOD LEADERSHIP

It is a historical fact that those conditions have brought untold tension and conflict between the Master and his disciples over the centuries. Particularly in this postmodern age, we are confounded by so many imminent threats to the life and to the entire world. Among those threats, Warren Bennis, the founder of the Leadership Institute at the University of Southern California, underlines the leadership crisis: "Humanity currently faces three extraordinary threats: the threat of annihilation from nuclear accident or war, the threat of a worldwide plague or ecological catastrophe, and a deepening leadership crisis in most of our institutions. Unlike a plague or nuclear holocaust, the leadership crisis . . . is the most urgent and dangerous of the threats we face because it is insufficiently recognized and little understood."

Mr. Warren is absolutely correct about the impending "leadership crisis," especially inside Christianity. We find many pastors leaving the ministry each month because of moral failure, spiritual burnout, or conflict in their churches. So many churches are closed every year, largely because of a lack of leadership.

Throughout our lives, we have been watching and witnessing many of our neighbors and friends shining in public as very good politicians and diplomats, including many priests, preachers, teachers, and church elders honored and esteemed popular and glamorous at the pulpits, podiums, and in front of the audience. But we too have noticed some of them being cursed and humiliated in public. Surely all these spotlight people once started well in their career, and they were counted as blessings from the Lord. But at one time, they can be turned out as curses and contemptible in the eyes of God. Many times, we are shocked to see such worse turning points happening in the lives of so many of our elders, priests, leaders, and teachers.

We naturally ask the legitimate question "Why?" The answer is simple: We have been impeding the eternal process God had ordained to create leaders according to his will. We read in church history that sometimes, at some places, many incompetent, ignorant, and reckless bullies have occupied the prestigious position of leadership. Many of them have been criticized by the public that they were suffering from acute senility and being incapacitated by thick fossil layers inside their hardheadedness, or because of early dementia, they become cowards toward progress and renovation. At the same time hiding these disorders, they act out publicly rude and cruel bullies. Some others behave as jumped-up playground toddlers, pushing around others much smaller and weaker than themselves, making others believe they were the chosen "whistleblowers" and "guardians" of morality and even faith.

As a result of such stained leadership, the church of Jesus has become so eroding that it has lost its original vigor, vibrant life, and shining light. The one who writes this—that is me—and those who read this book may feel remorse that too many years have been squandered by lies, double-dealings, and other words and actions contrary to Jesus's Gospel values. Our perennial discipled leadership's predicament recalls a scene in Ernest Hemingway's novel *The Sun Also Rises*. "How did you go bankrupt?" one character asks another, who responds, "Two ways. Gradually then suddenly." So it is with our leadership ministry. The problems we face in this dignified ministry are self-inflicted, that looked temporary and manageable have been compounded over time and are reaching a crisis point. Given the "grace time" offered to us by the just and merciful God, there is still a second chance to come back to our truthful life of discipled leadership.

THIS BOOK DOESN'T OFFER ANY QUICK-FIX SOLUTION

As Dave McCollum wrote about the true identity of deacons in his series of online articles on "The Biblical Deacon," we can attest in the light of Jesus's Gospel that every discipled leader, in whatever roles designed for them in the church by the Master, is called to be "an attendant, servant, waiter, or one who runs errands." An immediate question follows: for whom should they be so? Undoubtedly, it is for none other than the Master Jesus Christ in his Kingdom. Such an incredible call to be Jesus's discipled leaders certainly demands those who are ready to accept this call not only to know what they are and their roles but also to be aware of what they are supposed to perform as their responsibilities. I feel the book I am handing to my readers today may assist them in this regard.

My faith spurs me to declare that it was the life goal of our Master Jesus to reform the unholy and unjust leadership of the past and recreate it according to his Father's will. This is why I try my best in this book to unravel the deeper meanings of what the Master had proposed to all his disciples in the church leadership. I too include my personal testimonies of how I have incorporated them into my own life together with the role of pastoral leadership and, consequently, the immense gain I covet despite my pain.

I am both liberal and conservative. I am liberal as I go and glow with the Spirit wherever he takes me in my faith deliberation. I am conservative as I never leave even a single assertion, statement, or reflection on discipled leadership without scriptural augmentation and the church's traditional view—reformed, renewed, and reinterpreted according to the signs of the time. In this, I follow as much as possible the footsteps of Church Fathers, particularly St. Augustine, St. Thomas Aquinas, St. Gregory the Great, and many others, who have paved the correct way to interpret our today's Christian life in the light of the revealed Word of God in Jesus. The amazing matter I discover in their voluminous writings is they never skip any one of their argument or statement about our life with God in Jesus without quoting relevant scriptural verses to augment their holdings. They indeed followed a remarkable rare-blend journalism of both conservative and progressive integrated.

THIS BOOK IS ABOUT GOOD AND EFFICIENT LEADERSHIP

In my youth years of formation and education, I had developed within me a standard greatness of what a priest should be, and that is "being good." In the first year of my pastoral life, once, my bishop came to my rural parish for a pastoral visit as well as for administering the sacrament of confirmation. While I, being an associate pastor, was very busy in arranging parish programs, liturgical and social, the bishop came to me and asked, "Where is your pastor?" I replied, "He may be inside his room." To show off myself,

I added, "Bishop, he is a good pastor." The bishop stared at me and retorted, "He is good but not efficient." Though at that moment I felt ashamed of my "big mouth," soon, I learned that the statement of the bishop, though tiny, was full of meaning.

Unquestionably, true leadership requires being, deep down, a good person. Nonetheless, real leadership requires more than that. As one online writer accentuates, "It requires knowing how to amplify your deep-down goodness through the policies you pursue and the decisions you make." The discipled leadership I discuss in this book must be one of such good but efficient kind. All discipled leaders in the church are expected by their Master that their interior goodness, which has been bestowed, shipshaped, and developed by the anointing of Jesus's Spirit, must be magnified and enlarged through their planning and implementing of projects at their service territory.

I long to see all of you, my fellow discipled leaders, who are strongly attached and affiliated to Jesus's abode, to covet the abundant results of our discipleship to Christ, the one and only Master of mercy, truth, justice, and love. This is the sole aim of this book: It should assist as many disciples as possible in their leadership journey with Jesus's Spirit.

I am fully aware of the fact that Gospel writers and other letter writers brought home to the followers of Jesus as many demands of their Master as possible. Because of this book's page limit, I select "a few of the indispensable takeaways from his missives for Christian leaders." I divide the content into three sections: Two of them delve deeply Jesus's demands with their explanations and interpretations from both scriptural and traditional insights, certainly adding my personal inputs to them. Before I treat those demands of the Master for his discipled leaders, in the first section, I discuss first the nature and identity of the age-old traditional term "Christian discipleship," its origin and goal, plus the context and content of the "discipled leadership."

In brief, I can dare say that the entire content of this book can be reckoned as a detailed expounding of the remarkable exhortation given by Peter to all discipled leaders: "I exhort the presbyters [the officially appointed leaders of the Christian community] among you, as a fellow presbyter and witness to the sufferings of Christ and one who has a share in the glory to be revealed. Tend the flock of God in your midst, overseeing not by constraint but willingly, as God would have it, not for shameful profit but eagerly. Do not lord it over those assigned to you, but be examples to the flock. And when the chief Shepherd is revealed, you will receive the unfading crown of glory" (1 Pet. 5:1–4). I think it would help my readers for their easy understanding and comfortable grasping of the Master's intransigent mandates in their discipled leadership journey with him.

In the midst of leadership tensions,

Living joyfully in the vine as a tiny branch,

Only because of his uninterrupted graceful allowances.

—Rev. Benjamin A. Vima

SECTION I: GENESIS OF DISCIPLED LEADERSHIP

FOLLOW ME . . . COME AND SEE

CHAPTER 1: WHAT IS "DISCIPLESHIP"?

As I have pointed out in the introduction about this book's title, *Discipled Leadership*, it is some sort of nuanced usage of modern preachers and Christian writers for portraying the Christian leadership in the church. Before we discuss about it, we should first clarify the intrinsic connections between the noun "leadership" and the adjective "discipled."

VAMOOSE FROM A FAKE DEFINITION OF DISCIPLESHIP

In this postmodern era, as the world has turned out to be a global village, to lead a social life, all humans born in it are to carry with them some kind of ID cards in the form of "driving license," "passport," or at least a "note of attestation" signed duly by an authorized person in the political arena. This is very much needed specifically when humans attempt to climb the ladder of development and plan to covet a bigger position in life. This sort of norm demonstrates the humans' belongingness, their background, and many times, their personal and social values and views.

Unfortunately, as in every undertaking, in the Kingdom of God on Earth, there are some humans who try to hold fake identities and hide their true IDs under fake exposure. For example, some claim they are "disciples of Jesus," but sadly, in reality, they aren't. They may hold external ID cards and even titles and positions attached to discipleship, but in fact, their inner values and views are fake and counterfeit. This is why, as we treat here the genuine Christian discipled leadership in the light of Jesus's Gospel, we should discuss about what intention Jesus had when he called many humans as his disciples.

Dictionaries define the term "disciples" as those who are followers, supporters, devotees, and students to a master who is esteemed by them as their life's guide, teacher, and role model. In various religious and spiritual traditions, we trace out different kinds of masters who were the founders of certain religious faiths, or as the spiritually matured guides, or as some wise and enlightened teachers of God's revelatory truths, plus some who were experts in certain elements of human life's development and management.

TRADITIONAL MEANING OF DISCIPLESHIP

To throw more light on these references about "mastership" and "discipleship," let us go to the eastern part of the globe, where most of the world religions originated. The Sanskrit term "guru" used in India is equivalent to "teacher" in English. It also means "master" of any one or many subjects or arts. The term "guru" is composed of two syllables: gu + ru. "Gu" means the "darkness," and "ru" means the "remover." A person who removes the darkness from one's own life and others' is called a guru. In ancient religions like Hinduism, a "guru" has been venerated not just a teacher but also one next to God. According to the Indian tradition, a human's life is incomplete without a guru. None can attain salvation without the guidance of a guru, from whom spiritual teachings are transmitted to his/her disciples. Most of the knowledge related to human spirituality, physicality, and arts and science is imparted through the developing relationship between the "guru" and the "disciple." It is considered that this relationship based on the genuineness of the guru and the respect, commitment, devotion, and obedience of the student is the best way for subtle or advanced knowledge to be conveyed. The ultimate goal of this relationship is the disciple eventually masters the knowledge that the "guru" embodies.

In keeping with this traditional backdrop of the definition of "discipleship," the Judeo-Christian religion preserved a genuine understanding of this term by the light of revelation as it has been evolved over the centuries. In Judaism and Islam, great persons like Moses and Joshua are revered as God-given patriarchs, judges, leaders, and teachers whose teachings and guidelines have been admired and followed by their people as committed disciples. Then came gurus in the form of prophets like Isaiah and kings like David to take the people in right and safe path to their life's destiny. Following the footsteps of these leaders and messengers of God, Jesus of Nazareth claimed himself as the holistic Leader, Teacher, and Master because he recognized fully himself as the Son of God.

JESUS'S VIEW ON DISCIPLESHIP

When we go into the life of Jesus as narrated in the NT books, we realize Jesus of Nazareth, from the onset of his public ministry, was very keen on getting followers around him. As Matthew puts it, Jesus invited the first group of disciples from his followers and hearers, saying to them, "Come after me," adding an attractive pro-jingle, "I will make you fishers of men" (Matt. 4:18–22). Luke goes a little further and explains that Jesus's invitation to his discipleship was not a sudden and abrupt one. He includes a story before this historical call about a miraculous deed of catching a large bulk of fish, which made all astonished and overwhelmed (Luke 5:1–11). This was another strategic catch of Jesus. Only after solving the initial troubles, the guru began seriously his instructive lessons of discipleship.

We are aware of Jesus's intention that his disciple is to be a student. There is no doubt on this. But the genuine concept of student is skewed by the modern classroom experience. It simply recognizes there are different ways of approaching the learning experience. We often think of a student as a person sitting in a classroom, listening to a teacher, and taking notes as fast as they can. This is an information-based model. It has as its core the transfer of information from the teacher to the student. Its goal seems to be only to increase and enlarge the information stock in the student.

But being a disciple, according to Jesus, is about more than gaining information; it is about transformation. The difference between a modern student and a disciple of Jesus is the difference between listening to a teacher and working alongside a craftsman. The craftsman expects his disciples to gain knowledge, but both the information and the experience are meant to change the students. The goal is to make the students craftsmen as the teacher.

Jesus called his disciples to leave everything they owned and knew to follow him. The disciples lived with him, and he expected them to become different people by the end of their time together. It wasn't about giving out more information; the Pharisees could do that. In fact, Jesus chastised those who simply wanted more information without the transformation. Jesus wanted his disciples to become craftsmen, to be like him. They too followed their teacher everywhere because they were afraid the teacher would say or do something that would be valuable and they did not want to miss it. They lived with the teacher because they were intent on patterning their lives after the teacher. Studying and living with a master craftsman led to more than just information.

A DISCIPLE IS MORE THAN A STUDENT

In that vein, all followers of Jesus are supposed to be his "disciples," meaning more than being his "students." I agree with D. Mike Henderson (www.gotquestions.org), who has defined discipleship very beautifully: "Christian discipleship is the process by which disciples grow in the Lord Jesus Christ and are equipped by the Holy Spirit, who resides in our hearts, to overcome the pressures and trials of this present life and become more and more Christ like." He means that Christian discipleship is not simply referring to "doing discipleship," which may sound very passive, but it is also not something "being received."

The Greek term for "disciple" in the New Testament is *mathetes*, which means more than just "student" or "learner." A disciple is a "follower," someone who adheres completely to the teachings of another, making them his rule of life and conduct. Consequently, the phrase "being a disciple" has become a common one among Christian preachers and teachers in their reference to all Christ's followers. Every "discipled person" goes through a continuous process of learning their Master's crafts and values, from Jesus's life and teachings, as duly recounted by his disciples, with the inspiration of his resurrected Spirit.

NOT EVERY BELIEVER IS A DISCIPLE

In the light of what we discussed above about the true meaning of Christian discipleship and from our daily experience, we can accentuate that every disciple is indeed ineludibly a believer of Christ but not necessarily every believer is a disciple. We should keep in mind the eternal and biblical fact that the true identity of Christian disciple is not merely being a learner at the school of Jesus, listening, reading, and even meditating the Master's teachings; rather, he/she should be one who drinks every Word of Christ, digests it in mind and heart, making it as part and parcel of his very self, plus mainly to apply it in day-to-day life. The Master has been very transparent and unequivocal in this matter: "Not everyone who says to me, 'Lord, Lord,' will enter the kingdom of heaven, but only the one who does the will of my Father in heaven" (Matt. 7:21). Apostles like James continue to highlight it in their exhortation for followers of

Christ: "Be doers of the word and not hearers only, deluding yourselves. For if anyone is a hearer of the word and not a doer, he is like a man who looks at his own face in a mirror" (James 1:22–25).

In the Gospel narratives, we see Jesus offering first and foremost an invitation to every human through his first short but very powerful homily to accept his Gospel: "This is the time of fulfillment. The kingdom of God is at hand. Repent, and believe in the gospel" (Mark 1:15). Then we are told by the Gospel writers that great crowds started traveling with Jesus, who perceived that those people had started believing and accepting his Gospel message in principle. At the same time, he, being the Son of God, "would not trust himself to them because he knew them all, and did not need anyone to testify about human nature. He himself understood it well" (John 2:24–25). He detected majority of them were following him by being attracted by his popularity and his prophetic style of preaching and performing miraculous deeds. He wanted to eliminate those who were following him for such wrong reasons. Hence, we find the Master laying out some requirements to all those who were following him in crowd (Luke 14:25–35). That was his "Magna Carta" that deliberately thinned out the ranks of discipleship. They became the absolute requirements for any follower to be chosen by Christ as his own disciple.

SECRECY IN THE CALL TO DISCIPLESHIP

In the following pages of this book, we will discuss the multifarious ingredients of Christian discipleship such as its cost price, its heavy demands, and its survival techniques. Anyone who wants to be a daredevil in choosing to be a genuine disciple of Christ primarily should keep in mind at the start that a true "disciple" in the company of Jesus is one who has been duped by the Lord somewhere sometime in his/her life.

Have you ever had an occasion of being on fire with God and his values? Have you been mocked and scolded by your loved ones that you were out of your mind in making certain decisions for God and his Kingdom? If so, you are joining with the multitude of those victims who have been duped by God over the centuries. God won over Moses at the burning bush and Mary, the sister of Lazarus, at her household works. Inevitably, every person who has been chosen to be the Lord's disciple has been groaning and mourning for being seduced by God as Jeremiah: "You duped me, O Lord, and I let myself be duped. You were too strong for me, and you triumphed" (Jer. 20:7). Those disciples had been crying in their life as their heartbeats: "My soul is thirsting for you, Lord my God. For you my flesh pines and my soul thirst like the earth, parched, lifeless and without water" (Ps. 63:2–4).

Jesus indeed was never exempted in this. Throughout his life, he felt the same inner burden hanging over him: "Zeal for your house will consume me" (John 2:17). "Why were you looking for me? Did you not know that I must be in my Father's house?" (Luke 2:49). "My food is to do the will of the one who sent me and to finish his work" (John 4:34). Jesus was consumed and burned with the love for his Father and was thirsting to do God's will even in the midst of opposition and death. On the Cross in those hours of agony, he could cry out, "I thirst." He was literally blinded by the love of God the Father. There was nothing in his life besides this. So he could separate himself from his mother and loved ones. He couldn't care about his safety and security, food, and shelter. He was mad, truly mad, because he had been literally "trapped" by the love of his Father Almighty.

Jesus loves to see in the hearts of his disciples the same experience of "holy trap" in their lives. Unfortunately, most of his disciples preferred more to be friends and equal partners of God in Jesus than to be seduced, to be burned, and to be duped by him because getting into this sacred seduction of God takes the toll of the entire life of a disciple.

Being trapped is not anything strange for any human. As a matter of fact, almost all of us are seduced in one way or another by different powers. Are we not seduced by the desire of "making money"? Are we not trapped by the ambition of "getting popular"? Are we not seduced by the craving of sex, food, and other pleasures? But the most profitable seduction would be to be duped by the One who is our Creator, Redeemer, Giver, and Rewarder. Paul rightly underwrites that all things work for good for those who love God (who are duped by God), who are called according to his purpose (Rom. 7:28). We read in church history that God seduced many saints at an early age of five, some in their youth as in the life of St. Francis of Assisi, and a great number of them in their middle age like St. Augustine.

CHAPTER 2: DAZING OBJECTIVES OF DISCIPLESHIP

After knowing well the intrinsic relationship existing in the disciples who follow Jesus to learn and the apostles who are appointed to take the role of messengers of the Master, now let us discuss the main purposes of this noble appointment. According to Mark's Gospel, it is for three purposes: "to be with him and to be sent forth to preach and to have authority to drive out demons" (Mark 3:14–15). The disciples who are recruited and appointed by Jesus to be his apostles are supposed to fulfill three goals or dreams of their Master: (1) to be with him as an intimate friend, (2) to be sent forth to preach, and (3) with his authority, to drive out demons from humans and ultimately from out of the world.

PURPOSE 1: BEING WITH THE RISEN JESUS

Master Jesus has expounded the first goal of his discipleship in his farewell discussion with the Twelve. Using an agricultural metaphor, which all his disciples easily could understand, he said, "I am the vine, you are the branches" (John 15:5). When he asserted this goal of discipleship to be as vine and branches, he was at the edge of his physical life journey. Logically, a conclusion can be drawn that through the use of this allegory, he insisted everyone who would be following him, including his Twelve, after his ascension must be with him spiritually, morally, and much more so ontologically.

I have a personal liking toward the concluding doxology in the canon of the Catholic Mass—"Through him, and with him, and in him"—which to my view spells out most splendidly the first order of our Master in our following him. This is why I have dedicated a separate chapter in my book *Catholic Christian Spirituality* (Ref. p. 190 ff.), where I have stressed that the lifeline of the interior process of the disciples' spirituality is to live, move, and have our holding and performing anything and everything as spiritual deeds— interior as well as exterior.

UNBELIEVABLE YEARNING OF THE MASTER

Jesus expects the disciples to esteem their relationship with him as intimate, instructive, and lively as the ontological connection existing between the vine and the branches. In using this metaphor of a plant, Jesus Christ never intended to deny the disciples' human freedom. While he was highlighting the ontological connection between him and them, he showed his full awareness of their independence and individuality. Therefore, in his parable of vine and branches, he adds that the disciples have the capability of disowning him and drifting away from him with their will (John 15:1–2).

The Master calls himself the vine and those united to him the branches to teach his disciples how much they will benefit from their union with him. When the disciples join to him, as branches to a vine, they share in his own nature. However, their union with him depends upon a deliberate act of the will; on his part, the union is effected by his grace. Those who are joined to the Lord as vine and branches, in the words of Saint Paul, are one spirit with him. "Life in Jesus Christ means we live in him and he in us."

Undoubtedly, our Master declared his eternal wish about his disciples that they should be in his presence, in his team, and going with him wherever he goes. This doesn't mean he desired his disciples should be present with him under the same roof because he didn't have any such roofed place or shelter of his own even to lay down his head, nor did he indicate that they must be moving around him physically before his Jewish eyes because we hear about his second intention of sending them far and wide to perform his Gospel works in his physical absence. His total ambition was they should behave like himself as he dealt with his Father. He told his parents, who were so worried about his absenting from them, "Why were you looking for me? Did you not know that I must be in my Father's house?" (Like 2:49). What he underlined was that his disciples must be totally and holistically present every moment of their life in the spiritual Realm/Kingdom he has established.

All his disciples, like Paul, must take their first step in their appointment in their baptism of water and the Spirit to express their longing to be with him. "We were indeed buried with him through baptism into death, so that, just as Christ was raised from the dead by the glory of the Father, we too might live in newness of life. For if we have grown into union with him through a death like his, we shall also be united with him in the resurrection" (Rom. 6:4–5).

This kind of unique stay put with him, who is immaterial, can be accomplished by earthly humans only "in Spirit and in truth." And Paul later on would describe this goal by another tangible metaphor that is very close to each one of us. In his letter to the Corinthians (1 Cor. 12:12–31), though he uses it to portray the unity existing among the disciples, he emphasizes the disciples' closeness and union with their Master: "Now you are Christ's body, and individually parts of it" (v. 27). In later years, Church Fathers deliberated this union between the disciples and Jesus as "mystical."

Jesus therefore dreamed of such indissoluble togetherness between him and his disciples. He too assured us that he would be with us till the end of ages. He knew he would never fail in his promise and the same way he desired us to be closely related to him. He knew our weakness and frailty to fight against Satan's battle and to pursue our ultimate goal of reaching the glorified Son in his mansion, so he exhorted us to be always with him in mind, in memory, in words, in actions, and in every step of our vocation. We are very mean to be forgettable or careless about his dream. So he compelled us to persevere in quality prayer every day at quality time and quality place. During the time of prayer, he advised us to repeat our profession of faith in him as the Son of God: "Whoever acknowledges that Jesus is the Son of God, God remains in him and he in God" (1 John 4:15). If we lose our faith in Jesus, that is the end of our ontological and mystical connection with him.

IMPOSSIBLE RELATIONSHIP BECOMES POSSIBLE

Besides the personal longing of the Master to be eternally with his disciples, we know our limitations in performing all our duties as the Master directed us. Our spirit is strong, but the flesh is weak. We want to do good things, but we are unable to do, and we find it hard to stop doing bad things even if we long for it. However, when we abide in him, everything is possible. "Remain in me, as I remain in you. Just as a branch cannot bear fruit on its own unless it remains on the vine, so neither can you unless you remain in me. Whoever remains in me and I in him will bear much fruit, because without me you can do nothing" (John 15:4–5).

When Jesus purposed his choosing his disciples for being with him, we can conclude its inference as his longing to befriend them for good. We can derive this conclusion from his own farewell statement: "I no longer call you slaves . . . I have called you friends" (John 15:15). C.S. Lewis said that friendship is one of the greatest gifts we can be given in life. True friendship, he said, begins often with a common interest, or a shared experience, or a collaborative project. The friendship between Christ and his disciples is the joy of discovering each other. At the heart of friendship is knowing the hearts of other people. This is the heart the Master possesses, and so he longs to be intimately connected to his chosen ones as his true friends.

To be close to Christ, to be with him as vine and branches, the only strategy is to possess a pure heart, to be innocent of wrongdoing, and to avoid seeking useless and vain things. Who may go up the mountain of the LORD? Who can stand in his holy place? "The clean of hand [who is innocent of wrongdoing] and pure of heart, who has not given his soul to useless things, what is vain" (Ps. 24:3–4). That is what every disciple of Jesus hears in their inner sanctuary day in and day out.

PURPOSE 2: BEING SENT FORTH TO PREACH

The Gospel writers and Paul vividly stress that Jesus chose from his pupils certain persons, not at random but at the will of his Father, plus with his understanding of how sincerely they tried to be doers of his Gospel demands, to be sent as his messengers to extend his messianic mission through them (Mark 6:7–13). First, we hear from the Gospels that Jesus sent out the Twelve. Second, we see him sending out seventy-two more of his pupils (Luke 10:1). Indeed, he first empowered all the pupils he sent out and commissioned them to preach and expel demons (Mark 3:13–19). Luke, adding other seventy-two disciples being commissioned by Jesus like the Twelve, tells us that "the Lord appointed seventy-two others whom he sent ahead of him in pairs to every town and place he intended to visit." All for what? Mainly, these disciples would go to different parts of the land proclaiming his Gospel values, mainly, "Repent, the Kingdom of God is at hand."

We quoted at the beginning of this chapter Jesus telling his disciples that he has recruited them "to go and bear fruit that will remain" (John 15:16b). That is the basic reason why Jesus chooses and appoints his disciples to be sent out. Preaching his Gospel both by words and by life-giving acts will bear abundant fruits in his Kingdom. He does not deny that his disciples are becoming very productive through their IQ, talents, and other natural gifts. But he too had in mind as he appointed his disciples to be sent out that their activities should be eternally fructifying, to be valid and solid in the eyes of the Master. Becoming effective and efficacious "fishers of humans" totally depends on upholding the Master's dream of "bearing fruit that will last."

PURPOSE 3: BEING SENT OUT TO HEAL THE SICK

This purpose of Jesus appointing his followers as his messengers is found extensively in all the NT books. All Gospel writers expose this mind setup of Christ as he sent his messengers on his behalf: to go forth not only preaching but also driving out the evil spirits from the people and curing their every disease and every illness (Matt. 10:1; Luke 10:1–20). Imagine how glad and astounded would have been those ordinary disciples at the miraculous deeds of healing they could perform with the divine authority of their Master. This has been the historical glory of Christianity from the day of its inception. As Luke inserted the episode of the seventy-two disciples being commissioned by Jesus, biblical scholars contend he took this episode from Q Source to represent the Christian mission in his own day.

We too read in the Gospels and Acts this third purpose of Jesus for his sending out his disciples being well emphasized in many pages. To the Twelve, Jesus had said, "Cure the sick, raise the dead, cleanse lepers, and drive out demons" (Matt. 10:8a). Mark, on his part, adds this dream of the Master at the end of his Gospel. Before the Master ascended to heaven, he told his disciples, "These signs will accompany those who believe: in my name they will drive out demons, they will speak new languages. They will pick up serpents with their hands, and if they drink any deadly thing, it will not harm them. They will lay hands on the sick, and they will recover" (Mark 16:17–18). This is why we uncover in Luke's Gospel all the instructions given to the Twelve and to the seventy-two are similar.

CHAPTER 3: UNIQUE RANK AND FILE OF DISCIPLESHIP

In the previous chapter, we discussed about how Jesus commandingly recruited his first disciples. We know in his words that Christian discipleship is his choice and not ours, and in fact, we too know in this recruitment, he called, and continues to call, many, but out of them, "only a few have been chosen." This is how Jesus and his prime team of disciples claimed the sole authority of the Master toward choosing the discipled leaders in his regime. Now let us try to fathom out with what purpose in mind the Master has been recruiting his disciples.

THE UNBELIEVABLE REASON FOR CHOOSING US

Once the Master recruited his disciples, as a Pro CEO in his Kingdom, he immediately bestowed to them first and foremost a clear insight on for what purpose he had recruited them. The Gospel writers were very much concerned about this matter because, as they were completing their Gospel scripts, so many people who have not been living at the time of the Lord joined in Jesus's team. Plus, it was a dark age for Christianity during which so many of the disciples were persecuted, murdered. Being downhearted, the disciples were asking the elders, "What do you want us to do as the disciples of Jesus?" Going back to the time of the Master, inquiring so many who were living still from that time, getting the help of some manuscripts left safe, the Evangelists exposed some vivid answers to those questions, mainly about the right purposes for which Jesus chooses humans to his discipleship. To answer those questions, it is good to know first how Jesus and his Spirit categorize the rank and file of Christian disciples.

We discover through the NT books how Jesus ranked his disciples. While the Greek word *matheteuo* means "student, learner, or pupil," the Greek word *apostolos* (apostle) indicates the position of "a delegate, messenger" and "one sent forth with orders." If we go deeper analysis of NT verses that speak of disciples and apostles, we can easily find out how Jesus's Spirit portrays the intrinsic rank and file of his disciples.

Undoubtedly, Jesus calls all humans to be his disciples from the day he began his public ministry in Palestine. In ancient times, since very few higher learning institutions, those who wanted to learn the trades for right, better, and productive living attached themselves to a journeyman or a teacher and spent significant time with them and tried to acquire the best they could. In the case of learning a philosophy or a religion, the students would follow the teacher for years, traveling wherever they would go, and the teacher would expound as they walked, teaching the intricacies of the faith. This is what the disciples of Jesus did. Wherever Jesus went, these learners would follow, and Jesus would teach them as they moved across Palestine. They were certainly named as Jesus's followers or disciples.

APOSTLES ARE THE PRIMARY GROUP OF DISCIPLED LEADERS

One thing is sure: Jesus had a large number of such disciples during his ministry, but not all of them were "apostles." As the term used in NT, an "apostle" is a disciple who is sent out. The Twelve were chosen out of a wider group both to be with Jesus as disciples in his close circle and to be sent out to preach and teach as apostles. Mark, in his Gospel, writes about Jesus appointing the twelve apostles: "He appointed twelve [whom he also named apostles]" (Mark 3:14–15).

While John and Luke avoid using the term "apostles," only "the Twelve," Mark and Matthew profusely mention about the predominant position of the Twelve among the disciples. This is to emphasize the grand status of the Twelve, who were exclusively chosen and appointed by the Master both to be closely connected to him and later to be sent out to continue fulfilling his messianic mission. Thus, while the term "apostle" refers persons in terms of their purpose or *mission*, the "disciple" emphasizes the relationship of the followers of Jesus as learners, hearers to him as their teacher.

In the case of the twelve apostles, all of them were indeed disciples. Some of them like Andrew and John were already following the great teacher John the Baptist. Thanks to their teacher's testimony about Jesus of Nazareth (John 1:35–39), plausibly, they left him and followed Jesus. Then came an array of Jews starting from Peter and James and Matthew and Nathanael, following Jesus, listening to him wherever he was journeying. As the categorical statement of Jesus's Spirit through the Gospels, we are sure everyone who decides to follow Jesus is primarily his "disciple."

Then follow other positions as Jesus wished and entrusted to those disciples. Among them, the number 1 appointment was to be an apostle, in other words, to be sent as his messenger. As earlier mentioned, the Twelve were the first team of Jesus's apostles. In Luke 6:12–16, we read Jesus choosing the twelve apostles from a larger group of disciples. All the Gospel writers testify to this historical fact. Paul and his disciple Luke confirm this too. However, as the Kingdom of God through Jesus's Spirit being evolved in the proper direction of its fulfillment, history proves the church preserved the primary position of the Twelve as the Master's first choice to be his apostles.

THE HISTORICAL PARADIGM SHIFT IN THE DISCIPLES' RANK AND FILE

Surprisingly, Jesus's code of discipleship—to be with him and to be sent to preach and to heal—though it was specifically for the apostles, has been followed by the Master for appointing other disciples. While both Mark and Matthew emphasize this code as strictly for the appointment of the Twelve, Luke adds the other disciples and their appointment by Jesus in the same way as the Twelve were: "The Lord appointed seventy [-two] others whom he sent ahead of him in pairs to every town and place he intended to visit" (Luke 10:1–12).

This doesn't mean Luke disparaged the "first rank of the Twelve" among the disciples. His main thrust was this historical appointment of discipleship has been shared at the second level by any members who have accepted Jesus as the Lord and Savior. Therefore, Luke portrays in Acts (1:13–15) that at the dawn of the church before the day of Pentecost in the upper room besides the Twelve and Mother of Jesus, there were 120 men and women who would have surely recruited by Jesus and accepted by the primary Twelve into their team of discipleship.

However, the Master's will has been demonstrated from the beginning of Christianity that every one of his disciples can be and should be appointed by his Spirit and his church to carry on his messianic mission around the globe. That means to go out as apostles. Such a magnanimous will of the Master was revealed when Saul becoming Paul began testifying that he was also appointed by the Master as his apostle despite nonmembership in the team of the Twelve. In all his letters, he emphasizes that he is also an apostle elected and appointed to be sent for the Gospel of Jesus, not in any way belittling or ignoring the principal position of the Twelve. Discussing about the risen Lord's appearance, as the basic requirement of being an apostle, he confirms that he is eligible to be called an apostle. He states, "Jesus appeared to

Cephas, then to the Twelve. After that, he appeared to more than five hundred brothers at once, most of whom are still living, though some have fallen asleep. After that he appeared to James, then to all the apostles. Last of all, as to one born abnormally, he appeared to me. For I am the least of the apostles, not fit to be called an apostle, because I persecuted the church of God. But by the grace of God I am what I am, and his grace to me has not been ineffective" (1 Cor. 15:5–11).

When Jesus brought Paul into the nascent church as the "last one" having found favor with him, in the Spirit of the resurrected Lord, Paul was assured to be recruited into the team of the Twelve as well as the other 130 disciples and appointed as Jesus's disciple exclusively to be sent to the pagan world. Paul acknowledges this appointment in his own words: "I was appointed preacher and apostle (I am speaking the truth, I am not lying), teacher of the Gentiles in faith and truth" (1 Tim. 2:7). "I am grateful to him who has strengthened me, Christ Jesus our Lord, because he considered me trustworthy in appointing me to the ministry" (1 Tim. 1:12). Thus, every disciple of Jesus today firmly believes that any human, who is recruited by Jesus for his discipleship through his good-willed and trustworthy delegates, is also appointed to be his apostle.

This amazing historical paradigm shift in naming the disciples of Jesus as "apostles" besides the Twelve up to this day holds good in front of God, whose clarion call of every human to become not just learners but also being appointed as his Son's messengers. In this light, if we attentively read the NT books, we will discover the risen Lord paved the way for such appointment of apostles to be neither inclusive nor exclusive. It has become a universal fact that, from early church days, preachers like Barnabas; holy women like Magdalene, Mary, and Martha of Bethany, who were continuously following and serving the Master; Paul's coworkers such as Andronicus and Junia; to this day social workers like Saint Mother Teresa and world-famous leaders like Saint John Paul II; missionaries like Saint Francis Xavier; priests like John Maria Vianney; nuns like Saint Teresa of Child Jesus and Saint Mother Cabrini; and laity like Saint Juan Diego and Saint Gianna Beretta Molla have been appointed and sent out as disciples of Jesus in extending his Kingdom.

In the biblical sense of the term "apostle," one who is sent forth, the Master also can be called as the First Apostle sent by his Father from heaven as he claimed; God the Father sent him to the world to take into his hands the eternal redemptive mission of God. Consequently, anyone who decides to be an apostle being sent by the Master to continue the same mission first must join Jesus's team of pupils-disciples and learn from him all the content of this divine mission, plus clearly understand the conditions or demands such an august mission requires.

ALL DISCIPLES ARE TO BE JESUS'S MESSENGERS

As we mentioned earlier, the similarities existing between the apostles and the disciples are that both of them have been sent out to be witnesses for Jesus Christ. This is absolutely commanded for all believers and not just the original apostles and Jesus's disciples. However, those twelve disciples who would later be sent out by Jesus possessed a unique identity as the apostles to become the first church planters of the Christian church. Besides them, Jesus had hundreds of disciples; undeniably, all were sent out as ambassadors and witnesses for Christ to the ends of the earth. The later, as one preacher writes, can be identified as apostles (with little "a") because they too have been commissioned by the Master to be his witnesses wherever they went.

CHAPTER 4: WHO ARE THE DISCIPLED LEADERS?

As we have deliberated in the previous chapter, every Christian who is willingly and consciously baptized in the name of the Trinitarian God is named the discipled follower of Jesus. In addition, to put it bluntly, every follower of Christ is called to be a leader in human community. I simply echo the daring statement of St. Augustine who, referring to his own role as a pastor, has written in one of his sermons on the "pastors," "I must distinguish carefully between two aspects of the role the Lord has given me: A role that demands a rigorous accountability; a role based on the Lord's greatness rather than on my own merit. The first aspect is that I am a Christian; the second, that I am a leader." And he said directly to his people, "I am a Christian for my own sake, whereas I am a leader for your sake; the fact that I am a Christian is to my own advantage, but I am a leader for your advantage." However, we know well not all take the role of such prestigious leadership immediately after their baptism. It takes a certain intensive process designed by the Master.

LEADERSHIP IN THE VIEW OF THE WORLD

Over the centuries and millennia, the world has been changing in many ways, but the leadership the human society demands is the same forever. Perhaps it is a yearning for a savior or a liberator, with the hope for change. All social media declare that people of the postmodern age around the world have been tired of leaders who are all similar to one another. They look for special, dominant, and strong-minded leaders to be elected as their governing heads. We are also given a list of leaders recently chosen around the world, such as Vladimir Putin in Russia, Xi Jinping in China, Viktor Orbán in Hungary, Rodrigo Duterte in the Philippines, and Donald Trump in the USA.

These politicians in a world of democracy get their leadership position from millions of people by applying various strategies. For example, to create an image of power, Putin's aides intensified his mystery willfully and copiously before and after he had been elected. His stone-faced countenance on TV screens and on Instagram memes was spread rapidly by and to millions of Internet users. Plus, through the same social media, Putin's workers propagated fake news of the world's grievances against the existing political establishment in different continents, especially the Western world. His party leaders and well-wishers sold thousands of Putin T-shirts, the most popular one featuring him as a smirking, sunglasses-wearing macho and with tattooed torso. This is because he was keenly aware of the power of images through photo ops and he wanted to project himself to the eyes and ears of his well-wishers as the tough guy to knock down the imaginative existing disorders in the world. The political history of the world tells the age we live in is not alone in this sort of stories of public's longing for macho leaders and of how those who stand in the political fray act out for victory.

THE MEANING OF LEADERSHIP AS REVEALED BY GOD

Undebatably, God's sovereign leadership owns everything that exists, and we are merely stewards or managers of our Father's property. And he is the maker, owner, proprietor, and possessor of them all. At the same time, the Bible reveals to us that the same benevolent God entrusted a share of his own leadership to humans. While he governs the entire heavens, he offered us the earth to be ruled by us: "The heavens belong to the Lord, but he has given the earth to the children of Adam" (Ps. 115:16). The only difficulty is how we, with our feeble and vulnerable humanity, can govern as God who is the God of genuine leadership. We are told about God: "He shepherded them with a pure heart; with skilled hands he guided them" (Ps. 78:72).

Leadership, being shared by the Creator as his prominent gift, is much more than an art, a belief, a condition of the heart, and a set of things to do. The visible signs of artful leadership are expressed ultimately in its practice of servant attitude. The uniqueness of leadership is that the entire process happens within the will, plan, priority, and purpose of the Almighty God as revealed in the Holy Scripture and is grounded and operates under the lordship of Christ. It is from this source that leaders derive qualifications, objectives, principles, and methodologies. There is no finer example for leadership than our Lord Jesus Christ. He declared, "I am the good shepherd. The good shepherd lays down his life for the sheep" (John 10:11). It is within this verse that we see the perfect description of a leader. He is one who acts as a shepherd to those "sheep" in his care.

At the most basic level, a leader is someone who leads others. We don't think of leadership as some set of indefinable, intangible character qualities that some people are born with and others are not. We think of leadership as the performance of behaviors. The character and skill of performing these behaviors can be learned, developed, and refined by anybody. Consider some of the world's recent great leaders. Nelson Mandela, Mother Teresa, Steve Jobs, Bill Gates—they all used their leadership talents, diverse as they may be, to make lives better in some way such as achieving freedom, improving living conditions in low-income communities, making advanced technology available to all of us, and creating a global foundation that propels the idea that all lives have equal value. If you have the desire and willpower, you can become an effective leader. Good leaders develop through a never-ending process of self-study, education, training, and experience.

God in Jesus esteemed the leadership he bestows to the followers of his Son as greater than political and social leadership. Paul, exhorting his Christians how to esteem his leadership entrusted to him by God, writes, "Thus should one regard us: as servants of Christ and stewards of the mysteries of God. Now it is of course required of stewards that they be found trustworthy" (1 Cor. 4:1–2). Leadership in the church therefore is simply a stewardship and servantship first and foremost to God, and it should be accomplished in a trustworthy way in front of God.

Elaborating his definition of leadership, Paul advises how a bishop, who is called to such resplendent stewardship, should behave worthy to it: "For a bishop as God's steward must be blameless, not arrogant, not irritable, not a drunkard, not aggressive, not greedy for sordid gain, but hospitable, a lover of goodness, temperate, just, holy, and self-controlled, holding fast to the true message as taught so that he will be able both to exhort with sound doctrine and to refute opponents" (Titus 1:7–9). To confirm that all the abovementioned revealed characteristics of leadership are to be upheld in any kind of leadership ministries found in the church, Peter writes, "As each one has received a gift, use it to serve one another as good stewards of God's varied grace. Whoever preaches, let it be with the words of God; whoever serves, let it be with the strength that God supplies, so that in all things God may be glorified through Jesus Christ"(1 Pet. 4:10–11).

CHRISTIAN LEADERSHIP IS TO BE DISCIPLED

While we discuss in this book the leadership in the Kingdom of God, a legitimate question arises: is it the right way to approach the discipled leadership? From the definition of discipleship, discussed in the previous chapter, we can forthrightly say no. Being discipled is the first phase for leadership in the Kingdom of God.

A basic description of any leadership is the duty and call of the person who is in charge to take charge with courage and character and to risk leading his/her people where they need to go and how they need to be led. That means once the followers of Christ have been well-discipled after getting forgiveness and purification from the Divine, and consequently have been included into the team of Jesus's leaders, they, in turn, would begin to strengthen others (Luke 22:32) in the waiting list and in the process of being discipled and groom them into the Christian leadership. Peter splendidly summarizes how the amazing leadership process is to be handled: "Therefore, brothers, be all the more eager to make your call and election firm, for, in doing so, you will never stumble. For, in this way, entry into the eternal kingdom of our Lord and savior Jesus Christ will be richly provided for you" (2 Pet. 1:10–11).

The "discipled leadership" is a position that seeks vision, opportunities, and needs and then motivates others to get it done through the resources, talents, and time they can contribute. It evolves from the great mission of the Master. His mission in this world had been twofold: to bring liberation and salvation to every human being and to recruit men and women to be his disciples who can abide by his Gospel values and carry on his salvific work. Choosing and training people for his mission was the major preoccupation and occupation as well in his three-year public life. Every word he uttered in front of the public, every good work he performed for the needy, and every step he took toward his summit of accomplishing his Father's will was totally a teaching in action and formation in visual, especially for those trainees.

Though Jesus was very mild and soft in his teaching and doings toward the commoners, we can observe him so harsh, sometimes angry, at those elite groups who were already holding a certain responsibility of teaching God and religion, namely, the Pharisees, Sadducees, and scribes as well as the apostles and disciples who would be his future coworkers in his Kingdom. If we read the Gospels keenly, we would discover all his hard sayings targeted not merely or exclusively to the apostles, who were his first team of "evangelizers," but also to all his followers to be baptized in water, Word, and Spirit. He put forth his "discipleship demands" to them, sometimes in public and other times in private and intimate occasions. We will discuss about it in detail in the coming chapters.

EVERY CHRISTIAN DISCIPLE IS A LEADER

It was the willing command of our Master Jesus that those whom he recruits as his disciples are to be leaders in his Kingdom. Every follower of Christ who decides to be baptized in the church to demonstrate his/her willingness to join in his team of disciples is being offered by the Lord this amazing leadership role. Commonly, we might think the sacrament of baptism first of all is a source of cleansing our soul from sins. There is no doubt about it; however, even more importantly, and what comes through in the Scriptures more clearly, especially through the NT books, is that we become sons or daughters of God. "For through faith you are all children of God in Christ Jesus" (Gal. 3:26). Plus, we too are resurrected from old self to new one. "We were indeed buried with him through baptism into death, so that, just as Christ was raised from the dead by the glory of the Father, we too might live in newness of life" (Rom. 6:4). In other words, through submitting ourselves to the baptismal ritual established by Christ, we become Jesus's disciples, promising God to follow his Son's way of truth for life.

Besides all mentioned above, there is one more very important thing happening in baptism. Every baptized person is being ordained by the Triune God to perform a remarkable triple role of leadership in God's Kingdom. In the baptismal ceremony, there is a breathtaking part when the minister anoints the one being baptized with the oil of chrism with the words "Just as Jesus was anointed priest, prophet, and king, so may you live always as a member of his body sharing everlasting life." This means each one of us at our baptism was anointed like Jesus as priest, prophet, and king. Those are nothing but the "leadership roles" that we are to carry out then in following Jesus. All the baptized therefore are designated to rule and reign with Christ (Eph. 2:6) as kings and priests (Rev. 1:5–6).

Although there are certain ministerial positions in the church designed by Jesus and developed by the promptings of his Spirit over the centuries, to pay special responsible attention to the different dimensions of church governance and discipline, the "triple leadership of every baptized disciple" holds good to have the right and responsibility to discipline one another: to confess their sins not only to a minister but also to one another, to pray for one another (James 5:16), to not only rely on the discipline of the elders but also to exhort one other so they don't become hardened by their sin (Heb. 3:13), and to discern a sound doctrine with the anointing of the Spirit (1 John 2:20, 27). Though pastors and teachers are uniquely called to build up the body into spiritual maturity (Eph. 4:11–13), every baptized person is called to help build up the body into maturity by "speaking the truth in love" to one another (Eph. 4:15), plus to fight and defeat the flesh and the devil (cf. Eph. 6:11–18; James 4:7; 1 John 2:27, 4:4, 5:4).

THE HISTORY OF EXCLUSIVENESS IN DISCIPLED LEADERSHIP

Over the centuries, many leaders and preachers made us misunderstand Jesus's hard sayings as if they were exclusive for certain elite groups of monks and religious and ordained Christians. Those elite people, taking a public oath to strictly adhere to and abide by the three counsels of Jesus, namely, poverty (to be poor materially and spiritually), obedience (to obey willingly their superiors and many specific precepts promulgated by their congregations' founders), and chastity (to live and love God and neighbors totally with no double mind). Those precepts have been labeled as "the evangelical vows" or "the evangelical counsels."

In church tradition and history, we notice that the "life of the evangelical counsels" at the beginning of the third century has been the intrinsic involvement of the Spirit to enhance the holiness of Christ's church through the stringent observance of the Gospel demands proposed by the Master. According to this goal, the Spirit inspired certain men and women and chose them for this remarkable purpose and assembled them as religious institutes in the church to be the role models for fulfilling Jesus's discipleship demands. For this purpose, those who decide to join in those "institutes" must make the three vows of "obedience, chastity, and poverty." Such religious profession is well-defined in the 1983 Code of Canon Law of the Roman Catholic Church (see the Code of Canon Law, canons 599ff) in relation to members of religious institutes as follows: "By religious profession members make a public vow to observe the three evangelical counsels. Through the ministry of the Church they are consecrated to God, and are incorporated into the institute, with the rights and duties defined by law."

The church also states that any Christian can make such public profession of the three evangelical counsels even without being members of a religious institute: "A hermit is recognized in the law as one dedicated to God in a consecrated life *if he or she publicly professes the three evangelical counsels, confirmed by a vow or other sacred bond, in the hands of the diocesan bishop and observes his or her own plan of life under his direction."* One of the church evening prayer intercessions states, "Remember those who have consecrated themselves to serve you in the religious life: Enrich them in their poverty, love them in their chastity, and lighten their hearts in obedience to you."

When spiritual leaders like St. Benedict and St. Ignatius of Loyola were stirred by Christ's Spirit to form groups of resolutely committed disciples of Jesus, their main focus was at every moment of their daily life, they should strictly, with no compromise whatsoever, follow the demands of their Master Jesus. Thus, as church historians underline, the exclusive tree of disciples blossomed and branched out over the centuries and the Spirit's charism directed them both to hold and observe faithfully the demands of Jesus.

That is how a very large chasm occurred between the ordinary baptized followers of Jesus and these selected men and women. There started a misunderstanding among the church members that all that our Master proposed as his demands for his discipleship are meant for those "esoteric groups" and they in no way proposed to them or they can be easily compromised as humans are incapable of observing those demands. This sort of misconception was even justified quoting from the NT, particularly misinterpreting Matthew 19:21, where Jesus says, "If you wish to be perfect . . ."

Some others continue to interpret Jesus's demands or counsels for perfect discipleship are not binding upon all Christians and hence not necessary conditions to attain eternal life. The observances of Jesus's evangelical demands are only some acts of supererogation that is beyond what is required or expected of a disciple. In other words, to attain Jesus's ultimate goal of eternal life, it is enough to minimally obey the biblical commands, but for "better" results, these evangelical vows can be observed by the elite.

There is nothing wrong about taking an oath or a vow because it is a solemn and worthy act of a person. It is an expression of the person's ultimate desire to fulfill something that is of great value or importance that would bring about something great. It affirms, confirms, and strengthens the truth about something. The covenant that God made with humanity is a promise, an oath, and a vow to love us no matter what we become and who we are.

PROMOS AND ELEVATIONS IN GOD'S KINGDOM

Many Christians are being vexed to see that while they are ignored and put aside, many discipled leaders are being chosen, *promoted*, or *elevated* to dignified roles and statuses. It must be well-noted that there is a common factor that a person is esteemed a leader when he/she influences other people for good or sometimes for bad. Generally speaking, human leadership is qualified and graded on a single scale of how one causes change to others in their holdings, behaviors, and attitudes by his/her example or persuasion. It indeed needs certain basic skills for leaders. But in the Kingdom of God, besides natural and social resources, those of us who come out in their climbing the leadership ladder are interiorly empowered by the Spirit through prayer and discipline; they work hard to be well-groomed and developed in persuasive communication skills in word and deed. Stunningly, some of those leaders who judge sincerely their lack of such skills are strenuously and deeply involved with some other skillful people relationally and make the best use of them in influencing others.

This is the history of "proms and els" in the discipled leadership campus. But one eternal truth is this: A discipled leader becomes renowned in God's Kingdom not by mere promos and els but much more by his/her adherence and commitment to the Master's purposes and demands, above all, with deep love for the Master.

CHAPTER 5: RECRUITMENT OF DISCIPLES TO LEADERSHIP

NO RED-TAPEISM IN APPOINTING A DISCIPLED LEADER

In our human development process, almost all of us have gone through so many interviews and tests given by our leaders, organizers, directors, and superiors to select us as well-qualified and superbly suitable employees to their concerns, causes, businesses, firms, and projects, plus making us tiresomely to fill in their application forms with attachments of our credits, IDs, accomplishments, and of attestations from some important community leaders so that we are checked thoroughly in our "profile" and "background." The last one has been the most crucial factor because the interviewers intend to make sure we who are appointed are rightly fitting into their clout as apt members.

Every appointment process is very hectic and a seamlessly lengthy one. Most of us would not be granted immediately with the job or opportunity we strive for. It takes countless hours, days, and even months to find the results. Some label this as "red-tapeism," meaning it may be the bleeding every interviewee sheds by the unbearable bureaucratic system of requiring excessive paperwork and tedious procedures of "roundtable" conferences among leading and organizing teams or of several buzzy one-to-one conversations among the high-rank chiefs.

In the Kingdom of God, where Jesus was designated to take charge of recruiting and appointing his disciples, the appointment process is a bit messy in the eyes of righteous "red-colored" people. He never willed any other humans put their finger into this process, nor did he like humans think they have freely chosen him and his team. "It was not you who chose me, but I who chose you and appointed you to go and bear fruit that will remain" (John 15:16a). He knew what was in humans; he couldn't trust them because he was fully conscious of his fellowmen's stumbling, denying, betraying, lying, cheating, and, worse, some well-established bosses claiming stupidly and senselessly they are the ones who grant appointment in God's Kingdom. There is no "red-tapeism" in Jesus's appointment procedures. Unquestionably, he conducts interviews for his recruits but in private, in the depth of individual's heart. He doesn't need any team of humans to counsel him in this process.

AMAZING STARTING POINT OF RECRUITMENT OF DISCIPLED LEADERS

Before Jesus called his discipled leaders being intimately related to his Father, he too knew who were designated by his Father. The unthinkable fact is, even before their birth, Jesus's recruits are being chosen by his Father, as we read in the lives of prophets like Jeremiah and Isaiah, and he chooses them in our mothers' wombs: "Before I formed you in the womb I knew you, before you were born I dedicated you, a prophet to the nations I appointed you" (Jer. 1:5). "Before birth the LORD called me, from my mother's womb he gave me my name" (Isa. 49:1). Paul, with immense exuberance and gratitude, testifies many times in his letters how God of Jesus recruited him with these words: "God from my mother's womb had set me apart and called me through his grace" (Gal. 1:15).

We know well enough only through human relationship we can reach God and God reaches us. In all those human interactions, bad or good, hurting or pleasurable, God speaks to us and reveals to us certain truths about himself, about us, and about others. That revelation will be understood and grasped only by certain people: They should have been fully anointed by the Lord as prophets, namely, chosen by God to be his words. This anointing should have already happened when they were in their mothers' wombs. They should have become grown-ups.

Just one single example: We read in John, "Jesus saw Nathanael coming toward him and said of him, 'Here is a true Israelite. There is no duplicity in him.' Nathanael said to him, 'How do you know me?' Jesus answered and said to him, 'Before Philip called you, I saw you under the fig tree'" (John 1:47–48). He too knew in farsighted vision how every one of his disciples would walk, stumble, but rise again in their discipleship. The Master knew Peter would deny him thrice (Luke 22:31–34; Matt. 26:33–36; Mark 14:29–31; John 13:37–38), but he would wake up in remorse and confirm thrice that he loved his Master more than anyone else (John 21:15–17). Next to Peter, the genuine role model for discipled leadership was Saul, who became Paul. He sincerely confesses his deviated life of his past, which his Master, despite knowing it, overlooked and admitted him in his discipleship: "You heard of my former way of life in Judaism, how I persecuted the church of God beyond measure and tried to destroy it, and progressed in Judaism beyond many of my contemporaries among my race, since I was even more a zealot for my ancestral traditions" (Gal. 1:13–14). Jesus also knew how his disciple would die at the end of his discipled leadership journey (Ref. John 21:18–19).

THE AWESOME ACTION PLAN OF THE MASTER

In the history of humans being recruited for discipled leadership, we observe each disciple has been chosen not because of his/her own accomplishments but as Paul underscores what happened in his recruitment: "He saved us and called us to a holy life, not according to our works but according to his own design and the grace bestowed on us in

Christ Jesus before time began" (2 Tim. 1:9). Surprisingly, we too notice God's benevolence in admitting into his company so many like Paul despite their sinful past.

At the onset of recruiting his disciples, Jesus followed a phenomenal action plan. He recruited them in different ways: First, he straightaway orders them, saying, "Follow me" (Matt. 9:9) and "Come after me" (Mark 1:17). Second, he exposed to them his power and holiness and made them attracted to him, and once they were in excitement, he ordered them to follow him (Luke 5:1–11). Third, he used some of his close friends like John the Baptist (John 1:35–37) and his own trustworthy disciples like James and John (John 1:40–42) to testify to his would-be disciples about his greatness and his "greater cause" as eyewitnesses and then called them for his discipleship.

There is one more surprising strategy of Jesus in his recruiting his chosen ones. While all the Gospel writers place the call of first disciples in the beginning of their Gospels, John alone excludes the call to Peter in his story, but he adds it at the end of his Gospel (John 21:15–19). I am personally inspired by this writing style of John because it corresponds very closely to my own life as the Lord's discipled leader. Peter, the leader second to Jesus in his team of disciples, was found by the Master as not yet ready for his full-fledged discipleship. We may be wondering how this is true.

OUR CHOICE IS PRIMARILY HIS CHOICE

Jesus's words continue to ring in our heads and hearts whenever we think of our recruitment into his team: "It was not you who chose me, but I who chose you and appointed you to go and bear fruit that will remain" (John 15:16a). Undoubtedly, Peter behaved as dedicated and trustworthy to his Master for three years and even professed Jesus's messiahship identity in the name of other disciples. Jesus too welcomed it and appreciated Peter's gestures. Nevertheless,

Jesus never directly told him, "Follow me," as he did to other disciples.

The main reason—from my own experience I can testify—is that all that Peter was speaking and doing was merely exterior and not from inside his soul. Jesus knew it well that he was noncommitted and still wishy-washy in his spirit of discipleship. Hence, Jesus takes time, gives a long rope to him, and finally caught him in his hands as the professional "catcher of men." In this connection, let us remember the words of the Master to Peter. Predicting Peter's reckless denial of the Master, Jesus told him at the Last Supper, "Simon, Simon, behold Satan has demanded to sift all of you like wheat, but I have prayed that your own faith may not fail; and once you have turned back, you must strengthen your brothers" (Luke 22:31–32).

It is the way the Master dealt with me. I did so many wonderful things for the sake of Jesus and proclaimed his Gospel in season and out of season, but very sadly, my heart was not put to the discipleship as demanded by the Master. It took me nearly thirty-five years to prepare my inner soul according to my Master's will. One day I truly reconciled with him as Peter did, and peace and contentment was settled in my heart. Praised be, my Master Jesus, for his forbearance and mercy. If at all I am what I am now, thanks to his friendly understanding and compassion.

During those awful years, like most of my friends, I had cried out to Jesus many times, "Why God doesn't want me?" My mentors had consoled me by reminding me that I was in good company of shuttering Moses; tiny boy David with his sling; Hosea being troubled by his prostitute wife; Amos, a humble worker of tree pruning; Jacob, a liar; David, an abominable sinner; Solomon being hoarded with riches; Naomi, a widow; Miriam, a gossiper; Noah, a drunkard and, in the NT, Jesus, the poorest vagabond; Paul, a murderer; Timothy with his ulcers; Peter, the timid man; Lazarus, the dead; and so on and on. In these people's lives, I discovered the heavenly truth, and that is our God doesn't require a job interview. He's not prejudiced.

Undoubtedly, there may be lots of reasons God shouldn't want us. But if we are truly in love with him, if we hunger for him, he'll use us despite who we are, where we've been, or what we look like. That is history, and that has been my story of life. I am sure this too may be any one of you who are reading this book. Cheer up! Many are called, but few are chosen, but you and I who strive to be God's children surely are included in the team of Jesus's disciples.

The only thing we have to concentrate on in daily life is to "redo" or "revisit" our life choices and renew them according to the Master's heartbeats. Every one of us has a choice to make at every moment of life for our survival and success in earthly life. The same is true with our life in the company of Jesus. We have decided once for all at our baptism that we should know, love, and serve God, and we too have determined at a time of our youth that we would follow Jesus in fulfilling our covenantal love deal with God. That means now we have to make the right choice between to live for ourselves and to deny ourselves, to ignore the cross and to take it up, to seek to save our life and ultimately lose it and to lose our life and ultimately find it, to gain the world and to forsake the world, and to lose our soul and to preserve it.

CHAPTER 6: VARIOUS ROLES OF DISCIPLED LEADERS

U sually, in a well-organized church environment—be it mega or small, urban or rural—there is a clear-cut description of each role. That is called job description. A job description is a broad, general, and written statement of a specific job based on the findings of a job analysis, which contains certain details of the duties, purpose, responsibilities, scope, and working conditions of the "role" offered to a discipled leader, along with its title and the name or designation of the person to whom the employee reports. In practical life, we know well how important is such job description for the discipled leaders to work as effectively and peacefully as they should.

In this book, we are not discussing about those official job descriptions of the roles to be performed in a church. It all should be referred to the church a disciple is called to be affiliated. We too must know not every church is endowed with all the above-listed roles; rather, their number differs from one church to another in accordance with its social and structural nature, identity, and capability. This means a sincere disciple should acknowledge the providential hands of God in the quality and quantity of every church. Here therefore we try to consider the common code of performance of every role in the church, though it may be small or great, performed at forefront or in closed doors, as the workers in the vineyard of the Lord.

DIFFERENT FORMS OF DISCIPLED LEADERSHIP

Unquestionably, there are different forms of leadership service in Jesus's Kingdom. Even in our Lord's earthly journey, we find he designated a few special services to his apostles; for example, Judas was given a portfolio of taking care the team's finance. And from the days of church inception, Paul draws out in his letters (1 Cor. 12:4–11; Eph. 4:11–12; Rom. 12:6–8) a list of roles the discipled leaders were performing at his time. To sum, his list contains ten and more ministries: as apostles; as prophets; as teachers; as pastors; as missionaries; as healing ministers; as administrators; as charismatic ministers of mighty deeds and speaking in different tongues; as stewards of treasure, talents, and time; and as counselors and consolers and so on. The apostle affirms that these different kinds of roles have been allocated by Jesus's Spirit.

This sort of variety of roles among the discipled leaders continues till this day in the church milieu. Generally, those roles can be categorized as the following: pastors, deacons, church administrators, associate pastors, office managers, church secretaries, directors of adult education, youth directors, coordinators of religion classes, ministers of children's ministry, ministers of evangelism and outreach, ministers or directors of church music, organists/pianists, prayer team leaders, church board members and trustees, church council members, church finance committee members, church fund-raising coordinators, receptionists, church accountants, bookkeepers, computer technicians, directors of counseling centers, licensed and license-eligible clinical counselors, maintenance workers, ushers, and more.

THE UNIQUENESS ABOUT THE DIVERSE ROLES IN THE CHURCH

The primary source, as well as the ultimate goal, of the different roles we are accomplishing in the church is, as Peter writes, none other than God: "As generous distributors of God's manifold grace, put your gifts at the service of one another, each in the measure he has received. The one who speaks is to deliver God's message. The one who serves is to do it with the strength provided by God. Thus, in all of you God is to be glorified through Jesus Christ" (1 Pet. 4:8–11). Plus, the amazing factor of this variety of church services, either being remunerated or voluntary ones, holds a uniqueness in them. "The Spirit of unity in diversity." In emphasizing this breathtaking truth, Paul points out in his first letter to the Corinthians that they are all bonded together by Jesus's Spirit, who is the one who bestowed every bit of roles found in the church. Plus, the apostle also indicates that such varieties of gifts shared with them are meant for performing different forms of services only according to the Spirit's move: "There are different kinds of spiritual gifts but the same Spirit; there are different forms of service but the same Lord; there are different workings but the same God who produces all of them in everyone . . . one and the same Spirit produces all of these, distributing them individually to each person as he wishes."

Paul didn't end up with that. He experienced the horrible disunity existing in his first-founded churches and foreknew the same perennial problem would be found in future churches. In a website, I came across a sincere but heartbreaking organizational situation existing in today's churches underlined by a writer: "The theory that clergy and laity are competing for 'power' takes energies—the salt and light and leaven of Christianity—that are meant to be directed towards the world, for its transformation, and turns them inwards, to be consumed in sterile and at times acrimonious debates about church organization and structures and functions." This is the reason Paul added to his discussion on various roles in the churches an admonition that underscores that both the individual gifts and roles bestowed by the Spirit to the discipled leaders, ordained or laypeople, employed for inside works or outside accomplishments are for "common good": "Now to each one the manifestation of the Spirit is given for the common good" (1 Cor. 12:7, NIV).

Writing to the Ephesians, Paul explains what he meant by "common good." He says that all discipled leaders with their gifts and specific portfolios must perform their ministries being focused on equipping the whole people of God for their own individual work of ministry as Jesus's disciples (Eph. 4:12a). Plus, all leaders in the church must possess one purpose in their ministries, namely, "to build up the body of Christ, until we all attain to the unity of faith and knowledge of the Son of God, to mature manhood, to the extent of the full stature of Christ" (Eph. 4:12b–13).

Indeed, the church is the outward sign of God's Kingdom on Earth; however, it is made of human flesh and blood, a typical human institution. The discipled leaders who have been chosen to take the roles of leadership at every level are supposed to maintain the church's inner integrity and responsibility of bringing transformation in and around the world they move and work; they cannot make the church as a closed system, where humans pursue a deliberate fight for sharing power as the disciples of Jesus contested in the time of the Lord. As Pope Francis frequently points out, we should not be narcissistic in our attitude about our church, the bride and pride of Jesus Christ. She exists not for its own sake but for the sake of the Gospel, for the sake of the world, to bring the message and work of our Master to the whole world. If we focus our attention more on the "role" rather than on the "power" each discipled leader is called for, plus, if we are convinced that the true goal of our participation and involvement in God's Kingdom is to be effective instrument of evangelization, the age-old problem of disunity and infight will be solved.

IN CHRIST, NO LAITY OR CLERGY

The main brutal problem of disunity exists largely between two sections of the church: hierarchical and laity or the clergy and the commoner. The role of ordained priests, bishops, and cardinals, including popes and deacons, had been overwhelmingly expounded over the centuries by Church Fathers, by church councils, and by old and modern theologians that it is nothing but a ministerial role of service, primarily to the people of God. We are also informed by the teachings of the church and tradition that while the ordained leaders perform their roles of administering the sacraments, preaching the Word, and pasturing the flock of Jesus both in the inner campus of the church as well as on the streets and marketplaces, they should in no way go beyond their priestly unctioned life and try to behave in a secular lifestyle. The same policy holds good that when the laity recognize their responsible roles of leadership in the church as baptized disciples, they fail or degrade it in two ways: either they try to make the church's identity more secular, political, and earthly, or they ignore the Lord's vision of discipled leadership as equally shared but hierarchically performed.

Undebatably, in the Spirit of Jesus, we can never consider to divide the church into the hierarchy in which certain elite men and women take the higher levels and the laity where so many remain at the bottom step of the church ladder. No way. There is one and only church where the baptized move and have their being in Jesus as his followers, his disciples, and surely his leaders. As all the bodily organs make the whole body, all members of the church make one hierarchical church. That means every member, though small or big, do make the church.

We discussed and affirmed clearly in the previous chapters that all those baptized in Triune God are to be recognized as discipled leaders who have been granted a share of Jesus's leadership of Ruler, Prophet, and Priest. However, there are some among us being re-anointed called to be "ordained" in the name of Jesus by his church only for being role models of possessing and performing those triple Christic functions in front of other discipled leaders so that those unordained people of God may pursue to be engaged in their leadership performance as the Lord calls them to do. Nothing more or nothing less.

Vat. II clearly and profoundly states today's church view about the "unordained" leaders' vocation: "By reason of their special vocation it belongs to the laity to seek the kingdom of God by engaging in temporal affairs and directing them according to God's will" (Lumen Gentium 31). They have "to animate the world with the spirit of Christianity" (Gaudium et Spes 43), "to sanctify the world from within" (LG 10, 31), and "to permeate and perfect the temporal order with the spirit of the Gospel" (Apostolicam Actuositatem 2; c. 225). The council also exhorts the "unordained leaders" of the church: "The laity are given this special vocation: to make the Church present and faithful in those places and circumstances where it is only through them that she can become the salt of the earth" (LG 33). "The characteristic of the lay state being a life led in the midst of the world and of secular affairs, laymen are called by God to make of their apostolate, through the vigor of their Christian spirit, a leaven in the world" (AA 2).

Jerome, one of the fourth-century Church Fathers, wrote (Jerome, Commentarius in epistulam Pauli ad Titum 1:5), "Before splits appeared in our religion through the stimulation of the devil, and before it was spoken among the people: 'I belong to Paul, I to Apollos, and I to Cephas himself', the churches had been governed jointly by councils of presbyters. As soon as each of them started considering those he baptized his own, and not Christ's, it was decided all over the world that one man, chosen from among presbyters, should be set over the rest to take care of the whole church.

In this way the seeds of schism were done away with." And he too has underlined that this setup of hierarchical positions was a tradition of the church, inspired by the Spirit.

DISCIPLED LEADERSHIP PORTFOLIOS FOR COMMON GOOD

God and his Son deliberately recognized in the Bible the necessity and importance of human leadership as God's proxies for God's people. Paul contends in the Spirit that human leaderships are the establishment of God and he orders his Christians to obey and respect them: "Let every person be subordinate to the higher authorities, for there is no authority except from God, and those that exist have been established by God. Therefore, whoever resists authority opposes what God has appointed, and those who oppose it will bring judgment upon themselves . . . respect to whom respect is due, honor to whom honor is due" (Rom. 13:1–7).

This human leadership can be one to one or one to a group, two to a family, and one or a group to a community, kingdom, country, and surely the church. The leadership style has been developed and improved over the centuries either for worse or for better. Nothing is wrong in accepting humbly the flaws and failures of leadership that existed and will be existing inside the church/churches. Nonetheless, our Master entrusted with his church a perfect solution for lessening or even erasing those flaws and mistakes occurring in handling human leadership among the people of God. God's Spirit inspired Paul to deliberate such solution in his letters. He emphasizes love should be the base and process in handling and saluting leadership: "Let love be sincere; hate what is evil, hold on to what is good; love one another with mutual affection; anticipate one another in showing honor" (Rom. 12:10).

He too urges all disciples to possess the humble and selfless attitude of the Master: "Do nothing out of selfishness or out of vainglory; rather, humbly regard others as more important than yourselves, each looking out not for his own interests, but [also] everyone for those of others" (Phil. 2:3–4). Especially when he talks about the various gifts and portfolios found in the church, he portrayed the right solution to avoid struggles and tensions between hierarchy and laity as to consider: "Everything is given for common good" (1 Cor. 12:7). His claim is if everyone in the church circle acts with the esteem that all baptized Christians are called to be discipled leaders in various situations, through various portfolios, and with various objectives but for realizing one "common good-goal of salvation" of the entire humanity, then the realization of peace and success is possible in the church.

We read St. Gregory of Nyssa in his writing about the formation of the religious who take "living in obedience to their superiors" as one of their vows and points out that "Jesus's demand of self-denial means that we never seek our own will but God's, using God's will as a sure guide; it also means possessing nothing apart from what is held in common. In this way it will be easier for the religious to carry out their superior's commands promptly, in joy and in hope; this is required of Christ's servants who are redeemed for service to the brethren. For this is what the Lord wants when he says: Whoever wishes to be first and great among you must be the last of all and a servant to all."

The same saintly writer includes also a beautiful exhortation for those who handle leadership as superiors: "One who is in such a position must be subject to everyone and serve his brothers as if he were paying off a debt. Moreover, those who are in charge should work harder than the others and conduct themselves with greater submission that their own subjects. Their lives should serve as a visible example of what service means, and they should remember that those who are committed to their trust are held in trust from God. Those, then, who are in a position of authority must look after their brothers as conscientious teachers look after the young children who have been handed over to them by their parents. If both disciples and masters have this loving relationship, then subjects will be happy to obey whatever is commanded, while superiors will be delighted to lead their brothers to perfection. If you try to outdo one another in showing respect, your life on earth will be like that of the angels."

In conclusion of this chapter, let me write this: All the disciples of Jesus are bound by a singular demand of our Master to be with him intimately and to go out to be the salt and light in the world so that all humans may glorify our Father in heaven. It is simply to share in the power and mission of Christ so as to infuse their own earthly life and the world around them with his Spirit. This is nothing but to lead all humans to their salvific destiny, and it is this "discipled leadership" we discuss here in this book. In exercising our leadership, each one of us is gifted and anointed with specific charisma, particular portfolio. It is such a singular cause and goal that preserves safely the Christ-intended unity in our diversities.

SECTION II: JESUS'S PERSONAL DEMANDS FROM HIS DISCIPLED LEADERS

Whoever wishes to come after me must . . .
—Matt. 16:24; Mark 8:34; Luke 9:23

CHAPTER 7: IMITATE GOD IN JESUS

THE BIG SHOE TO FILL IN

Once at the first week of becoming a pastor to a very big parish, I attended the wake of one parishioner of that church. As I was brand new and not yet offered Mass in the parish, many were staring at me. However, one elderly lady with her smiling face came to me and said, "Welcome, Father, to the parish. You may have some big shoes to fill in." I smiled outside, but in the heart, I said to myself, "My dear lady, being born and bred in a semitropical land of South India, I hate to wear shoes all my life. I prefer only sandals and slippers."

When I felt that way within me, I was fully aware of the historical and geographical facts of Jesus who moved around with his disciples in Palestine with mere sandals. At the same, I too am deeply conscious of the mightiest power and love of the Master whom no other can equal in his greatness. I agree completely with the assertion of John the Baptizer about the Master: "The one [Jesus] who is coming after me is mightier than I. I am not worthy to carry his sandals" (Matt. 3:11b). In this chapter, let me share some of my thoughts regarding our imitating Jesus in our leadership ministry.

AS THE LEADERS, SO THE FOLLOWERS

Beginning from childhood through adulthood, all humans are stuck to the perennial truth of "as the elders, superiors, or leaders, so we have been, and we are still." All habits, good and bad, in all organizations and systems—small as families, medium as villages, and big as nations—flow down fast from the top. Underscoring this age-old fact, many modern journalists try to prove it through portraying what is happening currently in some of the international leaders' inner circle of their staff and advisers. As "spot winning" champions, these leaders' lifelong habits to covet the attention of the public are to improvise, to attack, to deny the undeniable, and to leak. In such malignant atmosphere, whoever joins these leaders is succumbed and sucked into its ferocious and unprecedented whirlpool. Commonly, many of them, as they start their journey with these fake self-centered leaders, go through a cycle of being enamored of their leaders' larger-than-life persona but then become frustrated by the environment the same leaders create and allow, followed by anger at their self-destructive tendencies.

The rancorous behaviors of superiors and leaders have become the day-to-day practices of most of their staff as well as of members of their family, political parties, or religious systems. In general, we notice in any human organizations the followers, except a few, not only support and imitate their leaders' undisciplined conducts but also sit and stand with eternal and blissful silence to oppose such shameful and contemptible situations as they had done against other leaders. They disregard the traditional rules of the road; they continue with no qualms the staff-on-staff infighting as the leader's style breeds internal factions; and following their leader's disgraceful culture, they thrive in upholding a boorish attitude: "It's every man for himself; do what's best for me, and not for the organization."

GOD CONDEMNS SUCH MALICIOUS LEADERSHIP

In human history, this sort of leaders have been living and still leading people to perdition as our biblical prophets have condemned and cursed. These leaders spent their past life creating their own reality inside their heads and wasted enough time working with that bogus self, and it becomes hard to resist seeing the world their way. Those who refuse to do so wind up lashing and leaking. That's why in the Bible, we are advised not to place our entire life in the hands of vulnerable leaders. Especially, we get a sincere and divinely revealed exhortation on this matter from David, who indeed was chosen to be a leader for God's people. He emphasizes in two Psalms why and how we, the disciped leaders, should treat our higher authorities and powerful superiors: "Put no trust in princes, in children of Adam powerless to save" (Ps. 146:3–5). "Better to take refuge in the Lord than to put one's trust in mortals. Better to take refuge in the Lord than to put one's trust in princes" (Ps. 118:8–9). Through Prophet Jeremiah, God bluntly underlines the curses and blessings to be encountered by mishandling of our trust: "Cursed is the man who trusts in human beings, who makes flesh his strength, whose heart turns away from the Lord. He is like a barren bush in the wasteland that enjoys no change of season, but stands in lava beds in the wilderness, a land, salty and uninhabited. Blessed are those who trust in the Lord" (Jer. 17:5–8).

In this God's admonition about reliance on human leadership, Paul, another godsent disciped leader, instructs and warns us as he advises his own disciple Timothy about the weakness of both human leadership as well as human followship: "But understand this: there will be terrifying times in the last days. People will be self-centered and lovers of money, proud, haughty, abusive, disobedient to their parents, ungrateful, irreligious, callous, implacable, slanderous, licentious, brutal, hating what is good, traitors, reckless, conceited, lovers of pleasure rather than lovers of God, as they make a pretense of religion but deny its power. Reject them . . . Wicked people and charlatans will go from bad to worse, deceivers and deceived. But you, remain faithful to what you have learned and believed, because you know from whom you learned it, and that from infancy you have known the sacred Scriptures, which are capable of giving you wisdom for salvation through faith in Christ Jesus" (2 Tim. 3:1–15).

THE "IMITATION" IN DISCIPLED LEADERSHIP PROGRAM

Our Master Jesus demands from his discipled leaders to uphold a remarkable ideal that seems to be very hard and undoable by fallible humans as we are. That surprising demand is be like the heavenly Father, namely, "Be perfect, just as your heavenly Father is perfect" (Matt. 5:48), and "Be merciful, just as also your Father is merciful" (Luke 6:36). Though the demand may be too idealistic, it is reasonable and certainly agreeable because we are God's children. Paul, one of the great role models to all the discipled leaders in Jesus's Kingdom, exhorts us: "Be imitators of God, therefore, as dearly loved children" (Eph. 5: 1). He is absolutely correct in his statement because we know well, "as the father, so the son." It sounds as a normal and inescapable process of human development where all human children learn proper behavior from their parents. If discipled leaders esteem themselves as the true and loving children of God the Father, they need to imitate their Father in walking his walk and in talking his talk. Our Master went one step further and indicated crystal clearly that his disciples should imitate their Father in his perfection, holiness, and mercy. And so should we be in our relationship with our Parent God, as Jesus proposes, to watch carefully how our Parent God is and what he does and then try to emulate him.

When the Master says that God the Father is perfect, we know he means his Father is the "best," indicating that God is a Supreme Being superbly greater, better and more than any being in the universe. Many theologians define the term "perfect" when it refers to God as something other than *model*, than that which lacks nothing, than that achieves its purpose, than that fulfills its functions, or than that is *harmonious* (Tatarkiewicz, "On Perfection: Conclusion," *Dialectics and Humanism* VIII, no. 2 (Spring 1981): 12). In the words of St. Augustine, God is "higher than my highest and more inward than my innermost self" (Conf. 3, 6, 11: PL 32, 688).

We also must understand the little trickery biblical translation of the term "imitate." The term "imitation" means to copy a person's life and behavior with the purpose of equaling or excelling him, to reproduce a more complete copy of a person who is esteemed as a role model, whereas the word "emulation" refers to a process of watching a person and observing the results of his actions rather than the details of the behavior involved. An emulator uses the model offered by his role model and, observing the effect of that model in gaining a reward, seeks to reproduce this outcome using his own efficacious actions, but an imitator copies the entire life of his role model and acts exactly as the role model to get the same results the role model achieved. In this sense, we can say our Master demanded from us to emulate God and not entirely imitate him. When we hear Paul advising us to imitate God, that thought was in his mind too; from all his deliberations over this demand in his letters, we can observe he expects us to emulate our Abba Father as his children and not to be hard on ourselves by trying to imitate him. We should try our best to emulate God the Father's attitudes and values as best as we can, though his ways are not our ways and our thoughts are not his.

BECOMING PERFECT IN "EXCLUSIVENESS"

In the Scriptures, we find sacred writers used this costly demand for different needs and implications. We hear God telling people through Moses (Lev. 20:25–26) that they should be holy for "I, the Lord, am holy, and I have set you apart from other peoples to be my own." He too asked them, as he has done to them, to set apart the clean animals from the unclean and use only the clean ones. These two demands correlate to each other that the Creator wished that his people must be always clean and pure in heart, mind, and body as well.

The Judeo-Christian culture thus promoted the "exclusiveness" mind setup among Jesus's followers. Even Paul could exclaim his unique identity as "chosen" and set apart exclusively for Jesus's Gospel. Accompanying him, Peter would vigorously write about how the followers of Jesus, because of the mercy of God, became a very exclusive group in his world: "You are 'a chosen race, a royal priesthood, a holy nation, a people of his own, so that you may announce the praises' of him who called you out of darkness into his wonderful light" (1 Pet. 2:9).

All discipled leaders therefore are to be convinced that we have been recruited and set apart by the Creator to be exclusively consecrated to him and him alone. No other humans or any other creatures and idols can be permitted to claim their ownership of them. As regards Peter quoting the same God's demand, he emphasizes that Jesus's disciples must be holy in every aspect of their conduct (1 Pet. 1:15–16). James offers a detailed meaning of Jesus demanding us to be perfect in perseverance: "And let perseverance be perfect, so that you may be perfect and complete, lacking in nothing" (James 1:4).

Undeniably, our Master wants us to recognize and appreciate the exclusive status of being his disciples and very specially his chosen leaders. Yes, we were once enslaved by various earthly things and persons, but you have delivered by God as remnants of the human race. Indeed, we were set apart from other humans as God's representatives, proxies, and agents. Yes, we have been gathered by the Master together for his mission purpose from different kinds of background, race, nationality, color, mind setup, IQ, disability, broken heartedness, roles and needs, and hopelessly hoping for better life. This is solely a gratuitous gift from God through Jesus. Therefore, being grateful and faithful to our Giver, we need to handle with care this amazing exclusive "opportunity" bestowed to us.

Sadly, church history proves that most of Jesus's discipled leaders, being succumbed to the evil's instigation and being ignorant and immature in our calling, make the worst use of the best gift. As I mentioned earlier in the first section of this book, every disciple of Jesus is born and reborn to lead others in one way or another, such as by ordination; by election, selection, promotion, and qualification; or by voluntarism. All these happen by the mere grace of God. Nevertheless, we are prone to glorify ourselves falsely for such gift as if we were its proprietors; we don't pay attention to God's holy dealings with humans in this regard.

In our daily dealings with our fellowmen, simply either ignoring or forgetting God's ways and attitudes, all of us possess the attitude of exclusiveness and inclusiveness. This may be because of being more safe and secure. We unjustly exclude some of our fellowmen from our dealings, from our environments, and even from our sight, or we include untruthfully certain kinds of people inside our company who are almost similar to us on certain common grounds, for example, class, caste, creed, opinions, and color of skin, language, and blood. The most atrocious behavior of many of us is to condemn mercilessly some of our family, community, or country or global members for the only reason that they don't talk our talk and don't walk our walk. Many times, we totally forget the perfection of God consists in his justice, truth, and love. When we intend to emulate God, he expects us, especially the discipled leaders, to follow some of his eternal strategies of truth, justice, and mercy in all dealings with others.

BEING PERFECTED IN LOVE

Mostly, what God does is he totally loves us, and we learn this love life from him slowly but intimately and try to lead that life. John strikingly writes about this truth in his first letter. Insisting the amazing fact that "God is love, and whoever remains in love remains in God and God in him" and that "God loved us first," John encourages to grow more and more in loving as God loves us. He also expresses the fragility of our love in its initial form as imperfect because it is influenced by fear. Rather, in our effort to perfect our human love, he advises us to look up to the Father, who has revealed his "qualitative" love by sending his only Son to us as expiation for our sins and follow him as our role model of love. And consequently, he assures us that that is the only way to bring our love to perfection (Ref. 1 John 4:9–17).

Paul, who, following the Master, advises the disciples strongly to imitate our God, speaks elaborately how to imitate him in practical life. We should imitate God in being "kind to one another, compassionate, forgiving one another as God has forgiven us in Christ" (Eph. 4:32). And little more in detail, he lists out how this imitation of God's love should be undertaken in our individual life: "Put on then, as God's chosen ones, holy and beloved, heartfelt compassion, kindness, humility, gentleness, and patience, bearing with one another and forgiving one another, if one has a grievance against another; as the Lord has forgiven you, so must you also do. And over all these put on love, that is, the bond of perfection" (Col. 3:12–14). Let us read again what Paul writes at the end of this passage: "Put on love, that is, the bond of perfection."

THE AUTHENTIC DISCIPLED LEADERSHIP

Proudly esteeming ourselves as an exclusively perfect group of church leaders, we often fail and fall to the pit as we perform our leadership roles of administering, preaching, teaching, exhorting, counseling, and son on. As the old saying goes, "Who you are thunders so loud that it drowns out your words." Every bit of our efforts turn out to be either unproductive or sometimes destructive. The main reason is, I know from my life and from witnessing others' too, that we don't walk with God in every moment of our life, especially at our "role calls." Walking authentically with God gives legitimacy to our leadership.

Being genuine discipled leaders of Jesus, we are certainly aware of our limitation and inability to walk with our heavenly Father, being perfect or holy or merciful as he is. However, in the light of Jesus's and his messengers' preaching, we know well this hardest demand of the Master is the ideal to be achieved, but his superbly idealistic demand has always an annexed statement: "Try your best and leave the rest in my hands, but never drift away from your climbing to the Highest."

THE PRACTICAL WAY OF IMITATING GOD

There are millions of us that still find it hard to digest and apply the advice of Jesus to imitate the heavenly Father in our life. We are therefore may complain to the Master about the hardship we undergo in this regard. But Jesus is never tired of exposing to us the right formula of tenderizing the demand. We should never forget how he encouraged us: "Come to me, all you who labor and are burdened, and I will give you rest. Take my yoke upon you and learn from me, for I am meek and humble of heart; and you will find rest for yourselves. For my yoke is easy, and my burden light" (Matt. 11:28–30). In other words, our Master plainly asks us to follow his footsteps as our only way, truth, and life.

Now another legitimate query arises in our hearts as it happened in his apostles (John 14:5–11): "How can we know the way?" and "Master show us the Father." Again, the Master was very clear in his claim: "Have I been with you for so long a time and you still do not know me, Philip? Whoever has seen me has seen the Father. How can you say, 'Show us the Father'? Do you not believe that I am in the Father and the Father is in me? The words that I speak to you I do not speak on my own . . . Believe me that I am in the Father and the Father is in me."

WE NEED TO BELIEVE JESUS AS THE IMAGE OF GOD

While most of the religions and cultures around us esteem Jesus of Nazareth as a created being "less than God," "one of many gods," "a high angel," "a good teacher," "a prophet," and so on, in Christianity, from the days of its inception, we uphold together with Paul and the other apostles and disciples of Jesus that Jesus, the Son of Mary, is "the image of the invisible God, the firstborn of all creation . . . For in him all the fullness was pleased to dwell" (Col. 1:15–20; Phil. 2:6–11; 1 Tim. 3:16; Heb. 1:1–14).

Paul and the other disciples of Jesus never started reciting, singing, and living up to this profession overnight. Either they had heard from the golden mouth of the Master or they saw before their eyes how thousands and thousands of their fellow Christians testify to this belief by their bleeding, by suffering, and even by undergoing cruel death. With them, we still hear what Jesus, the Master, said about his identity.

Every page of all the NT books is crowded with the deliberations on this demand of the Master. There are a couple of demands contained in that demand: "1. To believe in Jesus. 2. To believe him being in God." If we want to be social and religious leaders, claiming to be the "discipled leaders of Jesus," we should first and foremost profess with the entire throng of Christian witnesses that Jesus is Christ, the genuine icon of the Supreme Being. Fr. Richard Rohr defines in modern style the Greek term "Logos" as "the Blueprint." So we can join with Father Rohr and profess that Jesus is a concrete and personal embodiment of universal love. He is the blueprint of God's loving presence and plan in the economy of universal salvation. This truth was what the apostles and early disciples of Jesus held as the basis for their proclamation of Jesus's Gospel: "And the Word [blueprint] became flesh, and dwelt among us, and we saw his glory, the glory as of the only begotten from the Father, full of grace and truth . . . For of his fullness we all received grace upon grace" (John 1:14, 16).

There is indeed a valid reason to this primary step in shaping ourselves to fit into the shoes of millions of discipled leaders. Every bit of our leadership undertakings, missions, and responsibilities hinges on this profession about Jesus. Christian leadership has to start, proceed, and end in the discipleship as Master Jesus has demanded and instructed.

Jesus wants us to acknowledge in faith his genuine and holistic identity. This faith is a "naked faith" as Pope Francis labeled; many others may prefer to name it as blind faith, impudent faith, impolite faith, aggressive faith, and so on. Actually, Jesus, in his mother tongue, used the term "chutzpah" to mean such faith. That term covers all above listed and more. Chutzpah means a strong, persistent, and unrelenting confidence, trust, and fidelity toward God who was, is, and will be always invisible, unseen, unfathomable, and mysterious to human minds.

In many of his sayings and instructions on this kind of faith, he never denied the need of rationality. He desired that our obedience to his demands should not be merely blind and emotional, but precisely, it should be based on reasonable faith in the One who demands from us some hardest roles and performances in our leadership, especially in conceding to his crucial and utterly difficult demand that we should emulate God in his justice, truth, and love, as we discussed in the previous chapter.

Certainly, any master proposing such dazzling and dumbfounding demands cannot be mere human; it presupposes he should be more than an ordinary human being. He should know what he says, he should possess in himself all those extraordinary qualities, he should have proven them in his very life, and above all, he too must have the power to assist and uplift the weaklings in this regard. Our two-thousand-year adherence to the profession about Master Jesus as Christ, Lord, Savior, and the image of God enables us to listen and accept all his demands and walk his walk and talk his talk as if we were emulating God himself.

He too has guaranteed if we obey his demands, he, in his Spirit, would stay closely with us and enable us to accomplish as he did and even more than what he had done: "Amen, amen, I say to you, whoever believes in me will do the works that I do, and will do greater ones than these, because I am going to the Father" (John 14:12). Plus, having seated at the right hand of his Father, if we approach him for assistance, he promised us to bestow necessary strength and vigor in our limitations and disappointments in fulfilling his demands: "Whatever you ask in my name, I will do, so that the Father may be glorified in the Son. If you ask anything of me in my name, I will do it" (John 14:13–14).

It is understandable in the beginning of our discipleship journey that when we heard the Master telling us, "Follow me, I will make you fishers of men," it sounded cool to our ears. But then, like the first group of disciples, we would have failed and little more discouraged by our falters. However, once the Spirit of the risen Lord possessed those disciples, we know and read how they accepted willingly the demands of Jesus: "Follow me; that is the only way for imitating heavenly Father." Hence, they advise us, "For to this you have been called, because Christ also suffered for you, leaving you an example that you should follow in his footsteps" (1 Pet. 2:21). "Whoever claims to abide in him [Jesus Christ] ought to live just as he lived" (1 John 2:6).

Paul, who exhorts us to imitate God, instructs us to imitate him: "Therefore, I urge you, be imitators of me" (1 Cor. 4:16). "Join with others in being imitators of me, brothers, and observe those who thus conduct themselves according to the model you have in us" (Phil. 3:17). At the same time, he never missed adding how and in what we should follow him: "Be imitators of me, as I am of Christ" (1 Cor. 11:1). "Have among yourselves the same attitude that is also yours in Christ Jesus" (Phil. 2:5).

So here is the initial deal all of us should take to heart as we start our journey of "discipled leadership": With no confusion whatsoever about the terms "the Father" and "the Son," we relate ourselves to Jesus of Nazareth in fully unrelented faith as our God and listen to all his words as Godly Words, honor his mastership as the divine leadership, and follow his footsteps as walking on the "footfalls of the Supreme Being." If anyone of us falls short of this primary step, we should be pitied. For any high-priced job, there will be always some sort of "starting trouble." We should clearly understand that unless we overcome this initial trouble at the early dawn of leadership ministry, more and greater troubles will follow suit on the way.

CHAPTER 8: REMAIN IN AND WITH JESUS'S LOVE

After successfully dealing with the "starting trouble" and confirming firmly that Jesus our Master is "Emmanuel," God with us, we must now pay attention to how to conform ourselves to him as his "discipled leaders." As Paul writes, all of us who have been called by the Master to be discipled are predestined "to be conformed to the image of the Son" (Rom. 8:29).

TRUE FAITH INCLUDES SINCERE LOVE

Mere faith in his divine supremacy will not take us a long way in our attempt to conform ourselves to his image or in our leadership carrier. If God is love, Jesus, his image, also is love. Reaching out to this Lover and living with him forever requires love to connect ourselves to him. This is why Paul is never tired of repeating the phrase "in faith and love" as the motto for his life and ministries. When God is love, so also is his Son Jesus. It is not surprising therefore that he demanded love from his followers ferociously. His demand was very unrealistic, but that is the eternal truth.

Jesus stated, "Whoever loves father or mother more than me is not worthy of me, and whoever loves son or daughter more than me is not worthy of me" (Matt. 10:37). He meant that to be "worthy" of him is to receive him in a way that is "right and proper." He wished us to express our faith in him with excellent love. If we don't have it, we are not worthy of his love-based relationship. Paul asserts the valid reason why many among us are not enjoying the heavenly gift of salvation when he writes about the evil fate of wicked people: "They have not accepted the love of truth so that they may be saved" (2 Thess. 2:7–10). His citation about the love of truth undoubtedly indicates the love of Jesus, who is the Truth, Life, and Way. Merely hearing and preaching about the truthful teachings of Jesus is not what the Lord is looking for. Many say things about Jesus, but they don't love the One who said those things. According to Paul, this is why they are not saved.

COVENANTAL BOND OF LOVE BETWEEN JESUS AND HIS LEADERS

Being discipled in Jesus's abode consists certainly of listening, learning, and following the Master's teachings. Nonetheless, such difficult process presupposes an unbroken bond between the Master and the disciple. A learner or a follower should also be an adherent, a devotee to the Master. In this regard, love stands as a leverage. Indeed, Jesus asked his disciples to learn of him as the role model for restful and successful life. But when the first team of disciples approached him, seeking admission into his team, he told them, "Come and see." At that moment, I am sure his heart was beating within him, saying, "Stay with me." At the Last Supper, he explicitly revealed this mind-blowing demand: "Remain in me, as I remain in you" (John 15:4). He too immediately, with his ambitious love, added, "As the Father loves me, so I also love you. Remain in my love" (John 15:9).

Master Jesus was fully aware of Peter's weakness and impetuousness. At the same time, he knew the inner heartbeat of Peter to be one of his Master's inner circle of love. After his resurrection, before he entrusted fully his leadership to Peter, he wanted to make sure whether Peter had the most ultimate prerequisite of the discipled leadership (John 21:15–23). He asked only one question but thrice: "Do you truly love me more than these?" (v. 15). His question was extremely searching; indeed, it was the ultimate question in life. After, Peter answered very positively but controlling his self-tailored impetuous temperament, saying, "Lord, you know that I love you." Then the Master gave triple commands that Peter should handle his mastership or leadership in proxy.

Jesus's love expects from his discipled leaders an exclusive belongingness to him. The remarkable mystic, Thomas Kempis, splendidly writes about this fact in his classical book of *The Imitation of Christ*. This is the undivided love our Master longs for. First of all, we should never misinterpret his desire as some sort of slavery trade: "I buy you and you should be locked in with me to serve me." Rather, as he himself states, "I no longer call you slaves, because a slave does not know what his master is doing. I have called you friends, because I have told you everything I have heard from my Father" (John 15:15). Also, it is not merely an emotional and not even an intellectual relation but, above all, an ontological closeness. To expound this exquisite demand, he used a metaphor of vine and branches: "I am the true vine, and my Father is the vine grower . . . I am the vine, you are the branches" (John 15:1–5).

JESUS DEMANDS A LOVE WITH NO STRINGS ATTACHED

The discipled leaders are called to abide in Jesus's Spirit of love and not in a vulnerable and breakable religious milieu. We need to live and work in human communities and families. But that is not our licensed tents. They may seem like comfort zones that provide us safety, security, and pleasure, which would be temporary. As Paul makes remark about our human life on Earth, in all our human endeavors, we face corruptibility, temporality, many times unpredictability, and most of the time devaluating the spiritual efforts. For withstanding all the above and more hardships, Paul also offers a monumental support of Jesus's Spirit: "We know that if our earthly dwelling, a tent, should be destroyed, we have a building from God, a dwelling not made with hands, eternal in heaven. For in this tent we groan, longing to be further clothed with our heavenly habitation . . . Now the one who has prepared us for this very thing is God, who has given us the Spirit as a first installment" (2 Cor. 5:1–10). This first installment support bestowed from heaven is nothing but the spiritual abode of Jesus's love.

As we journey in our discipled leadership, we are wrongly pulled over on the sidetrack by some modern management teachers who advise us that, for an effective management and leadership in churches, we should pay more attention to the modern and popular trends of business and also no-profit organizational management. Trend-based leadership has been overemphasized as the standardized norm for even the discipled leaders disregarding all the scriptural traditional principles of the church. The core quintessential principle for fruitful leadership in this world is living in faith and love for the Master Jesus, who says, "Whoever remains in me and I in him will bear much fruit, because without me you can do nothing."

The word "meno," Jesus uses, carries the idea of sustaining a union with, continuing with, being steadfast, or enduring. That is what the Master required of us. In this perilous world, being surrounded by wolves and white-washed sepulchers and brood of vipers, to be calm and serene and well-balanced and to survive and succeed, we need to hold a loving and intimate and exclusive closeness with the Master, who has welcomed and promised us already: "Come to me, all you who labor and are burdened, and I will give you rest" (Matt. 11:28).

Whoever falls in intimate love with Jesus is filled with so much unimaginable and indescribable enthusiasm and stamina that they become "daredevils" to accomplish untold good things that the world cannot contain. That is the miraculous post effect of loving Jesus. Paul wrote on this mind-boggling effect: "For the love of Christ impels us" (2 Cor. 5:14). As one among millions who have been charmed by Jesus's love, he beautifully recounts the glory and power of this divine love: "What will separate us from the love of Christ? Will anguish, or distress, or persecution, or famine, or nakedness, or peril, or the sword? . . . For I am convinced that neither death, nor life, nor angels, nor principalities, nor present things, nor future things, nor powers, nor height, nor depth, nor any other creature will be able to separate us from the love of God in Christ Jesus our Lord" (Rom. 8:31–39).

SUCH UNTHINKABLE LOVE WITH JESUS IS POSSIBLE

As one who tries to be a discipled leader of Jesus's love, I tell you every morning I try to preach to myself while I am on my knees: "I like to be closely knitted to the team of lovers of the Master because I want to attain a deeper relationship with him, to walk with him, to enjoy all his blessings, including, of course, a life after death." Certainly, I know from my past experience, I cannot see him with my naked eyes. He is beyond my grasp. But still, I know he is there but beyond me, beyond everybody, and beyond everything. Even though I don't relish his physical absence all the time, recently, I have developed a taste for his absence. I have started loving his "eternal silence." While 99.99 percent he is absent and imperceptible, that .01 percent of his coming and going in the midst of my clouds, hubbubs, and even in stormy winds gives me great energy to move on through those dark days of my life. That dream about my Master, that vision about his glory, that hope and faith in his ever-loving presence take me through that major portion of my life in his absence. Prayer is not something I do, but it is a time I spent in his absence. While I spend .01 percent of my lifetime in his absence through prayer, I become his presence in the world for the 99.99 percent of my days.

I am convinced that kind of paradigm shift in my discipled leadership is possible. I read many events in many holy people's lives that they had intimate vision and intense conversation with Jesus in prayerful solitude. All the efforts of praying, conversing, imploring before the Master are certainly performed in spiritual level. It's all done in his impressive absence. I love it that way. Because the all-knowing Master knows my limitation at spiritual level, and so he takes full charge of that period of prayer. He is fully engaged in me.

As I come out of prayer time and begin to go through my physical and material leadership engagements, he begins to be present fully through my physicality. He runs the whole show. I affirm "prayer persons" outside their prayer circle are not the ones who are present. It's the Master who is physically present in my disguise. Prayer therefore is one of my most effective tools to grow in the intimate love of my Master. It is to me my conscious presence in my Master's absence, and all the rest I do is my conscious absence in my Master's presence. I perform all my duties. I play the roles I have to play in this world as if the Master does. I feel like Paul declaring boldly: "I live, no longer I, but Christ lives in me; insofar as I now live in the flesh, I live by faith in the Son of God who has loved me and given himself up for me" (Gal. 2:20).

Our job is not producing fruit. Our job is to abide in Christ (John 15:5–8), and if we do, the Holy Spirit will produce the fruit, and this fruit is the result of our obedience. As we become more obedient to the Lord and learn to walk in his ways, our lives will change. The biggest change will take place in our hearts, and the overflow of this will be new conduct (thoughts, words, and actions) representative of that change. The change we seek is done from the inside out through the power of the Holy Spirit. It isn't something we can conjure up on our own.

LIVING AND DYING WITH JESUS'S LOVE

While the Old Testament (OT) portrayed the second important command of God as "Love your neighbors as yourself," Jesus, the Redemptive Source, sent by God, enhanced the same commandment by adding, "Love your neighbors as I have loved you." And how did he love us? As he underlined in his Farewell Supper, "No one has greater love than this, to lay down one's life for one's friends" (John 15:13), he did die, underwent an ignominious death on the Cross for our salvation and for that of the entire humanity.

If we are offered such unbelievable death we are granted by God for the sake of our fellow humans, we are blessed. However, there are millions of his disciples who do not die that way who meet death in a daily basis for the welfare and development of our family members, our sinful community members. Those small and small deaths are taken into God's account of saving his humans universally, as Theresa of Child Jesus encountered and testified. The key qualification for this accomplishment of love is to be an exclusive love for Jesus that is characterized not merely by self-gratified devotion to him, not by mere emotional and ritualistic style, but more by our humility, dependence, and obedience.

There are many ways of dying daily deaths as living sacrifices for the love of God as Jesus demanded us. One of the most impossible deaths among them is to obey his command "Love your enemies." Whenever I recite some Psalms in my daily Liturgy of the Hours, I am astounded to notice how King David who wrote those hymns ventilates his agony, vengeance, and attitude of retaliation against his enemies-individuals as well as the nations. The imprecatory psalms such as 58, 69, and 109 and so on may sound cruel, revengeful, and "tit-for-tat" attitude against our enemies. Actually, the good thing I find in the Psalms is that David, who indeed exposes his natural human feelings of opposition against any evils or evildoers around him, places all his inimical thoughts at the feet of his Creator and the Redeemer and begs him to do the necessary punishment against his hostile neighbors. In other words, expressing his abhorring and disapproving against any kind of wickedness, he leaves the judgment and avenging of those wicked people to the Sovereign God.

Undoubtedly, the OT books include such imprecatory and hateful prayers and heartbeats of Israelites and their leaders and prophets, and as we said about David's Psalms, there are two important inspirational messages contained in the Bible. The inspired writers are not expressing personal vengeance for their enemies. And they are asking God to deal with his enemies according to his promise: "It is mine to avenge; I will repay" (Deut. 32:35). One more truth the same writers reveal to us, there were many occasions biblical heroes did forgive their enemies. For instance, Esau forgave Jacob (Gen. 33), Joseph forgave his brothers (Gen. 45, 50), Moses forgave the Israelites (Num. 12), David forgave Saul (1 Sam. 24–26, 2 Sam. 1) and also Shimei (2 Sam. 16, 1 Kings 2), Solomon forgave Adonijah (1 Kings 1), and the prophet of Judah forgave Jeroboam (1 Kings 13).

Amazingly, when we read the NT books, Jesus and all his disciples preached about the Gospel truth of forgiveness and consequently offered themselves as a living sacrifice of forgiveness till their last breath. Especially Jesus, from the beginning, his public life in recruiting his discipled leaders for his Kingdom taught and demanded them (Ref. Matt. 5:21–44) to "love your enemies," "do good to those who hate you," "pray and bless those who persecute you." Above all, as he was hanging on the Cross, enduring excruciating and ignominious humiliation, pain, and suffering, he prayed for his enemies: "Father, forgive them, they know not what they do" (Luke 23:34a).

When we meditate on our Master's demand of forgiving our enemies, we discover its validity. There is a certain crass, hypocritical attitude all humans possess within us: While we are very careless about our own sinful status, we tend to punish, retaliate, and never tolerate and forgive our neighbors' sinfulness. Forgetting that we are enemies of God by our sins, and that we have been again and again are forgiven by the Love of God in Jesus, we flare up and take weapons of revenge, retaliation, and even violence at the sight of noticing our neighbors' sinful status. This is why Jesus underlined, "If you forgive others their transgressions, your heavenly Father will forgive you. But if you do not forgive others, neither will your Father forgive your transgressions" (Matt. 6:14–15). And to clean up that mess we do against our Christic Spirit, Jesus taught us to frequently recite his own prayer in which he added, "Forgive us our sins for we ourselves forgive everyone in debt to us" (Luke 11:4).

I have read in an article published online, Politics (7-29-17), an unforgiving but retaliating words of a leader, who even claims as a staunch follower of Christ, who proclaimed his philosophy of how we should behave when it comes to being publicly attacked: "Get even with people. If they screw you, screw them back 10 times as hard. I really believe it." Undebatably, there exist many leaders in the society, even inside Christianity, identifying themselves that way in public. Our Master Jesus expects all his discipled leaders, keeping in mind the eternal mercy of God as the loving Father, to forgive and condone the evils others effect upon us through their sinful words and actions, to wait and endure patiently as our Father in heaven waits mercifully for the return of his and our enemies. As a loving God, he desires the salvation of all people, and certainly as a just God, in his time, he will condemn those who reject him. This is the truth Jesus exposed in his parable of "the weeds among the wheat." Permitting the evildoers (weeds) grow and move with the committed disciples (wheat), at the end of the day, which Jesus called "the harvest time," God would say to the heavenly harvesters, "First collect the weeds and tie them in bundles for burning; but gather the wheat into my barn" (Ref. Matt. 13:24–30).

Abbot St. Columban's prayer of love, found in one of his instructions, should become one of the daily prayers of all the discipled leaders: "Loving Savior, be pleased to show yourself to us who knock, so that in knowing you we may love only you, love you alone, desire you alone . . . Inspire in us the depth of love that is fitting for you to receive as God. So may your love pervade our whole being, possess us completely, and fill all our senses, that we may know no other love but love for you who are everlasting."

CHAPTER 9: BE CONSECRATED IN SPIRIT AND IN TRUTH

CON-SEGREGATED TO BE HOLY

The English verb "consecrate" is one of the translations of the Hebrew word "qadash" and the Greek word "hagiasmos." It has also some more synonymic words like sanctify, be holy, be saintly, and being set apart. A consecrated life to the Lord means to become totally as God's possession. Look at the vessels and other clothes we use at the altar. All are consecrated and dedicated to God for the sole purpose of using for God and by God. This means they become God's properties. Everything should be used according to his will.

In Jesus's discipleship program, the process of "being consecrated" is one of the pivotal concerns in accomplishing all the discipleship roles. This is why he begged his Father to consecrate his disciples as he himself was consecrated (John 17:17–19). Jesus had been growing in a culture where people were formed in the Mosaic law that God, who created the humans, is the Holy One and every human being, being formed in God's likeness and image, is blessed and obliged by God's utter holiness. Holiness is in God, and only from God can it pass to us, the crown of his creation. We are made in the image and likeness of God, and God's holiness, his "total otherness," is imprinted on each one of us. Human beings become vehicles and instruments of God's holiness for the world.

Therefore, in the Old Covenant, every human life is esteemed holy, sacrosanct, and inviolable. In particular, those persons like kings, prophets, and Levites, who have been delegated with the duties of serving people as God's proxies both inside and outside of the holy of holies, must be consecrated, namely, being separated from all evils. God shouts out in the Book of Leviticus, "I, the Lord, am your God. You shall make and keep yourselves holy, because I am holy" (Lev. 11:44a). God repeats the same in the OT so many times to make us understand how much he is longing for his people being consecrated. When God orders us, "Be holy because I am holy," he emphasizes that his holiness constitutes an essential imperative for the humans' moral behavior. This loaded statement describes best the vocation of every man and woman who is aspiring to be a discipled leader.

CONSECRATION OF INTERIOR SPIRIT

Holiness is a truth that pervades not only the whole of the Old Covenant but also the new one. Master Jesus testified it in his entire life, plus in his teaching and preaching. We know well enough, through his famous "Sermon on the Mount" (Matt. 5–7), how our Master's new definition of holiness was one of the bones of contention between Jesus and the Jewish religious leaders of his time. Advising us, "I tell you, unless your righteousness surpasses that of the scribes and Pharisees, you will not enter into the kingdom of heaven" (Matt. 5:20), he distinguished between the pharisaical teaching of holiness as "righteousness" and his enhanced doctrine of holiness as well-balanced consecration to God.

What we should understand from our Master's demand of righteousness is our first priority in our discipled leadership is to be a disciple more interiorly than exteriorly. Let me explain myself a little more. We know well that in Jesus's time, all the Pharisees, Sadducees, and most Jewish were meticulous in observing every bit of the Ten Commandments. They dressed wearing numerous images of their religion, including phylacteries, or miniature lists of the Ten Commandments hung from their headbands so that whenever they turned their head, they would fulfill the law: keep these commandments always before your eyes. They fasted. They said loud prayers for all to hear.

Unfortunately, they performed all those observances externally to give a good impression to the public. For Jesus, just to keep the law externally was not enough. He knew the hypocritical approach of the Jews of his time toward the observation of the commandments. He disliked completely their double-standard dealings in their religious life. Therefore, he said that his followers had to be holier than these holy Pharisees.

Jesus wanted his disciples to preserve a sincere spirit of consecrated love as the foundation of all their religious observances and obedience to moral commandments. To keep the law without such love is like having a body without a soul. Literally, to keep the law of God and of the church is not the same as being a good disciple of Jesus. Jesus advises that our external actions must be a reflection of what we really are like. If what we do is not a reflection of who we are, then we are hypocrites. It is not enough for others to see us performing the actions of Christians; rather, our whole attitude in life must be Christian.

INTRINSIC CONNECTION BETWEEN INTERIORITY AND EXTERIORITY

In the lives of disciples, both the exteriority and interiority of life must go hand in hand. Observing the Ten Commandments is for our social salvation through which we live a peaceful, healthy, and happy social life. Let's be very clear in this: Never any external observances will be the source of our personal salvation. It's only through consecrating ourselves totally to the holy of holies, the Supreme Spiritual Being, and changing and enhancing our attitudes individually that will take us to heaven.

Moreover, according to Jesus, a mere consecration of earthly goods and properties, animals, and humans, being set apart exclusively to God's worship and his temple use, would not be pleasing the Creator as much as the hearts and minds of the discipled persons in the Kingdom of God. This is why in many occasions in his life, he has detailed his longing for his disciples being holy as his Father, being sanctified by his Spirit, and being separated totally for the sake of his Gospel truth. We hear this more splendidly in his conversation with a Samaritan woman (John 4:23–24), when he plainly revealed one of his dreams about his followers and their performances in his discipleship.

He said, "The hour is coming, and is now here, when true worshipers will worship the Father in Spirit and truth; and indeed the Father seeks such people to worship him. God is Spirit, and those who worship him must worship in Spirit and truth." Undoubtedly, when Jesus mentioned about the worshippers and their ritual performances, he referred also the entire religious responsibilities of his disciples, such as spiritual exercises, sacramental acts, ritual practices, and all their good works for others, which include their discipled leadership. Anything we perform in the name of our Master must be done only in Spirit and in truth.

Following the holy footsteps of the Master, Paul, introducing his general instructions on Christian moral behavior, writes, "This is the will of God, your holiness: that you refrain from immorality." He continues then a detailed explanation of how that holy morality should be, especially in regard to immorality of lust and unjust exploitation of one's neighbors. He too separates all such discipled Christians from other Gentiles, confirming his statement: "For God did not call us to impurity but to holiness" (1 Thess. 4:3–8). Apostle Peter echoes the same mind setup of the Master when he writes to his first Christians, "Like obedient children, do not act in compliance with the desires of your former ignorance but, as he who called you is holy, be holy yourselves in every aspect of your conduct, for it is written, 'Be holy because I am holy'" (1 Pet. 1:14–16).

THE FOREFRONT LEADERS IN CHURCH'S UNIVERSAL CALL TO HOLINESS

Thus, Jesus's command of all his disciples being consecrated in Spirit and in truth continues to be followed strictly in the entire tradition and mission of his church throughout history. In the Vat. II Dogmatic Constitution on the Church, "Lumen Gentium," we read the clear traditional teaching of the church on the universal call to holiness: "[A]ll the faithful of Christ of whatever rank or status, are called to the fullness of the Christian life and to the perfection of charity; . . . They must follow in His footsteps and conform themselves to His image seeking the will of the Father in all things. They must devote themselves with all their being to the glory of God and the service of their neighbor" (5). Accentuating this church's holding, Pope John Paul II, in his apostolic letter "Novo Millennio Ineunte" at the close of the Great Jubilee of the Year 2000, invited all "to place pastoral planning under the heading of holiness," to express "the conviction that, since baptism is a true entry into the holiness of God through incorporation into Christ and the indwelling of his Spirit, it would be a contradiction to settle for a life of mediocrity, marked by a minimalist ethic and a shallow religiosity . . . The time has come to re-propose wholeheartedly to everyone this high standard of ordinary Christian living: the whole life of the Christian community and of Christian families must lead in this direction" (No. 31).

Pope Francis reiterated the same call of Jesus to all his discipled persons, especially the leaders of the communities, at a General Audience on November 19, 2014. He is quoted saying, "Holiness is not the prerogative of only a few: holiness is a gift that is offered to all, without exception, so that it constitutes the distinctive character of every Christian . . . Some people think that holiness is closing your eyes and putting on a pious face . . . No! . . . When the Lord calls us to be saints, he does not call us to something hard or sad . . . Not at all! It is an invitation to share His joy, to live and offer every moment of our lives with joy, at the same time making it a gift of love for the people around us." He too added, "The universal call to holiness is rooted in *baptism*, which configures a person to Jesus Christ who is God and man, thus uniting a person with the Second Person of the *Blessed Trinity*, bringing him in communion with intra-Trinitarian life."

BE POSSESSED BY THE HOLY SPIRIT

We read in the Bible all the leaders chosen by God had been consecrated in God's Spirit. He expected of them to be always living and moving in his Spirit. Otherwise, he proved they turned out to be prey to bad spirit. As in every age, humans, lived in the OT time, longed to see and listen to such consecrated souls in their midst and get their exhortations and directions to live a peaceful and fruitful life in this world. God too was fulfilling their desires by consecrating some of his chosen ones in his Spirit and sent them to his people. Except a few, most of God's consecrated leaders were genuine sources and tools in the hands of the Creator to preserve his people intact in their obedience to him. When those consecrated leaders breached out of his hands, he punished them by allowing evil spirit possessing them. In the life of King Saul, we see many references to this fact. Though Saul was the first king being anointed in God's Spirit, many times, he lost the sacred aroma of his consecrated anointing by his whimsical and undisciplined behavior: "The spirit of the Lord had departed from Saul, and he was tormented by an evil spirit from the Lord" (1 Sam. 16:14).

King David too acknowledges this spiritual encounter with the bad spirit (Psalm 51). He honestly confesses his terrible sins committed against God's will: "For I know my transgressions; my sin is always before me. Against you, you alone have I sinned; I have done what is evil in your eyes." Being aware of his loss of "God's Spirit" because of sin, he pleads with God to renew his original status of holiness: "Turn away your face from my sins; blot out all my iniquities. A clean heart create for me, God; renew within me a steadfast spirit. Do not drive me from before your face, nor take from me your holy spirit."

Following the footsteps of responsible leaders in the past who have been committed to their Master, we see John the Baptizer as not only a master of many of Jesus's first disciples but also a precursor and forerunner and in a way a role model to Jesus himself. John was a truly consecrated soul as God foretold of him to his father through an angel: "He will be great in the sight of the Lord . . . He will be filled with the holy Spirit even from his mother's womb, and he will turn many of the children of Israel to the Lord their God. He will go before him in the spirit and power of Elijah to turn the hearts of fathers toward children and the disobedient to the understanding of the righteous, to prepare a people fit for the Lord" (Luke 1:15–17).

In keeping with God's prophecies regarding his consecrated leaders and as John and other OT leaders, Jesus our Master fully abided to his Father's design and hope of his leadership. From the day of his conception, we notice God was generously and intensely anointing him with his Spirit. All prophecies were ultimately fulfilled in Jesus Christ, the perfectly consecrated One, who makes our own consecration possible. He was willingly undergoing the realistic baptism of blood and the Spirit-empowered consecration of sacrificing his very life for others. Jesus himself testified that the anointing of the Spirit that he has is not for him alone but also for us: "The Spirit of the Lord is upon me because He has anointed me to bring glad tidings to the poor. He has sent me to proclaim liberty to captives and recovery of sight to the blind, to let the oppressed go free and to proclaim a year acceptable to the Lord" (Luke 4:18).

Master Jesus, like himself, expected his discipled leaders to be consecrated in Spirit. As Peter taught the pagan Cornelius that "God shows no partiality" but offers this Spirit of consecration to all people because of Jesus Christ, if we beg God through Jesus in humility, honesty, and sincerity of purpose, he will certainly bestow his Spirit. Jesus Christ is the consecrated one par excellence, and that is why we are irresistibly drawn to him, and he alone is gifted to satisfy the deepest desires of our hearts. The more we belong to God and are consecrated to him, the more we become the visible signs to the others, and they will come to us searching for God's presence, action, and love in us.

Undoubtedly, we too are consecrated to God in Jesus Christ, and we too share in this same Spirit of consecration from the moment that we received the gift of faith in Holy Baptism. No matter the intensity of our pains and sufferings in this life or the gravity and number of our sins, nothing can take away from us this reality of being consecrated to God by the gift of the Spirit. We must let nothing take away from us the faith in this consecration, this sense of knowing that we and all, that we are and have, belong to God.

At the same time, we should know that our Christian life becomes qualified as consecrated or holy, not just because we undergo the sacramental ablution and consecration at baptism and confirmation. They are only signs and symbols of our lowering our fake self deep down to the Sheol of sufferings, sacrifices, and finally death in any kind as our Lord underwent. With mere human spirit, as Paul repeatedly exhorts us, we cannot move even a single step in our leadership undertakings. Exhorting his "discipled leader" Timothy to be attending to this profound issue of "being consecrated in the Spirit" in his leading roles, Paul writes, "I remind you to stir into flame the gift of God that you have through the imposition of my hands. For God did not give us a spirit of cowardice but rather of power and love and self-control. So do not be ashamed of your testimony to our Lord, nor of me, a prisoner for his sake; but bear your share of hardship for the gospel with the strength that comes from God" (2 Tim. 1:6–8). This exhortation indicates that the fact of our human spirit stays good and holy and powerful depends largely on how we live and move in and with the consecration done in the Spirit. If not, as we mentioned earlier, like King Saul, we can very easily become prey to evil spirit.

BE CONSECRATED IN TRUTH

At the Last Supper, we hear Jesus ambitiously praying to his Father, not ambiguously but crystal clearly. He meant that we too must be consecrated in the kind of truth, which is absolute as it is found both in the Scriptures and tradition. Since it is crucial but hard to be always attuned to such absolute and realistic truth, Jesus made a special prayer for this consecration of ours in the truth: "Consecrate them in the truth. Your word is truth. As you sent me into the world, so I sent them into the world. And I consecrate myself for them, so that they also may be consecrated in truth" (John 17:17–19).

WHAT IS TRUTH?

Jesus Christ identified himself as "'the Truth," saying, "I am the way and the truth and the life. No one comes to the Father except through me" (John 14:6). He too is quoted saying to those who believed and followed him, "If you remain in my word, you will truly be my disciples, and you will know the truth, and the truth will set you free" (John 8:31–32). Even at the horrible and cruel moment of his final hours in front of the Pilate, he asserted his identity and mission of truth: "For this I was born and for this I came into the world, to testify to the truth. Everyone who belongs to the truth listens to my voice" (John 18:37).

Either out of ignorance or pride and superiority complex, we hear the governor responding to Jesus with a question: "What is the 'truth'?" This might be in a sarcastic way or with some suspicion and doubt, but today the same question surely arises in the hearts of every person who desires to follow Jesus. "What does the Master Jesus mean by 'the truth'?" By analyzing the entire Scriptures, especially the NT books, we can sum up the meaning of the truth under three important factors:

The first dimension of the "truth" is that every human being is a sinner, offending God and his goodness, disobeying his commandments, and because of their sins, they undergo so many maladies, pains, and sufferings and lead unwanted, unpleasant, and unfair lives.

The second dimension of the "truth" is that the love and mercy of God presented itself in the form of the Cross and death of Jesus. The death of Jesus Christ is the performance in history of the very mind of God. There is no room for looking on Jesus Christ as a martyr. His death was not something that happened to him that might have been prevented. His death was the very reason why he came. If God does forgive our sins, it is because of the death of Christ. God could forgive us in no other way than by the death of his Son, and Jesus is exalted to be the Savior because of his death.

The third dimension of the "truth" is that all who hold Jesus as their Savior in that way turn out to be his citizens, and he becomes the Lord and King to them. This means even though I walk through the dusty and muddy road of earthly life, because of Jesus's death, I am cleansed from my sins; if I die the same death as his, namely, denying, detaching, and even losing my worldly and earthly pleasures and possessions, I am chosen to be his soldier, bodyguard, courtier, and even ambassador in my own territory. One thing is certain: the more I am consecrated in the triple truth, the clearer I can listen to Jesus. That is what he prophesied: "Everyone who belongs to the truth listens to my voice." He too emphasized that such consecration to the truth will set us free.

HUMAN DUALITY IS A MYSTERIOUS TRUTH

There is one more meaning to the demand of Jesus about his disciples being consecrated in truth. Members who belong to Jesus's Kingdom in this world are very human who constitute both soul and body, spiritual and physical, earthly and heavenly. This dichotomy of human existence is the reality of human creatures. A makeup of two elements is the truthful fact of humanness. So if we choose the one element and ignore the other in our dealing with humans, we are untruthful. Jesus emphasizes this fact, particularly in performing our religious observances, when he told the Samaritan woman that "the hour is coming, and is now here, when true worshipers will worship the Father in Spirit and truth; and indeed the Father seeks such people to worship him" (John 4:23).

When the discipled leaders lead or participate in any Christian worship, this truthful soul-and-body factor must be attended to, hence the necessity of rituals, which include involvement of all human senses, all human kinetic communications, and all aesthetic and artistic creativities. Humans, unquestionably, can worship God through meditation and recollection; they can also go so far as encountering mystic intimacy in Spirit; however, as God commanded us, we have to love our God with all our heart, with all our mind, with all our strength, and with all our being. He demanded from us a total and holistic worship.

Besides, Jesus Christ encouraged us to be together in prayer and worship as a family. It is there, he told us, he would be present, and he would grand whatever we request him. The church takes this wish of Jesus seriously and makes us gather together as one body, one community of disciples in a liturgical environment during which we sing, dance, kneel and stand, raise, and hold our hands together. We, the discipled leaders of Jesus, make sure that we don't participate in any liturgical services like immovable stone or dead cadaver but take strenuous efforts to involve both our soul and body in living, rejoicing, and communing with God and our neighbors.

HUMAN BODY IS TO BE THE AGENT OF TRUTH-FILLED CONSECRATION

When Jesus came into this world as human being, his heartbeat clamorously shouted to his Father: "Sacrifice and offering you did not desire, but a body you prepared for me . . . By this 'will,' we have been consecrated through the offering of the body of Jesus Christ once for all" (Heb. 10:5–10). By the merciful work of God's consecrating us by many miraculous ways, especially through his Son, his sole intention was to prepare us for his use by actually making us holy. We already said, as we are made of both body and soul, in his consecrating time, we firmly believe that he has prepared both our body and soul for being used in leadership ministry.

Nonetheless, what God does his work of consecration within us and outside of us remains half until we play our role in to complete it according to his will. It means truthfully, a complete consecration involves separating ourselves from evil by continually working with our heart so that we stay put to the presence of God and that we drink from the living waters that flow from Jesus the Master. This is, in truth, a practical, consecrated, holy living. While God will do his part, we just have to do ours. Practical holiness and the cleansing of God for holy use cannot be separated. One without the other is not possible.

The second part of our bodily consecration in truth is the most practical but hardest one. It would demand hardships and pains to complete it as Jesus paid for his own consecration. The author of the letter to the Hebrews writes about the secret connection existing between the Master Jesus and his followers: "He who consecrates and those who are being consecrated all have one origin. Therefore, he is not ashamed to call them 'brothers'" (Heb. 2:11). In other words, he calls all disciples of Jesus as consecrated ones as our Master Jesus. Paul and Peter, many times in their letters, announced that our Christian call is to be holy and consecrated to the Lord. Interestingly, the same author of the letter to the Hebrews points out the one and only way to get ourselves consecrated in the Lord is to follow Jesus's footsteps of love and truth for which we have to meet untold sufferings and sacrifices as he was. Indeed, the truth always hurts but, at the end, liberates us to unlimited joy and success.

As a lamp, even if it is consecrated outwardly or potentially by God and his representatives, it cannot give light without oil. Look at the sanctuary lamps. To shine at the altar, they need to be fed; though no rough winds blow upon them, they require to be trimmed. According to age-old church tradition, the oil to be used in the sacred lamps should be the best olive oil. However, there are some who use petroleum, produce of fish, or the extracted oils from nuts, thinking after all, we need light burning at the altar at all cost. With the same twisted attitude, there are many among us who consider the grace of light from disciples can be attained by mere natural earthly resources. But they are completely wrong. They only end in producing a sort of "pretended grace" from natural goodness, "fancied grace" from priestly hands, or "imaginary grace" from outward ceremonies. All consecrated leaders in Jesus's Kingdom should be filled with the holy oil we receive from the Spirit of Jesus. Then only we can stand near the holy of holies as well as walking in company with Jesus in the society as light bearers with the sacred beams of truth, holiness, joy, knowledge, and love.

JESUS'S PRAYERFUL DREAM ABOUT TRUTHFUL LEADERS

Quoting the words of Jesus at the Last Supper, "Consecrate them in the truth," Pope Francis rightly said in his homily during Mass at Quito's Bicentennial Park, Quito, on July 7, 2015 (ZENIT.org), "Jesus' dream can be realized because he has consecrated us. The spiritual life of an evangelizer is born of this profound truth, which should not be confused with a few comforting religious exercises. Jesus consecrates us so that we can encounter him personally. And this encounter leads us in turn to encounter others, to become involved with our world and to develop a passion for evangelization."

If we, the discipled leaders, are living and breathing the Truth, we will not act cowardly in front of any opposition or any kind of biased remarks from others. We will declare fully and fearlessly the Truth, nothing but the Truth, as Jesus did before the governor Pilate: "Can any of you charge me with sin? If I am telling the truth, why do you not believe me? Whoever belongs to God hears the words of God; for this reason you do not listen, because you do not belong to God" (John 8:46–47). In Paul's words, we are indeed charged with this "noble confession" of the Truth (1 Tim. 6:13). Besides, living "the truth in love," we would grow in every way into him who is the head, Christ (Eph. 4:15).

LEADERSHIP COMMITTED TO THE TRUTH, NOTHING BUT THE TRUTH

All great leaders at the laying down of authority articulate their plans for the future continuation of their mission or work through a speech or written communication. Sadly, most of the leaders, political and religious as well, have failed in their promises and still do the same. God knows the limitation of humans in handling properly the authority shared by him. Hence, through his revealed words, especially his Son, he offers some guidelines on how to apply our God-given power and execute it as he wants.

First, the Lord tells us we should always speak only what the "true God" commands us to speak: "If a prophet presumes to speak in my name an oracle that I have not commanded him to speak, or speaks in the name of other gods, he shall die." In other words, we, in our executing power of ordering or disciplining, must speak the balanced truth as God proposes to us and never rely on human authorities or power centers' influences. Listen to Jesus's words; they were not empty words. They had power because he made the wavelength between himself and his Father intimate. That is how his words got powerful and forceful.

Second, as Jesus, we should deliver our authoritarian speech or deed being accompanied with deeds of exemplary life and deeds of healing others and surely concentration on targeting to cast out evil spirits from others. "All were amazed and asked one another, 'What is this?' A new teaching with authority. He commands even the unclean spirits and they obey him." Unless and until we are attuned to the good Spirit of God, we can never discern the difference between good and unclean spirits.

Third, before exercising our authority or power on others, we must make sure our hearts are not hardened as hardheaded and hard-hearted people possess. We should listen to the inner voice of God as the Psalmist sings: "If today you hear his voice, harden not your hearts." The religion we personally follow must be one of "real religion" and not a fake one. This means our words and deeds, our inside and out, must be well integrated in truth. We should be never pharisaical in performing the religious duties of praying, almsgiving, and fasting. This is what our Master taught us (Matt. 6:1–18). We should preach what we live, and we should live what we preach (Matt. 23:2–7).

Being consecrated by the Truth and living and leading others in the same Truth as our Master dreamed of, all of us certainly find it hard to cope with this primary requirement. Knowing well of our human limitations, our Master promised to send his Spirit of truth to us who will guide us to all truth (John 16:13a). The One whom he sent will empower us, enlighten us, and accompany us in living out the demand of Jesus and leading others in Truth. Disciples like St. Polycarp not only wrote about such truthful behavior but also lived up to it. He wrote in his letter to the Philippians, praying for them, "May God the Father of our Lord Jesus Christ and the eternal high priest himself, the Son of God, Jesus Christ, build you up in faith and in truth." This should be the daily prayer of all discipled leaders for themselves and for their people.

TRANSPARENT LEADERSHIP

"Human but divine" and "Holy but sinful"—these are some of the paradoxical identities told of every disciple and surely of the church. I don't have any qualms about them. The inevitable duality exists in anybody or anything we produce and handle in this world. However, when we begin to dig into the admonition of the Master that we must be consecrated in Truth, there seems a discrepancy between his way and our way. As St. John writes in his letter (1 John 1:5–10), professing that we have fellowship with God who is light, if we still walk in darkness of sins, we lie and do not act in truth. Integrity, authenticity, and openness is the triple norm for any fellowship, be it with God or with fellow human beings. Because we are called to be holy, and because we are on the process of holiness, we should never hide any of our faults and imperfections in our dealings in the society.

We should not be masquerading our dark side with the put-on show. Pretending we are holy people while honestly we are not is the bad fruit of pride. Since it would be brutally

wounded by transparency, our proud self tries to hide our
imperfections at all costs. Our human reality is 100 percent
imperfectly perfect. For such transparent acceptance, the
virtue of humility is needed. That is why our Master insisted
all of us to be meek and humble in spirit. This is the only way
to be consecrated in Truth.

In the same vein, the church, being a community of
human disciples of Jesus, has to be humble enough to
recognize her holiness being desecrated by the imperfections
and sins of her members. Especially when her leaders are the
cause of such desecration, all the more, public transparent
confession, plus repentance, is called for. As some people hold
that this sort of transparency may destroy the identity of the
church, we can never support their assessment. God is her
Spouse; his Spirit purifies, shapes, molds, fills, and adorns her
when she is genuinely truthful, humble, and contrite.

According to Christian ethics based on God's
commandments and the light of Christ, "lying" in any
form is a sin. God's archenemy, the devil, is called the liar.
The act of lying is something we say or do to destroy not
only our neighbors' life but also their good name. Cheating
others deceptively is also a sinful act of lying. In addition,
we disagree with some old religious and moral admonition
in some cultures that points out that when we lie for the
sake of some ultimate good, it is not a sin. Discussing about
the catechism of St. Augustine on lying, Julia Fleming,
a professor of ethics at Creighton University in Omaha,
Nebraska, underscores that "Augustine condemns lying
under all circumstances. He sees lying as a violation against
God, who is truth. Human beings are to choose God above
all things, including our physical survival or other desirable
things." This means the ends do not justify the means. And
even lies that could save lives are considered by Augustine
"morally wrong."

We uphold about the nature of lying that just because everybody's doing it doesn't make it right and that a lie does not become truth when it is repeated by many in the social media. This morally wrong act of lying effects more serious results particularly when it is done by leaders of social institutions such as church leaders and so on. Even when, for the sake of the age-old notion of preserving the church's dignity and glory intact, our leaders in the church either hide or are silent regarding certain malefactors or abuses occurring continuously especially inside the church, they are morally wrong and going against the Truth with which they are consecrated. "Hiding oneself under the cover of diplomacy" is totally an untruthful behavior, taken for granted in organizational managements. This sort of "hide and seek" power game played under "holy diplomacy" has been contaminating the genuine identity of the church for centuries.

The same church of "discipled leaders" of Christ in the prompting of the Holy Spirit has been never tired of teaching that civil leaders must provide accurate information, which means ethically transparent and truthful in their communications to the public (Ref. Inter Mirifica, Vat. II Decree on the Media of Social Communications). This spirit of truth-based communications is to be witnessed more in the church leadership's words and actions for the very fact the church is the body of Christ, the Eternal Truth.

REPENT AND REPAIR ARE THE NEEDS OF THE DAY

The most urgent need in today's evangelical ministry of the church is that all church leaders, if they are truly the discipled leaders of Jesus, first, should begin to conduct themselves truthful to their call and commitment to their Master. Second, they should perform immediately two painstaking tasks: "repent and repair." As the new *Catechism of the Catholic Church* (#2487) cites, discipled leaders make reparations for their past behavior of lying and masquerading either through direct compensation or moral satisfaction in the name of charity. Plus, joining together in one heart and one mind, they should make an immediate move—visibly, audibly, and sincerely—of clearing up the mess of diplomatic untruthfulness in the entire church system and in their own individual leadership schemes. Consequently, as our Master dreamed, his church of today will stand on the hilltop as the beacon of the Truth who is still alive spiritually among us. Becoming and behaving as a credible and honest "Truth teller" in the midst of "fake news" is indeed a risky task.

The holiness of the church consists largely in the way she deals with her earthly roles of leadership. If such a mind setup is being possessed by every discipled leaders, certainly, that Truth will liberate us, and with its unflinching power, the same Truth will make us win in every task of our evangelical leadership ministries.

CHAPTER 10: BE A PRAYING PERSON

QUALITY PRAYER FOR QUALITY LIFE

We are taught by Jesus and his apostles to pray "ceaselessly," to pray "secretly" (Matt. 6:6), not to pray "babblingly" (Matt. 6:7), to pray "jubilantly" (Luke 10:20), to pray in "Jesus' Name" (John 16:23), and unquestionably, to pray "faithfully, hopefully and forgivingly" (Matt. 7:7–11, 6:14–15). Collecting all gleanings about prayer found in the Scriptures, we can conclude our Master expects all his discipled leaders to be perpetually praying persons inside and out.

The primary reason for such hardest demand is, as we described earlier, we, by ourselves, cannot fulfill all his demands of discipleship. In our plan of walking with Jesus as his disciples, we are fully aware of our inability to cope with all his demands. Jesus knew it well, and therefore, he offered us a support in our journey of discipleship. That is called prayer through which he hears the outcry of the poor and the fragile disciples who are longing to stay in his company. Hence, he wants every one of his followers to be a "praying person." There is no doubt about it; otherwise, we would not be his genuine disciples. We need continuous support from his Spirit of power, wisdom, and love. The act of praying is the most efficacious tool for gaining this heavenly spiritual support.

Sadly, not all prayer efforts reap the expected results. Most of us definitely pray at various times, in various occasions, and in various ways. In our "prayer time," we usually adore the Lord as our only God; we sometimes spell out to him what kind of God we worship. Whatever name we give him, we want to make sure we are present in front of him. We include in prayer many praises and thanks for his greatness, fidelity, and goodness. We express to him our weakness and mistakes and ask his forgiveness. In addition, we list out many petitions and intercessions to him. Some of us take seriously this prayer as their duty or as their daily need. Most of us take this as an extracurricular activity or as an appendix to the main humdrum affairs of earthly life. So many pray before they go to accomplish a certain serious and important job. Others pray only when bad and evil things occur as death, accident, separation, and deception. Because of such anomaly, faking, frustration, and silliness found in the countless uses of prayer, many among us have drifted away from any kind of prayer efforts. Also, some of us are feeling desperate that many of our prayer efforts become barren.

PRAY INSIDE DEVOTEDLY

Our Master desires his discipled leaders uphold a quality prayer for quality discipled leadership. His point is this: Whatever be our aim, style, mode, and kind of prayer, it must possess an important ingredient, which is called chutzpah.

Jesus expounded this core nucleus in our prayer efforts through his very life, plus by his parables, in particular, that of the "widow and the judge" (Luke 18:1–8). That hardheaded lady with all her strong formidable faith was disturbing or pestering the judge to get her settlement. Surprisingly, our Master requires from us this seemingly weird attitude of the widow and orders us to follow her footsteps in our prayer efforts. This widow's faith, which is a simple but strong faith in God as our Sovereign, our Designer, our Creator, our Provider, and our Abba Father, should be the basic and starting point for our prayer efforts.

Another dimension of Jesus's "chutzpah" includes our strong conviction about the power of prayer. In Sirach 35:17–18, we read, "The prayer of the lowly pierces the clouds; it does not rest till it reaches its goal, nor will it withdraw till the most high responds, judges justly and affirms the right." Prayer is so powerful that Jesus always resorted to prayer in his busy schedule. Knowing the important role prayer plays in his disciples' lives, he advised them, saying, "Ask it shall be given to you; seek and you will find; knock and the door will be opened to you. For every one who asks, receives; and the one who seeks, finds; and to the one who knocks, the door will be opened" (Matt. 7:7–8). Also, "Therefore I tell you, all that you ask for in my prayer, believe that you will receive it and it will be yours" (Mark 11:24). As Theophan the Recluse, a spiritual writer, wrote many years ago about prayer, "Prayer is the test of everything; prayer is the source of everything; prayer is the dividing force of everything; prayer is the director of everything. If prayer is right everything is right. For, prayer will not allow anything go wrong."

PRAY CEASELESSLY

In addition to this remarkable "faith," Jesus advises us to hold on to an attitude of perseverance in our prayer efforts. Frequently, Jesus emphasizes that we should pray with persistent faith. He wants that we must be persistent and constant in praying. He speaks about the necessity to pray always without becoming weary. This is what Paul means when he writes in one of his letters, "Pray unceasingly."

Many may have this question: "How to pray unceasingly?" If praying unceasingly means endlessly reciting prayers on our knees, we are in big trouble. However, if praying unceasingly means living, breathing, walking, interacting, laughing, and loving in a constant spirit of prayer, then this is achievable. And this is what the Spirit of the Master contends. Perseverance is the basics for the victory of Jesus's disciples in their process of becoming most worthy disciples.

In Jesus's life too, we see the same persistent prayer. He never ceased praying. He prayed day in, day out. He was praying alone, in a group, with the crowd, in the temple, in synagogues, and finally, on the Cross too. He was praying that his Father's rule must come and reign the whole universe. At the same time, he was busy with his daily schedule of family and other works as carpenter for thirty years. Later, moving around Palestine accomplished wonders for three years. He was found in the street corners, in the temple precincts, in meadows, on mountaintops, on the boat, and even on the Cross and inside the tomb. On one line, he was dealing with God intimately in a persevering prayer, and on another line, he was performing all his daily works in sweat and blood.

Victory in life can never go to the hands of people who are quitters and lazy bones. Here, we are talking about our total victory, winning this world and the world to come. The only possible way to succeed is to persevere and put our hard labor both on our human efforts and in prayer efforts. It is very true that most of our prayers are unanswered and remain in waiting list before the Lord. I think the only reason for failure in our prayer is on our side. Either we are not persevering in prayer with our total relying on God or what we ask is not in the plan of God.

I tell you, God considers most of our prayer efforts trash. Sometimes people who are timid, mentally sick, or have no backbone send us anonymous letters without signature or without "from" address. What do we do with it if we are smart enough? We simply do not read them, rather trash them or use it as our toilet tissue. The same way when our prayer is not signed with our violent, impudent, persevering, persistent, and consistent effort as Moses and the widow in Jesus's parable did, that prayer will be trashed by God. No wonder why Jesus said, "Ask, knock, and seek when you pray." Most of his sayings like this about prayer sound like nagging, begging, badgering, pleading, and cajoling.

GOD'S WORD IS THE BASIC SOURCE OF PRAYER

I know it is hard to survive in God's relationship without prayer, worse still, to persevere in prayer like this. This is why, as Paul writes to Timothy, we should largely support ourselves by the Word of God in the Bible and by the tradition handed down to us. Plus, as community of believers, we should help one another when we fail and lose heart in prayer. In the OT, we read about the typical "praying persons" such as the patriarchs, kings, judges, and prophets who became not only to Jesus but also to all his disciples as the best role models for our persistent prayer efforts.

For example is Moses who, according to the Bible, was the most loving person in the eyes of God among all human beings living in the world. From his life, we can dare to call him as the discipled leader of God's people. God entrusted to him the job of liberating and leading his people politically, socially, culturally, and spiritually. He offered him a wondrous staff as Harry Porter's magic stick and gave him power to do many miracles. Yet God wanted him to pray. Moses too prayed and petitioned in all times of needs and difficulties, and God granted his requests.

Nonetheless, once, even his devotional prayer didn't bring the exact result he was longing for. We read this in Exodus 17:8–13. While there was a horrible war going on down the hill, Moses, maintaining his persistent faith, climbed the mountain and prayed with his miraculous staff for the victory of Israelites over their enemies. Sadly, it didn't work. Moses never lost his heart. He persevered in prayer, lifting his hands. His style of praying may seem and sound funny and bizarre. Yet God granted finally a historical victory to his people because of Moses's perseverance in prayer. According to the

Bible, as long as Moses prayed persistently, God granted finally a historical victory to his people.

From Moses, we learn that no leader, however charismatic, can be self-reliant because no human leaders possess on their own the capability of leading others wisely and victoriously. Authentic leadership, especially regarding the spiritual mentoring that all of God's people need, begins in God. To that end, Moses gave himself over to God in prayer. Through this action, he acknowledged his utter reliance on God for the gifts and the grace he needed to be of good service to his people.

We have a common saying: "Tell me who your friend is or the book you read; I will tell you who you are." In the same vein, we too can say about our faith, "Tell me how you pray; I will tell you what kind of discipled leadership you hold." Take any saint or any holy person mentioned in the Bible. Their lives would tell us that they could not and did not achieve their aspirations to become worthy disciples till their death, but one thing is certain, and that is they were beloved sons and daughters in whom God was well pleased. God was pleased on what? Is it because they accomplished many things for Jesus? Or is it because they were with no interruption recited all possible prayers? No. The reason for God being pleased with them was that they persevered in prayer even in toughest times of their leading others.

FAITH-FILLED PERSEVERANCE IN PRAYER

Perseverance has got a lot to do in each one's life. Persistence and determination is the secret of success in any dimension of life and so in our spiritual life. A great Roman soldier named Sertorius served as a praetor in Spain in the first century BCE. He addressed his fellow recruits: "You see, fellow-soldiers, that perseverance is more prevailing than violence. Many things that cannot be overcome when they are together yield themselves up when taken little by little. Assiduity and persistence are irresistible and, in time, can overthrow the greatest powers." "Pray to God in the storm," urges a Danish proverb, "but keep on rowing!" Mahatma Gandhi has been credited with a similar piece of advice: "Spin carefully, spin prayerfully, leaving the thread with God."

Perseverance has been the basic element for the victory of Jesus's disciples in their process of becoming most worthy leaders. Their lives would tell us that they could not and did not achieve their aspirations to become worthy disciples till their death, but one thing is certain, they were beloved sons and daughters in whom God was well pleased. He was pleased not much on what they had accomplished for Jesus, nor on their "Guinness World Record" of reciting a thousand and one prayers with no interruption. The only reason for God being pleased with them was that they persevered in prayer and action.

About the role of perseverance in human life, Madam Swetchine, a Russian mystic, said, "There are two ways of attaining an important end—force and perseverance. Force falls to the lot of the privileged few, but austere and sustained perseverance can be practiced by the most insignificant. Its silent power grows irresistible with time." Victory, defeat, failure, success—all these are part of human lives. Prayer is not something that interferes the plan of God and changes God and his will. Rather, our prayer of perseverance indicates that our hearts are melted, open for God's grace, and ready to cope with whatever his will has designed for us. Let us remember what Jesus says today at the end of the Gospel: "When the Son of Man comes, will he find faith on earth?"

PRAY OUTSIDE TRIUMPHANTLY

As discipled leaders of Jesus, along with praying inside, privately with chutzpah and perseverance, we should also pray outside—I say triumphantly. Let me explain myself. At this moment, I do remember what the Master has cautioned us regarding the "showoff" praying habits of the Pharisees: "When you pray, do not be like the hypocrites . . . But when you pray, go to your inner room, close the door, and pray to your Father in secret. And your Father who sees in secret will repay you (Matt. 6:5–6). As biblical scholars have interpreted, Jesus's admonition to us is that we should always possess an integrated purity of intention. Whether we pray inside or out, our main attention is focused on the Almighty Creator and his beloved Son's Spirit.

We must know our Master never refuted or discouraged us in praying outside. Rather, as he himself did, he wanted us to pray out ritually, musically, liturgically, and in any other cultural forms. All for what? First, praying outside is a proclamation of what the leaders have heard from their Master in their inside prayer time. "What I say to you in the darkness, speak in the light; what you hear whispered, proclaim on the housetops" (Matt. 10:27). Second, when we pray together in group or assembly, our Master promised his presence would be full. "For where two or three are gathered together in my name, there am I in the midst of them" (Matt. 18:20).

Third, the honest act of praying outside bears testimony to our inner light, our spiritual joy, and our encounter of God's glory. "You are the light of the world. A city set on a mountain cannot be hidden. Nor do they light a lamp and then put it under a bushel basket; it is set on a lampstand, where it gives light to all in the house. Just so, your light must shine before others, that they may see your good deeds and glorify your heavenly Father" (Matt. 5:14–16).

The last but not the least, we hear Jesus emphasizing repeatedly that our outside prayer of praise and glory performed with "Alleluia spirit," especially during the hardest and toughest times of life, is the true witness to our glorification and complete joy benefitted from Jesus's resurrected Spirit: "Blessed are you when they insult you and persecute you and utter every kind of evil against you falsely because of me. Rejoice and be glad, for your reward will be great in heaven. Thus they persecuted the prophets who were before you" (Matt. 5:11–12). That is how Jesus, the apostles, and all Christian martyrs behaved and prayed outside joyfully and triumphantly while they were suffering for the sake of their Master: "After recalling the apostles, they had them flogged, ordered them to stop speaking in the name of Jesus, and dismissed them. So they left the presence of the Sanhedrin, rejoicing that they had been found worthy to suffer dishonor for the sake of the name" (Acts 5:40–41).

PRAYER AS A DOUBLE-EDGED SWORD

Being the discipled leaders in Jesus's team, we must pay full attention to the double-edged sword of Christian prayer. It must become our habit, our culture, and our very life. While we pray inside in private devotedly, lovingly, and intimately in the pure presence of the Master, we must never neglect the other side of prayer, praying outside triumphantly, joyfully, contently, and loudly with no blushing about it. We should never forget we are leaders and warriors for the people entrusted to us by God to win the spiritual battle, to strengthen the weak, and to consecrate the unholy through prayer. As one of the preachers writes, "Prayer does not fit us for the greater works; prayer is the greater work." In the mind of Jesus, prayer is the working of the miracle of redemption in every discipled leader, which produces the miracle of redemption in others by the power of God. Thus, we become role models in making our fellow Christians the true and effective "praying persons."

Indeed, there are some wonderful things happening inside every disciple's prayer: First of all, any kind of prayer, if it is addressed to the true God, expresses our human belonging to God, we show our leaning toward him in every step of our lives. We too indicate our longing for a better life, brighter tomorrow, and fuller life, namely, God himself. There is also another element hidden in our prayers, namely, we confess secretly our inability to handle and manage properly our own lives, and therefore, we request the support and help of the Big Boss.

The second thing that happens in prayer is we take one stronger step closer to God and heaven. This is what St. Augustine wrote about on prayer. He said, "Through prayer we make ourselves suitable to receive the greatest Gift God would be sharing with us. In prayer God makes our faith deeper, our hope stronger and our longing greater. Prayer enlarges our capacity to receive the Gift God has promised to us. 'No eye has seen it'; it has no color. No ear has heard it; it has no sound. It has not entered man's heart; man's heart must enter into it."

The third very important thing that happens when we pray is we silently begin to accept the Will of God in our lives. I recently read a commentary on this parable by Fr. Jude Winkler, who writes, "Do we change God's mind when we pray? A better way of describing the power of our prayer is that God trusts us so much that he invites us to join him in the decision-making process. It is not that God decides everything—or that we do. It is a union of the two (for God has called us to be his friends who assist him in his work for recreating this world in his image)."

As a final note to this chapter, I would like to quote Pope Francis's answer to a question asked by one of the priests during his visit to Southern Italian city of Caserta, about overcoming all the existential crises faced in Christian discipleship of witnessing: "As regards creativity, if a bishop who does not pray, a priest who does not pray, has closed the door to creativity." So let us continue to pray in whatever way our life situation invites us to do. Prayer is a wonderful support system God in Jesus offered to us for every discipled leader's victory.

CHAPTER 11: BE A DISCIPLINED DISCIPLE

The "discipling" in Jesus's Kingdom denotes the following of the discipline of the Master. He formulated and proclaimed his extraordinary code of discipline both by his life and teachings. Though we don't hear this code explicitly in the church circle, biblically and historically, we discover that the church had clearly defined boundaries within the structure of its organization and within the intangible fabric of the community of disciples. While the basic foundation of it grew from God's commandments, Jesus was sent by his Father to renovate and enhance the base with his "Gospel values" listed out throughout the NT books.

A WELL-DISCIPLINED RIGHTEOUSNESS

Jesus spelled out his demand from his "discipled leaders" that their life should be well-founded on his "discipline." It should be greater and more than what the scribes, Pharisees, and lawyers of his time followed. We hear him say in his Sermon on the Mount, "I tell you, unless your righteousness surpasses that of the scribes and Pharisees, you will not enter into the kingdom of heaven" (Matt. 5:20). In this book, the detailed version of Jesus's code of discipline is treated elaborately, mostly in the form of his demands. Therefore, in this chapter, let us discuss about the starting-up and post effect of Jesus's "discipline factors."

In the postmodern world, it is very difficult for most of us to continue listening on the exhortation, counseling, and guidance from another human like us. Admonishing sinners, instructing the uninformed, and counseling the doubtful are the hardest acts in this postmodern society. Recently, one of my friends asked about the difference between autobiography and biography; he knew both are about the lives of humans. But he didn't know about their publication deals. I explained to him the real difference. In our conversation, I commented that all of us born and grown in this world willy-nilly leave behind our death a living "bible" of our own. I too added that though all Christians have hold, read, and followed a "common Bible," all individually write our personal "bible" in which we fill in the events, words, anecdotes, experiences, and surely upholdings, values, and accomplishments relatively different from another individual's. Even though we don't publish our "bibles" as biographies or autobiographies, our posterity will inherit them either in blood, in memory, or in vogue and gossip.

DISCIPLINED JUDGMENT OVER OTHERS

This is the problem with the modern people. We know what our life is, what our weakness and strength is, what our worthiness and worthlessness is. We don't need anybody to come and impose their ideas, their values, and their judgments. We live in a culture of "I am OK, and you are OK" or "You may not be OK." As I hold the "bible" of my own values, others have their own personal "bible" of values. You respect my territory as I do yours. This sort of far-fetched "golden rule" empowers every modern mind. In this extreme utopian cultural environment, we would become most unpopular by living a life disciplined by our Master's values and by performing any sort of spiritual acts like admonishing, counseling, or instructing. Unquestionably, it is not stress-free to conduct ourselves in discipline. It takes a chivalrous attitude of faith, hope and charity, wisdom from God's Spirit.

If ever we plan to be a genuine disciple of Christ, we should first remove our proud and fake esteem of ourselves but adhere sincerely to three important tangible resources for growing in disciplined discipleship: Bible, sacraments, and guru. We can never survive in Christ's spirituality, only in Spirit. As we learned in the previous chapters, we need to act "in truth." I always consider the word "truth" Jesus used indicates not only the spiritual, inner, and invisible side of our life but also our truthful identity of humanness made of body and soul; we are little less than angel but dust and clay; and so on. This ontological truth about us must be considered in each and every act of our being. Nothing should be less nor more. This is why our sages and saints have advised us, besides holding on to spiritual sources of contemplation, meditation, ecstatic prayer in Spirit, to make recourse to visible, tangible, and appropriate resources outside of us: Bible, sacramental rituals, and reliable gurus close to the heart of the Master. Becoming a full-fledged disciple of Christ takes a lifetime disciplining oneself. Those three resources are a must in this lifelong effort.

DISCIPLINED HEARING ACCORDING TO THE SPIRIT'S PROMPTINGS

As one spiritual author and director writes, "You can become that person for others if you learn to really listen to the Holy Spirit in your own life first with the help of a spiritual director. Read the New Testament every day and listen to the Lord speaking to you there. Find a good spiritual director and listen to the Lord speaking to you through his or her wise counsel. Then, having learned to listen, you will be ready and able to listen deeply to others." We can find a good example of this in the lives of saints. We read about St. Faustina who, in her religious community, was apparently such a good listener she earned the nickname "the dump" from her fellow sisters because they were always dumping their problems on her (see St. Faustina's diary, 871). It's not hard to discover from her diary where she learned this art of listening. She learned it from listening to the Holy Spirit in prayer and from the same Spirit speaking to her through the guidance of her spiritual directors, such as Fr. Joseph Andrasz, S.J., and Blessed Michael Sopocko.

APPROACHING POSITIVELY TO GOD'S DISCIPLINE

One more thing we need to keep in mind: we should never approach the code of discipline of Jesus in a negative way. According to the Scriptures, far from being a dirty word, discipline is evidence of divine love. In Proverbs, we read, "My son, do not despise the Lord's discipline and do not resent his rebuke, because the Lord disciplines those he loves, as a father the son he delights in" (Prov. 3:11–12). Quoting these words of Proverb, the writer of the letter to the Hebrews goes on explicating them for our easy understanding. What the he indicates is that when we go through hardships in adhering to Jesus's hard conditions, we should fully be convinced that such time of psychological and even physical pain is a matter of God's discipline, and it is only because God, who is our loving Father, delights in his children. God's Son does so, first and foremost for our benefit, that we may share his holiness. Second, though his discipline seemingly causes pain and not joy, later, it would bring the peaceful fruit of righteousness to those who are trained by it (Ref. Heb. 12:5–12).

There are too many among us who have developed our Christianity along the line of our temperament, not along the line of God. Surprisingly, we forget mere impulse is a trait in natural life, but the Lord always ignores it because it hinders the development of the life of a disciple. Therefore, anyone who aims to be a discipled leader in Christ's Kingdom must make sure that one's own impulse is to be trained into intuition by discipline. As Oswald Chambers very well wrote, "Christian discipleship is built entirely on the supernatural grace of God. Walking on the water is easy to impulsive pluck, but walking on dry land as a disciple of Jesus Christ is a different thing."

LIFE MOLDED BY SELF-CONTROL

Besides, the effort of disciplining and controlling ourselves by Christ's "discipleship requirements" is some special endowment bestowed us from the Almighty. On this matter, Paul exhorts, "God did not give us a spirit of cowardice but rather of power and love and self-control" (2 Tim. 1:7). In other words, by observing God's Laws, especially the values of his beloved Son, we are groomed, we are chiseled, and our identity of being his leaders is enhanced in Jesus's godliness. We become modeled in the likeness of Jesus and consequently walk around in our leadership performances as role models. As Paul would ascertain, we can boldly advise those whom we guide and lead, "Follow me." There lies the bitter test for true discipleship. As discipled leaders among other disciples, we can walk the walk of Jesus; we can boldly but humbly state to fellow disciples, "When you see me, you have seen the Father." Ultimately, therefore, our disciplined discipled leadership life reaps and heaps ineffable rewards.

CHAPTER 12: DENY YOURSELF

In the Gospels we read, our Master proposes to his followers, "Whoever wishes to come after me must deny himself" (Matt. 16:24; Mark 8:34; Luke 9:23). To deny our very self is one of the most difficult conditions, which Jesus placed before everyone who wanted to be a discipled leader in his Kingdom.

WHAT JESUS MEANS BY THIS CONDITION

The term "deny" is the translation for the Greek word *aparneomai*, literally meaning "to completely disown," "to utterly separate oneself from someone or something." And the word "self" attached to it denotes, as Jesus himself has explicated, the "human life" made of both flesh and spirit. We read in Mark 8:34–37, "For whoever wishes to save his life will lose it, but whoever loses his life for my sake and that of the gospel will save it. What profit is there for one to gain the whole world and forfeit his life? What could one give in exchange for his life?" In other words, we are asked to put Jesus first in all things. The discipled leader of Christ needs to be set apart from the world. Our focus should be on our Lord and pleasing him in every area of our lives. We must put off self-centeredness and put on Christ-centeredness.

Self-denial is not in every aspect of who we are. Rather, the "self" to which we have to learn to say no is the composite of sinful habits that we brought into the Christian life. While Paul labels this "self" as sin and the "flesh," theologians and Church Fathers call it our fake self. This indicates there exists within us a genuine and real Self, which Moses describes in his narration story as the image and likeness of the Creator (Gen. 1:26–27). Hence, the combat happening within us is between the "Self" and the "self." Peter emphasizes this difference when he exhorts us, "Beloved, I urge you as aliens and strangers to abstain from fleshly lusts which wage war against the soul" (1 Pet. 2:11).

This inspires us to conclude that when our Master demands us "to deny oneself," he means to deny not everything about us, not our entire personal identity as an individual, but only those perverted and twisted attitudes and actions our "self" upholds for one's own gratification. It is wrong to believe that Jesus wants us to find every last thing about ourselves and just say no to it. His demand doesn't mean, for example, when a discipled leader at a parish tries to determine God's will regarding a place or role of ministry, saying, "I prefer to do the ministry for the Spanish immigrants" or "I like to serve as minister to outreach programs," and so on.

Jesus respects our individuality, our freedom, and our intelligence. The Bible says a lot about the importance of human individuality to the Creator and the Redeemer. One of the beauties of Christianity is that it is possible for every individual human to have a personal relationship with God through his Son Jesus Christ. Being the Creator, Provider, and Abba Father, God knows each one's name and every bit of one's individuality and its content, including even one's hair. Therefore, if he knows us in that kind of individual way, he's not going to turn around and ask us to deny every last thing there is about us.

THE INGREDIENTS OF SELF-DENIAL

Jesus's demand of self-denial contains the following: First, detachment from wrong motivation for our following him. We should never look for worldly comfort, convenience, and earthly possessions. Jesus has preached to us, "First and foremost seek the kingdom of God." He expects us to be like him "who had nowhere to rest his head." Second, detachment from our family, relatives, and friends. "Whoever loves father or mother more than me is not worthy of me, and whoever loves son or daughter more than me is not worthy of me" (Matt. 10:37). We will discuss more about this later. Third, detachment from our caste and race. Paul writes about this dimension of Jesus's self-denial positively: "There is neither Jew nor Greek, there is neither slave nor free person, there is not male and female; for you are all one in Christ Jesus" (Gal. 3:28). Fourth, detachment from our own flesh.

Jesus sounds seemingly very brutal regarding this dimensional part of self-denial: "If your hand causes you to sin, cut it off; and if your foot causes you to sin, cut it off; and if your eye causes you to sin, pluck it out" (Mark 9:43–48). Fifth, detachment from our self, even our very life: "For whoever wishes to save his life will lose it, but whoever loses his life for my sake will save it" (Matt. 16:25). Sixth, detachment from violence. Many times, Jesus strictly ordered and admonished not to divulge in violent activities: "Jesus rebuked James and John who wanted him to bring down fire upon his enemies and burn them to death" (Luke 9:54). Seventh, detachment from vain glory and pride. As this admonition of Jesus was so hard for his disciples to digest and apply in their life, Jesus repeatedly exhorted them: "One who wants to be number one among you must be others' servants"; "Learn of me, I am meek and humble." Eighth, detachment from even the laws.

Therefore, brothers, we are children not of the slave woman but of the freeborn woman. For freedom, Christ set us free, so stand firm, and do not submit again to the yoke of slavery (Gal. 4:31). "For freedom Christ set us free; so stand firm and do not submit again to the yoke of slavery. For you were called for freedom, brothers. But do not use this freedom as an opportunity for the flesh; rather, serve one another through love" (Gal. 5:1).

SELF-DENIAL IS HEARTBREAKING BUT VERY HEARTENING

But there is one thing we should understand well. Denying oneself is indeed an overwhelming effort for every one of us; the main reason is the "self" is nothing but our own birth partner. As many sages have stated, this effort, lasting till our last breath, is the last combat to be won by us. Disciples, like Paul, testified to this unavoidable human struggle. Naming it as a combat against "sin," Paul writes, "Sin, in order that it might be shown to be sin, worked death in me through the good . . . For I know that good does not dwell in me, that is, in my flesh. The willing is ready at hand, but doing the good is not. For I do not do the good I want, but I do the evil I do not want . . . So, then, I discover the principle that when I want to do right, evil is at hand. For I take delight in the law of God, in my inner self, but I see in my members another principle at war with the law of my mind, taking me captive to the law of sin that dwells in my members" (Rom. 7:13–25).

Paul also has been very clear of how this lifelong struggle goes on in every disciple. And therefore, he exhorts us in Galatians 5:16–17: "Let me put it like this: if you are guided by the Spirit you will be in no danger of yielding to self-indulgence, since self-indulgence is the opposite of the Spirit, the Spirit is totally against such a thing, and it is precisely because the two are so opposed that you do not always carry out your good intentions" (JB translation). He emphasizes also the horrific results of those who are unsuccessful in this combat: "The concern of the flesh is death, but the concern of the spirit is life and peace" (Rom. 8:6–9). At the time of his death approaching, Paul remembers his past fight, and in that same trust and hope, he authenticates, not that he procured full victory but that he has succeeded in enduring through it:

"I have fought the good fight, I have finished the race, I have kept the faith" (2 Tim. 4:7, ESV).

If we, the discipled leaders of Jesus, desire to win the battle against our sinful self, we need to imitate Paul. First and foremost, we should acknowledge that we have an acute need in our discipled life, that we fall short of the glory of godly leadership and admitting that we are being continuously taunted by Evil, and that there is no way of being renewed and reconciled to God by ourselves. And second, in this struggle of denying one's self, we need to preserve a principle that we always hide ourselves behind the "Cross" from where at least one single drop of our crucified Master falls on our sinful self and make its power diluted.

SELF-DENIAL IS FOR WINNING THE REAL VICTORY

In my personal view, this demand of Jesus is nothing but a practical advice for human survival and success in the midst of daily life's drudgeries of deception, disappointment, and rejection, especially the climatic and unbearable end of human life—death. In every step of combating and coping with this tragic life, humans have to uphold a certain kind of self-mastery over it. Generally, what humans do is to discover and apply some excuses, justifications, and surely strategies that can either tolerate or combat or even elevate oneself against those tragic moments. They don't want to lose their self-esteem or lower it hellishly to the nadir.

That is what the Master did as any of his fellow humans. He knew it well the comedy and tragedy of his earthly life, beginning from womb to tomb. He seemed to follow the "stoic" tactic, enduring such life's strains and struggles patiently, but he did it with some difference. Elevating every bit of his breathing moments as the "heavenly" bid designed by God the Father, he led his life restfully, resolutely, and positively under the haven of obeying God's will. He categorically denied that he led his life of doing his own will: "I came down from heaven not to do my own will but the will of the one who sent me" (John 6:38). He loved to repeatedly confirm that his daily food is to do God's will: "My food is to do the will of the one who sent me and to finish his work" (John 4:34). He was fully convinced by such obedience he was glorifying God: "I glorified you on earth by accomplishing the work that you gave me to do" (John 17:4).

It is on this basic attitude of self-effacement, namely, totally denying his own will and making God's will as his, Jesus accentuated his demand of self-denial from his disciples. There have been numerous disciples who considered this the most pertinent strategy offered by Jesus and demonstrated victory in their saintly lives. Developing their attitude as that of Jesus (Phil. 2:5), they could proceed in their life journey up to their death of any kind joyfully, contently, and exemplarily. I like Paul in his view and pattern of fulfilling this demand of Jesus. He writes in his letter, "For through the law I died to the law that I might live for God. I have been crucified with Christ; yet I live, no longer I, but Christ lives in me; insofar as I now live in the flesh, I live by faith in the Son of God who has loved me and given himself up for me" (Gal. 2:19–20). It is in this Pauline way, despite the continuous "tug-of-war" between the two real and fake selves, every loyal disciple will win the victory of fullness of life.

SELF-DENIAL IS FOR SOLVING THE PROBLEM OF EVIL

We all know life is not a bed of roses. It has got its own price to be paid. Life is not fair to us all the time, so what do we do? We try building up within ourselves a strong sense of "I." We imagine that on the strength of our bloated or inflated "self," we can resist all evils from outside. We draw clear-cut boundaries around "ourselves" so that nobody encroaches into our premise of the swollen self and destroys our peace. Of course, many times, we decide to be good and even better and the best, but that we do often by covering our weakness and faultiness with a religious shield. This is why we create or adhere to certain deliberate values for ourselves and our friends but different ones for others. Unfortunately, that also ends in failure. It is not surprising then this false sense of this individuality and truncated personal spirituality becomes a breeding ground for more evil within us.

If we look into the temptations of the Lord (Matt. 4:1–11), we can see very clearly that he was not tempted by the evil force to violate any of the Ten Commandments of the Lord. He was not asked to kill somebody, nor was he allured to commit adultery. Rather, the evil force demanded from him to use his individual perception of himself, namely, his Sonship for his own glory and selfish purposes. For thirty years, he was meditating, reflecting, praying, and obeying God through his parents. It was a very intense and long process. Finally, a time arrives when he is confirmed that he is the beloved Son of God. His inner conviction is very strong and his values secure. He is aware of his power, wisdom, and unthinkable identity. It is at this juncture that he was tempted to misuse his power, wisdom, and identity. But Jesus won.

We have to be aware of the fact that at any time, with any kind of strategy, the evil force within us can tempt us, attack us, and get the worst out of us. Especially when we feel we are sure about ourselves, when we build up within us a strong individuality of "I" and "me," the evil force will use us to the maximum for its maximum benefits.

In the early part of this century, a London newspaper sought the help of its subscribers in addressing the problem of evil. Readers were invited to send in their responses to the question, "What is wrong with the world today?" The best response of all was the briefest. It read, "Dear sir, I am. Yours faithfully, G. K. Chesterton." True to his Judeo-Christian heritage, Chesterton understood that the responsibility for the world's problems and the solutions to the pervasive problem of evil is not to be found in any myth or philosophical system. It is very easy to find out the culprit. Let each of us look at the mirror. The problem is none other than our own self. Consequently, most of the problems of evil we come across in our personal world do not come from without but from within. Sadly, most of the problems of evil that exist in our families and communities are not from bad people but mostly from people who think they are good when, in fact, they feel good only about their swollen ego or fake self.

SELF-DENIAL IS FOR FOLLOWING JESUS FREELY

God has been for centuries inviting his humans to become his discipled leaders in many ways. Nonetheless, he recommends only one way to respond to it and that is "detach and attach." When God's Son came to us, he did the same, inviting us, "Come and follow me." It was simply a loving demand to follow him, leaving behind all that may hinder and obstruct to attach ourselves freely to him and his Gospel values and ministries.

In this demand of "detach and attach," we notice in the Gospels our Master being very categorical and ruthless. Luke testifies to this through a set of three interchanges happening between the Master and the would-be followers (Luke 9:57–62). Though they liked to follow Jesus, they expressed their intention first to fulfill certain of their life's desires and holdings, which were logical and legal. But the Master forcefully demanded from them a single-hearted response to the call to follow him. He clearly stated to the one who held secretly in his heart that the Master had a cozy life that he too can share with: "I don't have not even a place of my own to rest my head. Are you ready still to follow me wherever I take you?" To the second who intended first to go and fulfill his filial obligation of burying his father, the Master underlined, "Let the dead bury their dead. But you go and proclaim the kingdom of God." And to the third one, who also communicated his longing to go back home to say goodbye to his family, Jesus said, "If you want to be fit in God's kingdom, don't look back what you plan to leave."

From the life and teachings of Jesus and his apostles, we clearly find that all the discipled leaders of Jesus are expected to detach ourselves from our family, relatives, and friends (Matt. 10:37). As Paul writes, we need to detach from our human artificial networks of caste and race, and so on: "There is neither Jew nor Greek, there is neither slave nor free person, there is not male and female; for you are all one in Christ Jesus" (Gal. 3:28); to be detached from our own flesh: "If your hand causes you to sin, cut it off; and if your foot causes you to sin, cut it off; and if your eye causes you to sin, pluck it out" (Mark 9:43–48); and as we discussed earlier, to be detached from our self and even our very life: "If anyone wishes to come after me, he must deny himself." "For whoever wishes to save his life will lose it, but whoever loses his life for my sake will save it." From all these demands, we understand our Master's will that we should be detached from wrong motivations for our following him. Namely, we must never look for worldly comfort, convenience, earthly possessions, and so on.

By enlisting the above-listed demands, Jesus intended that we would be free in attaching ourselves totally to God and to his service, freedom to be preoccupied with God and heavenly things: "Love your God with your whole heart, whole mind, whole soul, whole body and whole strength"; and to live single-minded in focusing on to heaven instead of Earth: "First seek the kingdom of God and then all others will accompany you."

By all those detachments, we would enjoy freedom to be controlled by the Spirit instead of the flesh. Being in the flesh, there is a great danger of following more the desires of our body rather than listening to the Spirit. This earthly attachment, in return, can take any form, like addictions, and produce results that in the long run become obstacles in following the promptings of the Spirit. The sole purpose of Jesus's demands of detachments is therefore to make us completely free for serving God instead of serving Satan; free for following him wherever he takes us, whenever he calls us, and whatever he commands us; and certainly being free for obeying his Gospel values in every moment of our life.

Thus, we too would feel it easier to belong to macro family instead of micro family as the Master demands: "Love your neighbor as yourselves. Love one another as I have loved you. Amen, I say to you, there is no one who has given up house or brothers or sisters or mother or father or children or lands for my sake and for the sake of the gospel who will not receive a hundred times more now in this present age: houses and brothers and sisters and mothers and children and lands, with persecutions, and eternal life in the age to come" (Mark 10:29–30).

SELF-DENIAL IS A DETACHMENT OF ONE'S HUMAN RELATIONS

Human life is a bundle of relationships through which we are made what we are. Once, we were in the womb of our mother, a lump of mere flesh and bones. But later as we grow, we became humans, thanks to the connections we established with our fellowmen. Actually, all religions, as any other natural helps, are meant to make those relationships stronger, more fruitful, and more successful. However, the same religions also demand us to relate ourselves to God the Creator. They stand as unique support to us in relating more fully and meaningfully to him and to sustain that divine relationship as a sole base on which other human relationships are to be constructed and maintained. Hence, together, with the commandment to love God with our whole heart, whole mind, whole soul, and whole strength, they established another commandment as the first: "Love your neighbors as yourself."

In secular and political world, people may refer this demand to "no more nepotism in public life." But in Jesus's perspective, its meaning is deeper and higher: discipled leaders therefore are demanded from the Master to uphold a relational bond being established and maintained between God and man and between man to man. This relational adventure gets its perfection and completion by mutual support of both parties involved. Jesus, as the Son of God, was very much concerned about his disciples' wholehearted commitment to him. He insisted their fidelity and love should in any way be distorted and distracted. So we hear him loudly say to us, "Any of you who does not give up everything he has cannot be my disciple" (Luke 14:33). We should detach from any other things or persons before we attach ourselves to him. He was quite explicit about the cost of following him. Discipleship requires a totally committed life with sacrifice.

According to our Master, all the relationships in discipled leaders, bonded on blood and social law, must take second place to the absolute dedication to him and his values: "If any one comes to me without hating his father and mother, wife and children, brothers and sisters, and even his own life, he cannot be my disciple" (Luke 14:25–26). Our worthiness in his crew largely consists in our total detachment from human natural love: "Whoever loves father or mother more than me is not worthy of me, and whoever loves son or daughter more than me is not worthy of me" (Matt. 10:37). In his uttering on certain conditions for becoming his discipled leaders (Luke 9:57–62), we observe some peculiar severity and the unconditional nature of Christian discipled leadership. Even family ties and filial obligations, such as burying one's parents, cannot distract one no matter how briefly from proclaiming the Kingdom of God.

Unquestionably, this crucial demand of Jesus will be like the burdensome cross he carried to his death: "If anyone would come after me, he must deny himself and take up his cross and follow me" (Matt. 16:24). This is why, sadly, not all of Jesus's followers were able to make such a commitment. There were many who left him after a while: "From this time many of his disciples turned back and no longer followed him" (John 6:66).

GENUINE INTERPRETATION ON JESUS'S DEMAND

One thing we should be clear about this demand of the Master. In the light of the interpretations many biblical scholars and Church Fathers shared with us, we conclude that when Jesus said, "Leave your relations and even very self," he didn't mean to desert everybody at home and all our friends and become a lonely person or an isolated island in the universe. On the contrary, he expected us to build up all our relationships in this world not by mere natural bases like blood and flesh, human laws, contracts, racial, creedal, national, regional, tribal, civic, and social foundations. Rather, every relation must be founded on supernatural, spiritual, above all, Jesus's Gospel. A true disciple of Jesus tries to build up his relationships on love of Jesus, justice of God, morality of innocence, human dignity of God's child, freedom of God's Spirit, peace, forgiveness, and joy of heaven. Any relationship we create in this world as spouses in marriage, parent and child at home, leader and follower in any social and political arena, CEO and other employees in corporate enterprises should not lack this Gospel foundation.

To explain such Gospel-oriented human relationship, there is a beautiful event described in Paul's letter to Philemon (1:8–20). He wrote from prison to his friend Philemon asking him to take back a slave, Onesimus, who had apparently done something wrong but who, under Paul's influence, had become a Christian. Paul speaks with the greatest affection of this young man: "Whose father I became while wearing these chains in prison." The boy, Paul also adds, is "a part of my own self." Paul asks Philemon to treat the young man Onesimus "not as a slave any more but . . . a dear brother . . . Welcome him as you would me."

BE CHOOSY BUT ALWAYS COMMITTED

One of my friends (a nonpracticing-religious person but philanthropist) used to say "You, Christians, are good to make promises and vows, but we are the ones who keep them promptly." In a way, he was right. Thanks to those wonderful nuns and missionaries from my early childhood, I made wonderful promises to the Lord and carried them in my diary. As the years passed by, I found out that not only was my diary filled with wonderful promises, but my heart was also loaded with the bulk of guilty feelings for not fulfilling them. So I stopped making such pledges to the Lord anymore. However, one of my spiritual directors advised me, "Vima! There is an old saying, 'Better to have loved and lost than never to have loved at all.' By the same token, it is better to have made promises and broken them than never to have promised at all."

I gave some serious thought to this advice. I noticed in my life every success as a student, teacher, preacher, administrator, CEO, chaplain, and so on largely depended on the commitment I made to my responsibilities. I had to make up my mind whether I wanted it. Once I made my choice, then I had to tell my body and the spirit that I will abide by the rules, codes, and obligations that my role offered me. I decided to endure whatever hardships arose while fulfilling those obligations. I did it. I won. I reaped the results. I found out that if we, the humans, want our lives to be successful, we have to commit ourselves to certain things that each one's life puts before us.

The commitment we place to our different roles in life—as a mother, father, friend, leader, member, and so on—enhances our total commitment to the entire human life we inherited. Willy-nilly, our life situations designate us for some roles to be played in the community. There may be certain natural liking for such roles. For example, a mother has a natural instinct to cling to her baby. But natural instinct will not endure in difficult times. Besides, making choices according to natural liking is not fully human. Even animals can do that. But if we want to be fully human, and to be matured persons, we have to commit ourselves to those choices with our free will and intelligence. Any hardship will never deter us from that firm commitment.

ALL FOR BEING GENUINELY FREE

Paul writes today, "For freedom Christ set us free; so stand firm and do not submit again to the yoke of slavery." This means we are freed to be free in attaching ourselves to God and to his service. It indicates freedom to serve God: "Love your God with your whole heart, whole mind, whole soul, whole body and whole strength," to be preoccupied more with heavenly things instead of earthly ones: "First seek the kingdom of God and then all others will accompany you," and to be controlled by the Spirit and not by the flesh. After listing out fifteen and more works humans would do by the insinuation of the flesh, Paul shares with us (Gal. 5:19–24) how we produce amazing fruits of the Spirit by the freedom we uphold from the fleshly influence: "In contrast, the fruit of the Spirit is love, joy, peace, patience, kindness, generosity, faithfulness, gentleness, self-control. Against such there is no law. Now those who belong to Christ [Jesus] have crucified their flesh with its passions and desires. If we live in the Spirit, let us also follow the Spirit."

Self-denial also is identified by our Master as the freedom to belong to macro family instead of micro family. He lived up to his own demand. We hear him loudly saying to his own kith and kin what his true family was: "Stretching out his hand toward his disciples, he said, 'Here are my mother and my brothers. For whoever does the will of my heavenly Father is my brother, and sister, and mother'" (Matt. 12:46–50).

Thus, Jesus expects all his discipled leaders to enjoy the true freedom in serving God, in following the Master and his Gospel values. Though many would like to follow Jesus, his primary demand is that first, they should leave everything they uphold as their near and dear ones, their life's desires and holdings. Indeed, the Lord Jesus demands a single-hearted response to the call to follow him.

CHAPTER 13: BE AN ALL-TIME VISIONARY

John Maxwell, a well-known preacher, pastor, and author who has written a number of books on leadership, has repeatedly included in most of his talks a thought-provoking statement: "Everything rises and falls on leadership." As the discipled leader, so is his congregation. If church leaders do not lead their people with certain vision, bestowed and supported by the Master, they will fail to reach God's destiny for their church. Therefore, Proverbs rightly underlines, "Where there is no vision, the people perish" (Prov. 29:18a, KJV).

UPHOLD A CLEAR VISION FROM THE START

A visionary is commonly defined as one who possesses and shows clear ideas about what should happen or be done in the future. In all walks of life, we observe most of the best leaders win their goals by creating some valid and doable visions and safeguarding them intact throughout their lives. Undeniably, the same is true with any discipled leaders in Jesus's Kingdom. Usually, on the onset of their leadership ministry, they are being provoked by certain vision in the form of an idea, shared the risen Lord's Spirit. This idea is often a mental picture of a possible future based on biblical principles combined with imagination or, possibly, an actual special revelatory "vision" from God.

This godly vision, as we come across in Scriptures, can originate, be evolved, renewed, and ultimately, authenticated by God in various manners. First, we can receive it directly from him in our intimate commune with him as it happened to Abraham: "I will make of you a great nation, and I will bless you; I will make your name great, so that you will be a blessing" (Gen. 12:2), and to Moses: "Now, go! I am sending you to Pharaoh to bring my people, the Israelites, out of Egypt" (Exod. 3:10). Second, God can propose and explicate to us his vision through his chosen elders while we are blinded and ignorant of what is what as in the case of Paul: "A certain Ananias, a devout observer of the law, and highly spoken of by all the Jews who lived there, came to me and stood there and said, 'Saul, my brother, regain your sight.' And at that very moment I regained my sight and saw him. Then he said, 'The God of our ancestors designated you to know his will, to see the Righteous One, and to hear the sound of his voice; for you will be his witness before all to what you have seen and heard'" (Acts 22:6–16). At the same time, God permits us also to clarify the vision he insinuates within us either personally or through some of his disciples or his messengers. All the Scriptural heroes and heroines, starting from Abraham, Moses, to Jesus, were not exempted in this authenticating process. Mary, the Mother of Jesus, for example, has been the number 1 role model in this regard. When the angel offered greetings as well as the breathtaking vision about herself and her Baby, she began questioning the angel and got all necessary clarification about that vision (Luke 1:26–38).

RECONFIRM YOUR VISION IN THE SPIRIT

And Paul was very intense in getting authenticated of the vision delivered by God through Ananias. So we hear from him the stringent procedure he undertook. Though he got revelation of the august vision that "he must proclaim Him to the Gentiles," he writes, "I did not immediately consult flesh and blood, nor did I go up to Jerusalem to those who were apostles before me; rather, I went into Arabia and then returned to Damascus. Then after three years I went up to Jerusalem to confer with Cephas and remained with him for fifteen days" (Gal. 1:15–18). Only then he convincingly declared what his vision for life and ministry: "For which I was appointed preacher and apostle and teacher."

This sort of godly-vision-oriented idea excites all genuine leaders or fills them with longing. They want others to see what they see and appreciate how cool it would be. A leader may not always develop a new, unique vision but may buy into another's vision. Some studies suggest that the best leaders are not necessarily the most creative people in a community, although they are usually more creative than average. In a secular political world, it can be said that whether the leader's vision is original or borrowed is unimportant. However, in God's Kingdom, that cannot be said and upheld regarding the vision of discipled leaders of Jesus. They, by all means, either at the outset or during their performing of leadership ministries, should have coveted personally from the Master such revelatory unction of specific vision and mission.

TRANSFORM THE VISION TO EFFECTIVE MISSION

I dare say it is not enough for them to correlate their claim of leadership to the electoral votes of certain people or to be proud of attaining assistance from the power of some hierarchical dignitaries. Those may help them to climb the ladder to own social rank and file or to enter into the clout of esoteric personages, but in no way they become fruitful and successful leaders according to the heart of Jesus without receiving God's gratuitous gift of his vision. Acting on discipled leadership is not to be performing leadership duties by some imaginary or certain impulsive feeling.

Indeed, as any other good leaders, they can practice ways to communicate their visions, tying future pictures to past realities, showing how such a picture is better than the status quo. They can explain why attaining such a vision justifies risk and pain. And consequently, the followers of visionaries find their excitement contagious and accept the leader's vision as their own. Nonetheless, in the regime of Jesus, without a vision being directly blessed by him, these followers will not find themselves highly motivated to attain any Jesus's vision, usually without much consideration of personal benefit. They would be involving in the mainstream of Jesus's mission only superficially and for self-gratification and worldly ambition.

WE CAN SHARE ONLY WHAT WE POSSESS

When we are appointed to lead God's people, we can fulfill such marvelous task only to the degree of the realization we have encountered in the journey of our Kingdom's vision. As have we traveled in the vision pursuit, so would we be taking people, entrusted to our care, from where they are to where they have never been before. From the Bible and in the history of humanity, we know our God is a God of adventure. He likes the same kind of adventurous people as his own. Being adventurous means taking strenuously certain ventures in life. God's chosen leaders never disliked engaging the unknown with faith and vision. For example, in the OT, we read when God told Abraham that he would take him to a strange place unknown to him, he obeyed immediately: "The Lord said to Abram: Go forth from your land, your relatives, and from your father's house to a land that I will show you . . . Abram went as the Lord directed him" (Gen. 12:1–4).

And in the NT, we see Saul, who became Paul, doing the same (Ref. Acts 9:1–20). While he heard and saw in a spiritual vision the Master calling him, he lost his physical sight. The Lord reminds Paul about his sinful past, but not revealing to him the details of the vision of his future, the Lord only directs him to go to Damascus, a neighboring city, and there he would be told about his future vision. In a breathtaking way, the Lord appears in vision to a holy man named Ananias and directs him to go and meet Paul in the place where he stays. Through this Ananias, the Lord shares with Paul all about his future vision: "This man is a chosen instrument of mine to carry my name before Gentiles, kings, and Israelites, and I will show him what he will have to suffer for my name."

In that process of revealing a vision of future to Paul, the Lord got him surrender his past, his strength and weakness, and his anxiety about the future totally to himself. As he opened his physical sight, he offered an envisaged prestigious but very risky future of being Jesus's "vessel of election." This historical event in the life of Paul instructs all discipled leaders that any vision of leadership ministry can be received and managed only by our total and honest surrendering to the Caller and his Spirit's promptings coming through many ways—elders, friends, Scriptures, sufferings, and surely signs of the time.

How does a person choose to follow another person as his/her leader? By experience, we know people want a candidate to become their leader to be respectful and ethically unblemished and, as Paul indicates, to be "irreproachable, temperate, self-controlled, decent, hospitable, not a drunkard, not aggressive, but gentle, not contentious, and not a lover of money" (1 Tim. 3:2–3). Plus, that would-be leader must possess a clear sense of direction. People are correct in making a choice of their leaders. They expect their leaders, in any situation and role of leadership, to direct the flock to achieve certain goals. They can be short term or long term, interim or permanent ones. Any goal demands a clear and effective process of implementation. To direct and engage people to participate in the goal-oriented process, their leader must first possess a clear vision of goal and process as well, and he/she also should have the ability to communicate his vision and process efficiently through his/her words and actions. As one of the quotes I read in a preacher's website, "A leader is one who knows the way, goes the way, and shows the way." For discipled leaders, this specific way is Jesus Christ, who is the Way of Truth to attain eternal life.

In this regard, discipled leaders should never become complacent with a wrong notion of "God will take care of everything." Yes, every bit of discipled leaders' move, including the result, belongs totally to God in Jesus. That does not maroon the fact that God chose us to be stewards and laborers in his vineyard to do all the best we can as our personal input into his designed creative and redemptive works. Hence, we should uphold and be serious about the common factor of any leadership being a process of common influence, which amplifies the efforts of others, toward the achievement of a common goal. God guarantees all blessings will be showered on those leaders who respect their leadership as a mind-blowing task of inspiring others to pursue a vision within the parameters set, to the extent that it becomes a shared effort, a shared vision, and a shared success.

This is why leaders like Warren Bennis beautifully states, "Leadership is the capacity to translate vision into reality." And joining with him, Peter Drucker writes, "Leadership is lifting a person's vision to high sights, the raising of a person's performance to a higher standard, the building of a personality beyond its normal limitations." Finally, let me close this chapter with a beautiful definition of "leadership" proclaimed by the United States Army: "It is influencing people, by providing purpose, direction, and motivation, while operating to accomplish the mission and improving the organization."

CHAPTER 14: BE A LIFELONG LEARNER

NECESSITY OF LIFELONG LEARNING

In Job, we read, "There is a spirit in human beings, the breath of the Almighty that gives them understanding. It is not those of many days who are wise, nor the aged who understand the right" (Job 32:8–9). It means that wisdom does not come automatically with age. This we know well by our daily experiences with the elderly leaders. While for many aged leaders, gray hair and a good head go hand in hand, we notice that so many others are, by the length of their life and of their leadership position, are only embedded with stubbornness, irritability, and careless ways of thinking and living. This second group of aged leaders may have matured physically and even some times intellectually and diplomatically, but without some long-term pattern of receptivity and intentionality, we discover their multiplied life experiences would only create more confusion than clarity, more unproductive and destructive than fruitful and useful. If such is the critical situation every political and social leader has to undergo, how much more it would be for the discipled leaders of Jesus? This is mainly because the stakes for us are even higher for cultivating holy curiosity and the mindset of a lifelong learner.

Teaching and learning are at the very heart of our faith. To be a "disciple" means to be a "learner." Our Master is the consummate teacher, and the central task of his discipled leaders in the local church is teaching (Titus 1:9; 1 Tim. 3:2, 5:17; Heb. 13:7; Matt. 28:20). It has been the eternal will and design of God that his family in this world should be a community of lifelong learners under the earthly guidance of leaders who are teachers at heart. It is not as most of us think that, once we undergo strenuously and complete in flying colors the learning process in Jesus's school of Scriptures, theology, spirituality, ecclesiology, and so on, our learning comes to a climatic end with being sent to teach and preach the same among God's people and then spend the rest of our lives drawing from that original deposit of knowledge. Rather, as our Master and his Spirit-filled disciples stated, the ongoing status of Christian life is inextricably linked to ongoing learning.

LENGTHY PROCESS OF LEARNING

Astonishingly, our lifelong learning process extends to the day of Christ arriving at the end of our life's journey. That is what Paul points out in his letter to Philippians: "I am confident of this that the one who began a good work in you will continue to complete it until the day of Christ Jesus" (Phil. 1:6). In other words, the discipled leaders' nonstop learning course doesn't close today or tomorrow but as Jesus delays. It is a lifetime curriculum. As God's mysteries are immensely beyond our human grasp, with our limited brain, we can understand them slowly, little by little, and gradually. Undoubtedly, we are not offered them all at once, but forever, we would be dealing with new, newer, and newest. Hence, as one spiritual writer would claim with Paul, "even in heaven and then in new creation we shouldn't expect that our learning will be done. Writing on this fact, we hear from Paul, in the ages to come God might show the immeasurable riches of his grace in his kindness to us in Christ Jesus" (Eph. 2:7).

THE SYLLABUS OF LIFELONG LEARNING

Now we should know the exact curriculum and syllabus of this learning. Surprisingly, there is one and only curriculum and single syllabus in our learning the mysteries of God. There is indeed something we take in a front-end load in our discipled leadership and continue to explore and go deeper into it. It is the "word" or "message" about Jesus, God's incarnate Word. Simply put, the focal point and center of our lifelong learning is the person and work of Christ. We are told in Colossians 1:17 "that all things are in him, through him, and for him." We can learn all the divine mysteries together with their implications, applications, and results from Jesus the Master, and his Spirit will assist us not get into complication and confusion. Being fully aware of his role given by his Father to lead us to the Truth, our Master deliberately ordered us to get learning from him and about him. Jesus's life is the syllabus for our lifelong study. In that syllabus, he unhesitantly included three lessons most necessary to our role of leadership in his church:

Lesson 1: How and why of being and behaving as a meek and humble leader. "Learn from me, for I am meek and humble [lowly] of heart" (Matt. 11:29). Etymologically, the word "meek" was always associated with the strength and courage that are expressed in gentleness toward God and all others. In its Godward glance, meekness means perfect trust, willing obedience, and lived faith; in its posture toward others, meekness means a force of character and inner strength that invites admiration and a desire to emulate such virtue. This is what our Master demonstrated in his entire life and taught us the same.

We are advised by our Master not only to believe in and obey him, not only to hearken to him as a teacher, not only to rely on him as a Savior, and not only to be subject to him as a governor, to be meek and humble in heart—meek toward all men and humble toward God. Whether we are delegated with the role of shepherding, governing, or teaching and directing his people, he expects us to live as he who has been most mild, gentle, and forbearing; kind and condescending toward all his disciples; directing them with tenderness, patience, and lenity in the way to pardon, life, and salvation; and not imposing on them any unnecessary burdens but being meek in bearing all kinds of injuries and being humble in condescending to do the meanest good offices to the meanest of mankind.

I say this as the number 1 instruction to us from our Master because it was from this messianic attitude and mind setup (Zech. 9:9) all his behaviors as Master and Leader were generated (Phil. 2:5–8). He wants the same remarkable fountainhead set up within us from the day 1 of our leadership ministry. We may claim and credit ourselves possessing all kinds of charism, talents, and aptitudes, but if we don't have the gift of meekness and humility, we will be rebuked, even to be cursed by our Master as he did in his life to the Pharisees who were harsh, overbearing, and oppressive in their leading people, being hardheaded in faith-holding but hard-hearted in their promulgation and implementation of God's laws unreasonably. The Jews have a saying, "For ever let a man, 'be meek as Hillell', and let him not be wrathful as 'Shammai.'" These two men were presidents of their universities during the times of Jesus. Quoting this saying, Andrew E. Hill writes in his commentary, but our Master says, "Learn of me, not of 'Hillell', or any of your doctors."

Lesson 2: "Being and behaving serviceable." In the early centuries, when there was no formal education through the school systems, in every neighborhood or town, there were elders who taught certain strategies of life's survival and winning livelihood such as hunting, planting, harvesting, and so on. The only payment a student studying under those gurus is not dollars or pennies; rather, they lived as servants of their gurus and did all household duties at their teachers' homes. That is how we see Jesus, a grand Teacher and Guru behaved when he washed the feet of his students, disciples (John 13:12–17).

However, we come to know he showed his powerful teaching technique of education in action. Every one of us has got our own unique mannerism, habit, and style. Each one has to belong to a culture of family, neighborhood, nation, tribe, race, and religion too. As regards religious cultures, every religion is a bundle of many cultures and habits, but there is always one cultural act or performance being held as the core and center of all their cultural activities. For example, in Judaism, as we hear from Moses in Exodus, the Passover Feast was the nucleus of their religious culture. "This day shall be a memorial feast for you, which all your generations shall celebrate with pilgrimage to the Lord, as a perpetual institution" (Exod. 12:14), The teachers and guardians of that religion left behind this "Passover Feast Practice" as their legacy to the future generations.

In the same way, Jesus Christ, as the Founder and Teacher of Christianity, handed on to his disciples a unique legacy of his own creation to be performed continuously by them. It is nothing but a love-based service to one another. Pope Francis, when he washed the feet of twelve disabled patients on a Maundy Thursday, was quoted saying, "Jesus' symbolic gesture of washing his disciples was like a parting gift and 'an inheritance' that he left out of love. This is the legacy that Jesus leaves us and he wants it to be passed down through people's loving service to others. It reflects the universal gesture of a God who became man, who serves all of humanity. We should think of ways how we can serve others better—that's what Jesus wanted from us."

This act of washing feet was done in the early centuries by the slaves to those who came to dine. In Palestine of Jesus's time, walking on the streets of dirt and earth created this issue that when guests entered into the house, it was necessary to wash their feet. Jesus's unique system of covenantal participation in earthly life was a serviceable participation. This is why he could declare in his life, "I came not to be served but to serve" (Mark 10:45). The entire control over his life was surrendered to his Father. His whole life demonstrated it. He was obedient to God, took the form of a slave, and took the Jewish body nature and culture provided. He humbled himself, becoming obedient to death, even death on a cross. Jesus also served his fellow men: his parents, his relatives, and his friends and especially those in need. He was always a good host, doing good wherever he went. Indeed, he was serving as a Good Samaritan. As a symbolic gesture of this serviceable system of new life, he washed the feet of his disciples and showed this unique dimension of God covenantal participation in life. Not only during the night of the Last Supper but also throughout his life, we encounter the Master becoming a servant, a Shepherd becoming a Lamb, and a guru becoming a disciple.

In our daily walk of life, he orders us to express, to practice, and to exercise the same kind of service to others with humility and simplicity and even ready to sacrifice our conveniences and comforts, even life if need be, to bring a better life to the needy. "Wash one another's feet as I have done for you." Though it is a slavish act of washing of the feet of fellow men by bending, lending, and spending his time, energy, and dignity, we know it was Jesus's command of instruction as a second lesson to us in our lifelong learning.

Indeed, it would give us a shock. What a shock it must have been to the disciples: Jesus kneeling before them to wash their feet, a task considered so demeaning that it was relegated to slaves. Jesus, the eternal Son of God and Savior of the world, kneels before us and humbly requests that we allow him to take away the sins and flaws that weigh us down. If we reflect fully and deeply on this, can we possibly consider ourselves "above" any act of service and love we are called upon to perform for the old, the young, the sick, the poor, and the defeated?

The persons who believe in God and religion are named in this modern world as dunce, fool, stupid, blockhead, bonehead, booby, cabbagehead, and so on. This term "fool" is an apt term to be applied to every discipled leader who intends to be serviceable like the Master. In Paul's writings, we hear him labeling all such leaders of Christ as "seemingly fools." He writes in his First Letter to the Corinthians, "We are fools on Christ's account" (1 Cor. 4:10).

Lesson 3: "Finding fulfillment only in self-sacrifice." I read a story about a ten-year-old son who, obeying his father, stayed there in a cabin of a warship, waiting for his father, who went to fight his enemies by submarine. His father, before he left, gave him an order. "Until I returned, you should stay where you are." The ship was on fire. People asked the boy to save himself, jumping with them into the lifeboat. He denied. When his father returned, he saw his son burned fully and gasping for breath. Before he died, the father asked, "Why did you not save yourself?" The son replied in a feeble tone but with unction, "I obeyed your order, Dad."

We know from the Scriptures that as a boy in the story, Jesus was fully committed to his Father's will and command and kept his own promises to God. He conducted his life as a covenantal participation in earthly life. He underwent all his passion and death upholding in his heart till his last breath this remarkable policy of covenantal participation in God's life. He willingly accepted the lethal and sacrificial demands of such covenant. Before he came from heaven, his Father commanded him to perpetuate in our midst his covenantal love and sacrificial participation in life. Jesus said OK to his Father as we hear from the letter to Hebrews: "For this reason, when he came into the world, he said: 'Sacrifice and offering you did not desire, but a body you prepared for me; holocausts and sin offerings you took no delight in. Then

I said, 'As is written of me in the scroll, Behold, I come to do your will, O God'" (Heb. 10:5–10).

One of the many characteristics of Jesus's covenantal life is an unimaginable sacrificial participation. He became totally a lamb to be sacrificed; as a vulnerable person, he underwent a cruel death; for thirty-three years, he denied himself, took up his own cross daily. As the Scriptures testify, he became fully the Son of God by his sacrifice of himself; he finally sacrificed his very life as a ransom for the sins of the whole human race.

Many of us may criticize him for his upholding and teaching as well of this unbearable demand of God's covenantal love. Before his final days, we hear him say to us, "The hour has come for the Son of Man to be glorified" (John 12:23–26). We may think it is a sort of foolhardiness on his part of emptying himself, stripping of glory and all his comforts. How can he dare enough to utter that he was glorified by his "bloodshed way of life," his "broken-bread sharing of his everything," a total annihilation and burial of his own glorious status? And amazingly, he recommends to us, "Do it in remembrance of me." However, if we go on reading what he spelled out after glorifying such treacherous matter, we can understand very clearly the positive and valid reason for such approach. He says, "Amen, amen, I say to you, unless a grain of wheat falls to the ground and dies, it remains just a grain of wheat; but if it dies, it produces much fruit. Whoever loves his life loses it, and whoever hates his life in this world will preserve it for eternal life. Whoever serves me must follow me, and where I am, there also will my servant be. The Father will honor whoever serves me."

QUITTERS CAN NEVER BE LEADERS

Any evil that is encircling us in earthly life—be it an ignominious passion, death, or total washout and disappearance like the grain of wheat—turns out to be the source of a refurbished, eternal life. No pain, no gain; no sacrifice, no fruits. In this regard, I have to add one more adage: "Winners never quit, and quitters never win." There are many disciples of Jesus who behave like the "Chicken Little." She thought the sky was falling. One little piece of bark fell off a tree as she passed under the limb, struck her on the head, and the rest of her story was one of perpetual alarm. All it took was one piece of injury. From that day forward, Chicken Little lived in a constant state of anxiety. She was prepared for the "worst." The only thing for which this paranoid little chicken was not prepared was for the "best." The sky did not fall.

Jesus hated to see his followers as quitters, especially those who desire to be and perform as his discipled leaders in his Kingdom. He abhors persons of such "Chicken Little" attitude and behavior toward facing occasions of sacrificing even their very self. In the Gospels, we see Jesus as a noteworthy winner, never quitting from his life situations that challenged his very life. Yet he did not quit. Such was our Master, a praiseworthy Winner. Through his teachings, he instructed us not to be so. In one of his parables, "the parable of the talents" (Matt. 25:14–30), he brings before us a notorious quitter who acts exactly like that Chicken Little. He is a fellow who by birth or by his DNA possessed very little resources, while his fellow citizens or his neighbors were gifted with abundance. That was his life situation, very much constrained in comparison with the others. Instead of making the best use of it by plowing with it to the maximum, the "Chicken Little," resented, terrified, insecure, became lazy, lousy, and maybe cranky too. Jesus is so vehement in denouncing such quitters. He repudiates this notorious quitter and even punishes him by confiscating what he has and giving it to the others who are not quitters.

The modern mind dictates to most of us: Is your wife not usable or becoming glamourless? Quit the marriage. Is your husband irritating and not appreciative? Just quit.

Does the color of your church sanctuary unpleasant? Quit and shop around for some other colorful churches. Do the pastor or the members of the parish councils and other associations or some members of community bother you with their continued crummy, crabby, cranky, lousy, and crafty behavior? Just quit from your leadership role.

I don't know how many among us are living a life of grumbling, isolation, and nagging grievances and are digging hole in our own life like the notorious quitter in the Gospel and as the Chicken Little in the story. Let us try our best to get rid of this modern destructive mind setup and play not quitters but winners so that we can hear from the Lord one day: "Well done, my good and faithful servant. Since you were faithful in small matters I will give you great responsibilities. Come, share your master's joy."

Ultimately, there are more lessons besides those three enlisted above we find in the textbook and workbook of Jesus's learners. When we say "learning in the school or ashram of Jesus," we don't mean of mere facts, information, and head knowledge. We mean all that "and more." We don't just learn facts and principles but of a person. We are lifelong learners in relationship with Jesus as we hear his voice in his word and have his ear in prayer and share in community with his body, all through the power of his Spirit.

THE RESULTS OF LIFELONG LEARNING UNDER JESUS

Those who live in this postmodern age, baby boomers, and millennials as well are esteemed as more pragmatic than our forebears. We always seek the final results of what we intend to do; we long to find out what we will gain here and now, instantly and immediately from all that we accomplish. Jesus foresaw this attitude would be creeping in among his followers. So when he ordered us, "Learn of me," he added the expected results coming out of our obedience to his order. He said, "Come to me, all you who labor and are burdened, and I will give you rest. Take my yoke upon you and learn from me, for I am meek and humble of heart; and you will find rest for your selves. For my yoke is easy and my burden light" (Matt. 11:25–30).

According to Jesus, the results of our lifelong learning of him are the following: First and foremost, our attitude will be changed into the likeness of Jesus, who is meek and humble of heart. As Paul writes (Rom. 8:9–13), we begin to live always in the Spirit of Christ. We will be no more in the flesh; we will not be debtors or slaves to the flesh, to live according to the flesh, but by the Spirit, we will put to death the deeds of the body, and thereby, we will live a quality life, an eternal godly life. As a consequence of "Christic learning," we would be continuously hearing a warning from the Master who resides always inside his committed students: "It is the spirit that gives life, while the flesh is of no avail" (John 6:63a). What the Master indicates is that the flesh counts for nothing. He too continues, "The words I have spoken to you—they are full of the Spirit and life." While the Spirit alone gives eternal life, human effort accomplishes nothing. In this way, Jesus stresses the ultimate result of our lifelong learning in his school is to be fully conscious of the eternal fact that our life is spiritual. And all that we accomplish through our physicality—body, emotion, and even brain-outsourced intelligence—are just a handmaid, if it is properly controlled by our Spirit-filled spirit. This view of our earthly life would be fully built up within as we progress in our learning of Jesus.

RESTING IN JESUS

Second, we get into the true restfulness of Jesus. We begin to live in genuine rest and peace. That is the promise Jesus makes when he invites us to his inner shelter: "Come to me, all you who labor and are burdened, and I will give you rest." It will be a permanent peace settled in our spirit, and that peace will not be as the world gives, but it will be a genuine peace.

While I was serving as a resident priest in a parish of the archdiocese of Chicago, I developed an admiration for an elderly woman in that parish. At a time when all the churches in Chicago decided to lock the churches during daytime except for services, this lady approached my parish priest and told him, "Father, I have two requests from you. One, I need a church key so that I can continue to come and visit the Lord and before him. Two, kindly allow me to clean daily the tabernacle and the altar so that the Lord may find his living quarter spotless." The pastor willingly gave her the key and granted permission to clean the sanctuary as she requested. I used to go to church for my daily visit during daytime. I often saw this lady doing that cleaning job perfectly. One day, out of curiosity, I approached her and asked, "Grandma, what makes you to come daily here and do this kind of job?" She responded, "My son, I see Jesus here. I get complete peace and rest in him."

I was indeed flabbergasted in awe of her attitude based on Jesus's promise. This would be the response we may hear from many of our present discipled leaders who, with no fuss and hoo-ha, have been serving the Lord in their parishes as altar angels, as organizers of socials, as catechetical teachers, as prayer warriors. They find certain restful and peaceful settlement in the presence of Jesus and his values.

Undoubtedly, this gift of peace and rest is totally a blessing from on High. It is holistically genuine, true, and stable. Jesus has promised so about this gift. When he instructed us to be humble and lowly, serviceable and sacrificial, he stated, "If I, therefore, the master and teacher, have washed your feet, you ought to wash one another's feet. I have given you a model to follow, so that as I have done for you, you should also do. Amen, amen, I say to you, no slave is greater than his master nor any messenger greater than the one who sent him. If you understand this, blessed are you if you do it" (John 13:14–17).

REMARKABLE GAIN BY PAINFUL LEARNING

Third, Jesus promised that we would start feeling all life's burdens easy and light: "For my yoke is easy and my burden light." Jesus's promise of an easy or well-fitting yoke does not mean that his followers would be freed of all challenges of unfairness of life or burdens of human roles and duties; rather, he did not bring a Gospel of prosperity or that of comfort. His compassion led him to take an entirely different approach. He promised to help the burdened to bear whatever load they had to carry through life. As a preacher said, "Because yokes were often built for two oxen, Jesus was, in effect, promising to be the yokemate of those who would come to him to rest in him." Jesus also assured believers that his burden will be light. When the burden is laid upon us in love and shared by a loving yokemate such as Jesus, then, as an ancient rabbi once said, "My burden is become my song."

There is one more great gain earned by our learning of Jesus: When we lean on our spiritual values, not only do we get true peace and restful life, but we also become an effective source for others' peace and rest. An incredible incident happened in 2004. A mother with her two children, an eight-year-old boy and a two-year-old girl, were caught in the middle of tsunamic waves and tossed around very badly. The mother was carrying her children on her shoulders and advised them to hold her neck tight. As they were drowning down into the waves, she found out a tree on their path, so she climbed that tree with her children. While they were on the top of the tree, safe and secure, she found out the tree could not bear the heavy weight of the three, and so she told her children to hold tight the branch of the tree and once the flood subsided, they should search for their uncle and join with him. As she was advising them and bidding them goodbye, she dropped herself into the waves and disappeared. The children were safe and were taken to their uncle, and the boy enumerated this remarkable story to the public.

In this incredible incident, we notice three of them were tossed around by the waves and lost their hope, peace, rest, and safety. But finally, they found out peace, rest, and safety in different ways. The children got rest and peace not just by holding first on their mother's neck and then the branches of the tree but also much more than that; it was the trust they held on their mother's love and concern for them. The mother was holding on to her spiritual value of love for her children and fully satisfied by settling them at a safer place. That was her source of peace and rest. This is what Christ invites us to hold on to if we need true peace and rest.

MOST EFFECTIVE EDUCATIONAL TOOLS IN THE SCHOOL OF JESUS

With no reservation, I should insist that the primary medium of lifelong learning of Jesus is the Bible. There is no second opinion about it. However, from the onset of Christianity, Jesus's Spirit moved us to add one more to it, and that is the church tradition that has been intensely penetrated by the same Spirit in the lives and teachings of the apostles and their successors and surely of every committed Christian from the day of resurrection of Jesus. To learn more of Jesus and his teachings and his traditional values and holdings, historically, discipled leaders made recourse to different communication media available in every age, such as silent, meditative prayer; as listening to pulpit or platform-based public speeches; as getting explanations and counsels through dialogues; and certainly through arts and theater media. Then came the printed media through which disciples began reading and digesting what the apostles and other disciples wrote and published.

Today, as we are born and bred in a postmodern age communication media world, we are blessed with so many powerful, instant, and elaborative communication facilities in our lifelong learning effort. Besides learning from personal conversations, reading books, and attending special classes and group discussions of likeminded discipled leaders, we too can watch educational videos. These videos provide the flexibility of watching at a time; they are most convenient to us and benefiting from visuals (diagrams, charts, body language). Using audio media, we can listen to recordings. It also gives the flexibility for multitasking (learning while driving or exercising or cleaning) and engages the mind in ways different from video instruction by leaning on the imagination to picture the teacher and the setting.

Also, there are so many (probably ninety-one) leading social networks worldwide, such as Facebook, WhatsApp, WeChat, LinkedIn, Google+, Twitter, through which we can gather amazing detailed, as well as pithy, descriptions of the teachings and instructions of Jesus. When we use them, we should, by all means, first evaluate the particulars of our particular season and need of life and choose the media and venues most conducive to our ongoing learning about God, the world, and ourselves.

LISTEN TO GOD IN JESUS'S OTHER LEADERS

In this communication process of learning, we must bear in mind that every discipled leader should be open-minded to other discipled leaders' suggestions, directions, and style of ministerial life. Our Master couldn't bear to see the same pharisaical attitudes and behaviors of the learned and skilled religious leaders at his time. He blamed them, sometimes even cursed them, for such perversion in leadership. The NT books narrate profusely the events of this sort occurring between Jesus and Jewish leaders. If we read carefully Jesus's parable of the rich man and Lazarus (Luke 16:19–31), we will discover the mind of God regarding our serious and continuous educative learning task in this world. At the end of the parable, the rich man begs Abraham to send Lazarus back to his hometown to warn his siblings (perhaps they too, like him, would have been very selfishly rich) lest they too come to the place of torment because according to him, if someone from the dead goes to them, they will repent. To him, Abraham replies, "If they will not listen to Moses and the prophets, neither will they be persuaded if someone should rise from the dead."

There are many such pharisaical leaders in our midst. While they research, study deeply, and teach the biblical instructions and commandments, they won't pay heed to what other discipled leaders preach and teach. Many of them, as soon as they hear or read about some leader is going to come to their jurisdiction or "so-called their territory," they make sharp criticism about him/her with the biased attitude, and sometimes they obstruct such leader entering into their "territory," or other times, they never attend to their meetings, preaching, or convention. There are some other leaders who actually go and participate in other leaders' conventions or classes, but their ears are closed or, much worse, their hearts are mummed. Instead, they raise some reasonable questions regarding the legitimacy of the speakers talking. On the contrary, our Master, as he indicates in his parable of the rich man and Lazarus, instructs us not to behave like pharisaical leaders, rather to be humble, simple, and open-minded to what the Spirit says through other leaders moving among them.

When we begin to be fervent, uninterrupted learners of the Master's life, words, and experiential intricacies we discover in our daily life, we will teach, preach, and perform all other leadership activities in a fruitful, efficacious, standard way. Our communications will originate from our guts, from our hearts, and not from papers. Our words and actions, plans and implementations, will be dialogical, synthetic, and solid. Our visionary proposals will be appreciated and received warmly by our congregational members.

SECTION III: JESUS'S OFFICIAL DEMANDS FROM DISCIPLED LEADERS

Your light must shine before others,
that they may see your good deeds
and glorify your heavenly Father.
—Matt. 5:16

CHAPTER 15: BE JESUS'S WITNESS

CALL TO BE LIFELONG MISSIONARIES

Though there are some discrepancies in the details of how, when, and where of Jesus's final moment of leaving this world to his Father, all the four Gospel writers (Ref. Mark 16:14–18; Matt. 28:16–20; Luke 24:46–49; John 20:19–23) are in the same mind to stress a singular fact happening at that moment: Jesus "sent out" his disciples with his "grand commission" of witnessing him and his Gospel values through miraculous power of healing, which he would grant them through his Spirit. Pope Francis, in his Angelus address on July 15, 2108, said that the unique missionary style Jesus proposed in his Great Commission had two dimensions: "The mission has a *center*," which he explained as Jesus's person as a center of reference in all missionary labors. And Pope also pointed out the "poverty of means," which is the typical "face" of missionary style Jesus demanded.

This evangelical mission applies not only to the "ordained" leaders but also to all the baptized, who, as we mentioned in the first chapter, are called to be disciples of Jesus. All disciples in Jesus's Kingdom are called to witness Christ and his Gospel in the different environments of life. Pope Francis emphasizes in most of his homilies and writings that "a baptized person who doesn't feel the need to witness Jesus' Gospel, through the life of poverty, isn't a good Christian."

The witnesses Jesus intended to choose for his purpose may be scrutinized by those to whom they are sent with some legitimate questions such as the following: Were they present in the company of Jesus? Did they see and hear him proposing his values? Were there some others with them while they were accompanying with him? And so on. We know if the 12 apostles and some other 120 holy men like Joseph, called Barsabbas, and women like Mary, Mother of Jesus, and Mary Magdalene (Acts 1:13–23) are present today in the public court, they would be certainly numbered as the legitimate witnesses to Jesus, responding rightly to the right questions. When Jesus left from this world, he assured this undebated fact, declaring, "You are witnesses of these things" (Luke 24:48).

The doubtful question arises when people like you and me allege that we too are witnesses to Jesus. Yet from the day of the church's inception, all discipled leaders of Christ, including some of the NT writers, assert they are genuine witnesses to their Master Jesus. How is it?

EVERY DISCIPLED LEADER IS A WITNESS TO JESUS

All discipled leaders, as we discussed in the previous sections, are the ones who listen and think and then, separating themselves from any worldly elements that are dear to them, follow Jesus, who would become then the most precious for their life. Jesus turns out to be the most valuable pearl. The discipled leaders uninterruptedly must remain with Christ and live and travel with him. From the NT books, we conclude that the same discipled leaders are the ones whom Jesus sends out on a mission.

In this mission endeavors, the primary project the discipled leaders are to implement, as Jesus intended, is to witness. Before ascending to his Father, Jesus said to his discipled leaders, "You will receive power when the Holy Spirit comes upon you, and you will be my witnesses in Jerusalem, throughout Judea and Samaria, and to the ends of the earth" (Acts 1:8). By this assertion, as the biblical scholars maintain, the risen Jesus was stressing the role of his discipled leaders as a body of divinely mandated witnesses to his life, teaching, and resurrection. In many versions of the Bible, we find the verse being translated as "You shall be witnesses" to emphasize more on disciples' act of witnessing as a command from the Master. Yes, all discipled leaders of Jesus, wherever and whenever they are designated by Jesus through his community to take the role of leadership, should keep this "grand commission" of the Master as their primary duty.

A witness is commonly known as one who spells out what he or she knows about a person or a given situation. The role of witnessing to Christ has been expounded in various ways by Jesus and the apostles, especially Paul, and other NT writers, such as being ambassadors for him (2 Cor. 5:20; Eph. 6:19–20), becoming fishers of men (Matt. 4:19), being his imitators (1 Cor. 11:1), being light of the world and salt of the earth (Matt. 5:13–16), proclaiming Jesus's teachings from the housetops (Matt. 10:27), testifying to the truth (John 18:37), and being coworkers in that truth (3 John 1:8).

Explaining clearly what we, as discipled leaders, should witness to, Jesus is quoted saying, "You are witnesses of these things" (Luke 24:48). This is what Jesus instructed his "missionaries" before he ascended to his abode. What are "those things" he expected them to witness to? Pooling all that have been proclaimed in the Bible, let me highlight here what is paramount in our today's role of witnessing to Christ.

As a witness for Christ, our life is a key part of our witness. We profess we are a new creation in and with Christ. This means our habits and lifestyle should reflect this unique life consecrated to Jesus Christ. Because of our human weakness, we may stumble from time to time as we try to walk the walk of Jesus, but getting forgiveness from him, we should rise and go steady in our witnessing to the below-listed truthful facts:

WITNESS TO JESUS'S ABIDING PRESENCE

The postmodern world insists through its various researches and studies that "religion is nothing but a fictional reality." As we read and see in so many novels, documentaries, TV series and films, and so on about the "Unsolved Mysteries" and "Secrets Unveiled," we are told the essence and existence of faith and religion remains surrounded by questions, rumors, legends, and wild speculations. Particularly when it talks about our faith in the existence and transaction of the risen Jesus, it cruelly criticizes us, saying we are simply weaklings supported by certain "social networks." Here comes the important role of every discipled leader to counteract to such outrageous ill-treatment of our faith in the risen Lord. Our Master forewarned us in this matter and also asked us to prioritize the duty of witnessing him in truth and Spirit as genuine reality.

Some years back, there was a humorous commercial jingle for Wendy's hamburgers. In it, a tiny old lady with a huge voice was portrayed getting a hamburger at one of Wendy's competitors. She looked at the little bun and screamed out, "Where's the beef?" Well, that's what many of our people bellowing in our leadership services. "Where's the beef?" Talk is cheap, as the old expression goes, but the beef will be seen when the discipled leaders do their best to add to their ministerial actions and talks their convincing testimonies of the risen Lord's marvelous deeds in their life.

Christ sent his disciples to fulfill the mission to bring to all people the joyful proclamation that salvation is not only closer but that the Savior can also be encountered through the presence of the disciples of the new life. This is the primary demand of the Master as he chooses, teaches, grooms, elevates, and sends them out. This means the uncompromised responsibility of all discipled leaders is to testify to the primacy and supremacy of the One who has chosen and sent them out. Plus, they should continue to encounter the risen Lord who promised he would with them till the end of ages: "And behold, I am with you always, until the end of the age" (Matt. 28:20).

Christianity, which Jesus intended, is nothing but a fact and transmits itself as a real encounter. And that fact is not some package of dogmas and rituals but specifically about an intimate relationship with a Person who died, rose, and lives among us, within us, forever. It must be remembered, as we pointed out in the previous pages, that the Christian disciple is above all someone called by God through a personal encounter. Strictly speaking, no one becomes a Christian for autonomous choice; he becomes so by answering to a call. There is, in fact, a love that precedes our response. This is the way it goes with any move a discipled leader takes out in the world.

Even in the narratives of the prophetic calls in the Bible, we notice the primacy of God is being witnessed adamantly. For example, take the story of Amos who was thrown by the call in a confrontation with the injustices of the political power. He must also contend with the cold considerations of the court chaplain, the priest Amaziah, who urged to flee away from the land. Amos said to the priest that at the root of his words, there is not a personal choice tied to his prospects. It is God himself who forced him with a precise call: "I was no prophet, nor a prophet's son; I was a shepherd and a harvester of sycamores; the Lord took me from following the flock, and the Lord said to me, 'Go, prophesy in the midst of my people Israel'" (Amos 7:14–15).

WITNESS TO HIS POWERFUL INTERACTION

The primary function of the disciples, sent by Jesus to lead his people, is to witness to him. This is because as we mentioned earlier, they have already had intimate knowledge of his life, plus personal encounter with him. However, this duty of witnessing to Christ would be incomplete without being empowered by the anointing of his Spirit. We know from the NT only after Pentecost Jesus's first group of disciples, who even lived, walked with him, and heard intimately many heavenly matters from him, were to be empowered fully by the Spirit for their leadership ministries. Their witness to Christ was not only empowered but also guided and validated by his Spirit (John 14:16–17). Thus, their full vocation of witnessing was realized only in the Spirit.

Claiming "All authority in heaven and on earth has been given to me," Jesus shared his authority with his disciples. Before he ascended to heaven, he promised them two things: one, they will receive his power: "You will receive power when the Holy Spirit comes upon you" (Acts 1:8a), and two, it was he who would send the Spirit: "Behold I am sending the promise of my Father upon you; but stay in the city until you are clothed with power from on high" (Luke 24:49).

The most important authority and power Jesus shared with his discipled leaders through his Spirit was to possess direct knowledge of the incarnate Word, and being sent out as authorized agents of the same Word, they provided the authentic interpretation of the life and teaching of Jesus. This is because their witness to Christ was guided by the Spirit sent by the Master.

Also, this empowerment in the Spirit was the genuine source of miraculous signs and mighty works they performed all their apostolic ministries: "These signs will accompany those who believe: in my name they will drive out demons, they will speak new languages. They will pick up serpents [with their hands], and if they drink any deadly thing, it will not harm them. They will lay hands on the sick, and they will recover" (Mark 16:15–18).

In the early nineteenth century, a plantation owner was moved by the sobs of a young girl, a slave, who was about to be sold on an auction block. In a rush of compassion, he bought her and disappeared into the crowd. After the auction, the clerk handed the girl a bill of sale on which the plantation owner had written "Free." Stunned by such unexpected kindness, the girl begged to know the identity of her liberator. "He has set me free!" she exclaimed. "I must serve him as long as I live!"

In our discipled life, there is a very intrinsic connection between ourselves and Christ Jesus. We are related to him very closely not only because he is our Teacher and we are his students; not only because he is the Shepherd, Leader, who leads us to green pastures; not only because of the nourishment he offers us spiritually and socially by the Eucharist and the church but mainly because as the girl in the story exclaimed, "Christ has set us free." This is what we hear from Paul: "For freedom Christ set us free; so stand firm and do not submit again to the yoke of slavery" (Gal. 5:1). Besides, as the same girl said, we too promised in baptism and confirmation that we should serve him as long as we live.

CHAPTER 16: DISCIPLE OTHERS TO THE MASTER

We know well the grand commission of the Master to his disciples was "Go, therefore, and make disciples of all nations" (Matt. 28:19a). These words resonate what he held as his initial motivation why he chose and called them: "[T]hat they might be with him and he might send them forth" (Mark 3:14–15). Even to those who had been charmed by the miraculous deeds he did to them and pleaded to remain with him and to accompany him in his journey, Jesus ordered, "Go home to your family and announce to them all that the Lord in his pity has done for you" (Mark 5:19). Then Mark adds, the healed man "went off and began to proclaim in his region what Jesus had done for him."

DISCIPLE-MAKING IS OUR PRIMARY TASK

Those of us in the role of leading others haven't completed our discipleship until we are equipped and motivated to engage in the disciple-making process. In other words, a disciple isn't a true disciple until they've become a disciple-maker. We should never forget if we want our friends under our leadership to realize everything God has for them, then we need to give them a vision of discipleship that extends beyond a sanctified version of the any sort of earthly dreams. We must help our people engage earnestly in the Great Commission as their primary calling in life. The Holy Spirit will only flow into them as much as they are willing to let it flow out of them into the lives of others.

The church's primary mission is to create disciples who create other disciples, just as Jesus intended us to do. The church, where we are elected or chosen to lead our people, is a community that is helping humans to follow Jesus, assist them being changed by Jesus, and then join them on his mission. We are committed as our first duty to state that vision again and again and again. Our friends may forget; they may drift in their thinking; they may get new ideas and want to explore different directions to take the church. But we should go on repeating the vision and mission of the church as handed over to her by the Master. As one writer calls, we are undoubtedly none other than the "vision casters" of Jesus. We should, standing on the housetop, speak loudly and constantly about the Christian duty of disciple-making in season and out of season. Consequently, that duty becomes the culture of our local church.

DISCIPLING MEANS ENCOURAGING INTIMACY WITH THE MASTER

There is a lot to be done in our undertaking the above-mentioned vision casting. As we proclaim the august duty of the disciples to disciple others, we also must form and train our people to listen and meditate Jesus and his values attentively and then to separate themselves from all that obstruct their connection with the Master, who unequivocally becomes the most precious pearl from above. We direct our people how to remain with Jesus closely and how to live and walk with him in daily life.

This vision-drive "discipling education" is the most needed process for any disciple to go out to fulfill Jesus's mission. Let us remember when the Master sent his disciples, he intended them to bring to all people the joyful proclamation that not only salvation is closer but also the Giver of that salvation can be encountered through the presence of his disciples of the new life. Christianity is a fact and transmits itself as a real encounter. Every Christian's discipled life originates from nothing but a divine encounter, which may happen in a different style and mode. Indeed, no one becomes a Christian for autonomous choice; he/she becomes so by answering to a call. There is, in fact, a love that precedes our response. This is what we are taught by Christ when he says, "It was not you who chose me, but I who chose you and appointed you to go and bear fruit that will remain" (John 15:16a) and by St. Paul when he says, "In Christ [the Father] chose us before the foundation of the world, to be holy and blameless before him in love" (Eph. 11:8). Already in the Old Testament, from Abraham onward, emerges the primacy of God at the beginning of each call. The initiative to start the story of the salvation of the people of Israel comes from the Lord: "Abraham, called by God, obeyed" (Heb. 11:8).

Even in the narratives of the prophetic calls, it is clear the primacy of God who calls. Exemplary is the story of Amos, who was thrown by the call in a confrontation with the injustices of the political power. He must also contend with the cold considerations of the "court chaplain," the priest Amaziah, who urged caution. Amos says to the priest that at the root of his words, there is not a personal choice tied to his prospects. It is God himself who forced him with a precise call: "I was no prophet, nor a prophet's son; I was a shepherd and a harvester of sycamores; the Lord took me from following the flock, and the Lord said me, 'Go, prophesy in the midst of my people Israel'" (Amos 7:14–15).

DISCIPLING DEMANDS SHARING A DEEPER EXPERIENCE OF THE RISEN LORD

Therefore, the discipled leaders must bear in mind no good will come out of any discipleship program unless and until each individual follower of Christ encounters the risen Lord. Many times, I myself, being a theater student and director, actor, and playwright, think and regret that most of my sharing Christ and his values to others, whether it is at the altar or in classes or in counseling sessions, seem as if I am acting out on stage for audience.

The main reason for such bitter convulsion within me is I know what I say, what I proclaim, and what I perform as sacramental leader, catechetical teacher, and pastoral counselor does not correspond to what I am engaged in natural life. In other words, anything I say or do is not authenticated truthfully by my personal encounter with the risen Lord. I am just rattling and exposing what the church taught me or orders me; they do not come from my guts but simply a kind of "lip service" or a "stage performance." Rather, I should have shared my faith holdings to my audience, my congregation, my clients, and certainly the nonbelievers with heart-filled conviction about the wonderful changes the risen Master has made in my life.

No matter how low our IQ and how much we fall short of creative artistic talents, as discipled leaders chosen by Christ, we have been empowered with the unique experience of the risen Lord. Testifying to it is sufficiently enough to disciple others to Jesus. Tantalizingly, we are prone to low-esteeming ourselves, thinking we don't really know enough or haven't been a good Christian long enough to make a difference. It is completely false. Church history bears out millions of followers of Christ—very rural, poor, uneducated, and even typically prodigal—have turned out to be disciples of Jesus, like Mary Magdalene, the torchbearers for the risen Lord alive. The one and only truth they witness is they have experienced the immense love of the living God through Jesus. That is exactly for which we select, groom, teach, and discipline as many as we can and disciple them for Christ.

DISCIPLING INCLUDES FREEING FROM IGNORANCE AND BLINDFOLDEDNESS

There is one more thing the discipled leaders must keep in mind as they disciple others. Many of the followers of Christ in our parishes are indifferent to be discipled as they wrongly think that it is something they are already doing; in fact, they are not. Simply going to church on Sunday or attending a few adult catechism or Bible classes or throwing some checks or cash envelopes in the collection baskets is not the full discipleship; maybe it is a part of it. Besides, most of the laity consider, especially those in Catholic churches, that the duty of discipling the humans belongs to only those who are ordained or those who have entered into religious life with three vows taken.

These views have become very obsolete long ago when the church had entered into the new age of enlightenment. Every follower of Christ is entrusted with the grand commission of Christ: "disciple others." Yes, the Lord explained the commission of discipling includes "preaching and teaching and healing." He too added to them the duty of baptizing. Go therefore and make disciples of all nations, "baptizing them in the name of the Father, and of the Son, and of the Holy Spirit" (Matt. 28:19). This is because, as the church tradition upholds, every Christian disciple, through baptism, participates in the role of the Master, being King, Prophet, and Priest. We will treat the sacramental aspect of this role later in this book. Here, let us be concerned only about the remarkable role Jesus handed over to all his discipled leaders.

DEALING WITH UNRECOGNIZED DISCIPLED LEADERS

We are demanded by Jesus to become "developers of leaders for Jesus's Kingdom." When a person is baptized and inducted into Jesus's team, he/she is not instantly made "disciple-makers." They should grow into an effective discipled leadership, but not everyone is gifted as a leader. This doesn't mean our local churches don't have leaders; they are already there invisibly, just underdeveloped or overlooked. The impending problem that exists among us is that most of us are too busy in implementing or accomplishing our given jobs and we find no time to look into the dignified but burdensome duty of developing the discipled leaders. Sometimes we hunt for already well-developed leaders in our community but fail because of the invisibility of disciples' potential. We should never look for a person who is jack-of-all-trades, who can cover all the ministries. There also we fail.

We read in Paul's letters how the early churches conducted their ongoing programs according to the Spirit of the risen Lord. There were many discipled leaders according to the local needs and to the human abilities as well: "Since we have gifts that differ according to the grace given to us, let us exercise them: if prophecy, in proportion to the faith; if ministry, in ministering; if one is a teacher, in teaching; if one exhorts, in exhortation; if one contributes, in generosity; if one is over others, with diligence; if one does acts of mercy, with cheerfulness" (Ref. Rom. 12:6–8; 1 Cor. 12:26; Eph. 4:11–12). In a good church system, we can notice it is run very effectively by a group of leaders with different leadership capabilities. That is what we should focus on as we discipling others to become discipled leaders.

Before crossing Jordan River, Joshua, as a strong and faith-filled leader delegated by Moses (Josh. 1:12–18), was addressing the Reubenites, the Gadites, and the half tribe of Manasseh that they should be the first groups to inhabit the Promised Land and that they too, as warriors, must cooperate with him in settling all other Israelites in the land God gave them. Accepting all he said, all those who joined in his warrior team pledged in one accord: "We will do all you have commanded us, and we will go wherever you send us. As completely as we obeyed Moses, we will obey you." The only part I don't like in their pledge is that they were ready to murder anyone who rebelled against Joshua's orders and did not obey all his commands.

This kind of hero worship can never be encouraged in the team of discipled leaders. We know what all the atrocities had been politically, even religiously, done around the world by such blindfolded, mere emotional clinging to human leadership. Whoever surrenders to the leadership of Jesus can never think and plan doing evil for evil in their fights. Therefore, the discipled leaders serving in a parish or any church institutions should in no way give any chance of such hero worship to those who are willing to cooperate with the leadership. They must be directed not to the human power and glory of the discipled leaders but to the all-good and all-forgiving heart of our Master. Let me quote a best direction from a best political leader, Theodore Roosevelt, on best leadership, which we can adhere to in our discipling efforts: "The best executive is the one who has sense enough to pick good men to do what he wants done, and self-restraint to keep from meddling with them while they do it."

CHAPTER 17: GO BEYOND

In the previous pages, I have quoted profusely the authoritative command of our Master to "[g]o therefore," which he spelled out as his grand commission not only before he was being ascended but also during his public ministry in Palestine as a sort of pilot program of mission to be performed by his disciples to the places and people where he wanted to go but couldn't because of so many natural and supernatural factors. One thing was certain: from the moment he began choosing people to his team of leaders, he intended that all of them, besides remaining with him spiritually, are to be sent forth physically (Mark 3:14–15). Admirably, as "God set forth in Christ, a plan for the fullness of times, to sum up all things in him, in heaven and on earth" (Eph. 1:9–10), Jesus handed over to his disciples this unbelievable responsibility that God had entrusted to him.

In order that we accomplish God's universal plan, Jesus, though he demanded us to stay with him intimately, ordered us to go out. When he ordered us to "go out," we can be sure what was in his mind. With Oswald Chambers, we can dare say, "Once the call of God comes to you, start going and never stop." Our acceptance and affirmation of this unique commission of the Master does not relate it to the historical factors of Jesus of Nazareth as being a Jewish, a Galilean rebel who lived some two thousand years back, or one sage who founded his own "Better Way" to reach the Supreme Being, nor as a feudal king who emerged in the beginning of the third century to counteract and topple down all then-existed rulers of the world. Rather, the primary reason for our submission to the grand commission to go out is that we encounter today the same Jesus, Mary's Son, personally and communally as the resurrected Lord in his Spirit moving and leading at his will around the globe; that this leader cannot be contained or restricted only to a few, even to the so-called Christians, but to every living creature with no discrimination or labeling or profiling; and that we are so proud of being inducted into this Jesus's church and share the same power and dignity of being assigned as the proxies of his leadership, plus the assurance of entering into his heavenly mansions.

GOING BEYOND OUR "SELFIES"

Among many implications contained in his order, number 1 is a very personal one. When Jesus says to his disciples to go, he means "come out." In other words, our Master desired that all his disciples chosen to be his leaders must get out of their so-called selfies, my territory, my clan, my race, my community, and surely my own family. We are chosen to perform the universal and global evangelism in the name of Jesus. In the previous section, we discussed about how our Master expected all his followers to leave their families and their own personal agenda and, if needed, even to deny their very self (Luke 9:57–62). Instead of acting like many self-oriented disciples, we are to depend on God and obey his sovereignty and seek our greatness and dignity through sacrificial service and humility. If we disobey and turn back from him, we may become like Lot's wife (Gen. 19:15–26), a salty, immovable, lifeless figures walking inside our ministerial territory.

With this hope-filled mindset, we are supposed to come out of our blues, depression, inhibition, perversion, bad attitudes, and so on, which as every human being challenged in earthly life. The Supreme Being predicted such liberation would be possible with his help: "Thus says the Lord God to these [dry or dead] bones: Listen! I will make breath enter you so you may come to life. I will put sinews on you, make flesh grow over you, cover you with skin, and put breath into you so you may come to life. Then you shall know that I am the Lord" (Ezra 37:5–6).

Jesus pointed out this mysterious reality by his miraculous deeds, particularly in the event of raising Lazarus from the dead using the same command: "Lazarus, come out" (Ref. John 11:43). Human resurrection is possible and real, not only in the resurrection on the last day as the "heavenly resurrection" but also here and now as "earthly or physical resurrection." Jesus confirmed this unbelievable fact in his discussion with Martha (John 11:17–27), and after praying to his Father, he ordered the dead man to come out from the tomb. Thus, today when Jesus commands us to "go out," he expects us first to come out of our darkened inner sanctuary that has been corroded into like a tomb. Our Master wants us to be liberated from our twisted personality, weird perversions, addictions, coldness of heart, procrastination to accomplish his duties, hatred and resentment, and surely prejudices. We have been blessed by our Master at the time of baptism, not only exhorting us but much more, helping us come out of our grotesque original fate of darkness (Rom. 8:8–11). Indeed, when we were called with special unction to share his leadership ministry in his church, Jesus desires we should to be reconfirmed in this brightened status and strive to conform to it daily.

While the abovementioned first act of "going forth" happens within ourselves, we are commanded by the Master to exercise it and proven it in our outward actions. As Cindy Wooden pointed out in an article she wrote for CNS on February 27, 2014, in Italian, the phrase "Go forth" is even snappier: "avanti." Pope Francis began his pontificate with that Italian word, avanti. Even before he was elected, he dreamed of "avanti." As the world's cardinals gathered at the Vatican in early March 2013 to discuss the needs of the church, before they entered the conclave to elect a successor to Pope Benedict XVI, "avanti" was at the heart of a speech by then cardinal Jorge Bergoglio of Buenos Aires, Argentina. He differentiated sharply the two kinds of church—church going out and church living within—we encounter these days.

Let me quote him: "'Put simply, there are two images of the church: a church which evangelizes and goes out of herself' by hearing the word of God with reverence and proclaiming it with faith; and 'the worldly church, living within herself, of herself, for herself.'" After many hours of meditation on those Pope's words, I loved to label this act of "avanti" as "going beyond."

GOING BEYOND OUR NATURAL JUDGMENTS

The clarion call of Jesus "to go beyond" pushes all his discipled leaders never to stop at the surface of things, especially when we are dealing with human persons. We are called to look beyond, to focus on the heart to see how much generosity everyone is capable. No one can be excluded from the mercy of God; the church is undoubtedly a "house that welcomes all with no barrier and refuses no one." Its doors remain wide open so that those who are touched by grace can find the certainty of forgiveness. The greater the sin, so much the greater must be the love that the church expresses toward those who convert.

In browsing human history, we discover that always, it is our second move or second thought that gets us into the second chance God imputes to every human in their fallen and skirmish foul plays. As soon as we come in contact with our enemy either in thought or in outside situation, our naughty brain claims vengeance, grinding of teeth, and escalated anger and hatred. But being a discipled and disciplined leaders of Jesus, our heart exhorts or pricks the brain to pursue another style of forgiveness, kindness, and tolerance. It pushes us to go beyond our natural human tendency to Christic mindset.

This is what Jesus intended to proclaim at many events in his life, especially when he forgave the sinful woman (Luke 7:36–50). While Jesus intuitively got sight of the interior love the sinful woman possessed, Simon the Pharisee, on the contrary, "could not find the path of merciful Way of Jesus." He stood firm upon the threshold of formality. He was not capable of taking the next step to go meet Jesus, who brings him salvation. Simon limited himself to inviting Jesus to dinner but did not really welcome him. In his thoughts, he invoked only justice, and in so doing, he erred. Consequently, "his judgment on the woman distanced him from the truth" and did not allow him even to understand the greatness of the guest he was hosting. He stopped at the surface; he was not able to look to the heart. But Jesus, through a small parable, tried to liberate the Pharisee from his hardheaded and wrong approach of being just and coaxed him to be turned toward love and forgiveness "to be right."

Every discipled leader of Jesus must behave the same way as the Master did. He intended our church has to go out of herself and to be engaged in the life of the greater society of which it is a part, especially with the poor and those who are far away. The church is missionary by her very nature; she is not self-enclosed but sent out to every nation and people. Her mission is to bear patient and loving witness to the One who desires to draw all creation and every man and woman to the Father. Her mission is to bring to all a love that cannot remain silent. In each of our neighbors whom we serve as their leaders, then we must see a brother or a sister for whom Christ died and rose again. What we ourselves have received, we have received for them as well. Hence, we need to go beyond our human motivations and agendas in our any dealing with our community members—be it spiritual, religious, moral, liturgical, and social.

UPHOLDING A UNIVERSAL OUTLOOK OF OUR MISSION

In Mark, we read Jesus commissioning his first team of discipled leaders: "Go into the whole world and proclaim the gospel to every creature" (Mark 16:15). The church never ignored this universal vision and mission entrusted to her. Not only had the apostles gone around the world of their time to venture Jesus's mission, but they also trained and sent out discipled leaders to do the same.

Every baptized one was encouraged to be a missionary in this regard. Certainly, a few journeyed from continent to continent, nation to nation, and community to community. Thus, thousands and thousands of priests and religious brothers and sisters, as international missionaries around the world, serve the physical, social, and spiritual needs of the natives despite their racial, linguistic, cultural, and color differences. It is about them the Scriptures say, "How beautiful are the feet of those who bring the good news!" (Rom. 10:15) They truly live out the mandate of the Lord to go and make disciples of every nation.

Nonetheless, most of the discipled leaders have been asked to choose or affiliate to one local community to fulfill their obligation of proclaiming the Gospel. However, as Vat. II stated, the local church or Christian community should never be isolated from the global church and her universal vision and mission. There should be an intrinsic connection between the local church and the global one. Here I am in no way drag the reader into the debate that happened in the early years of the twenty-first century between Cardinal Kasper and Cardinal Ratzinger.

My only contention is any disciple of Christ performing his/her duty of leadership even in a small little village parish of Uganda is supposed to be closely connected to the identity and mission of the universal church. We are what we are. We cannot be and do more than our Leader. Where the Master is there, the servant be. If any discipled leader loses this vision, he/she may be a social and community leader but can never be called a discipled church leader. This is why Pope Francis has been insisting persistently that every *land is a mission land*.

It is about the missionary nature of the entire church. Every baptized Christian has been entrusted with a grand mandate of Master Jesus: It is about loving, living, appreciating, and sharing one's faith that was given to us at our baptism. It is about being the salt of the earth and light of the world, no matter what our state of life is. It is about putting the Lord's teachings and values into practice in our daily activities, in our professional life, in our relationships, and in our homes. In today's second reading, Paul advises his disciple Timothy to act like him in faith sharing. He says, "Proclaim the word; be persistent whether it is convenient or inconvenient; convince, reprimand, encourage through all patience and teaching" (2 Tim. 4:2).

GETTING READY TO LAUNCH OUT INTO DEEP

In Luke 5:1–11, we read Jesus performing a miraculous act to attract the fishermen to get out of their natural life to a life of discipled leadership. Interestingly, at that instance, the Master offers them a command that if they obey, they would get its benefits thereof. According to Luke, three fishermen—Peter, James, and John—were fishing in the sea through the whole night but caught nothing. They were surely frustrated, tired, and desolate. Jesus reaches out to them and orders them, "Put out into deep water and lower your nets for a catch." When they obeyed, amazingly, they caught a great number of fish.

Jesus always takes pride in being a visionary, seeing through the victorious future. This is because he holds strong grip of his "present." As a remarkable leader, he is a passion fuser. He never stops bringing a sense of urgency, excitement, or passion in every commitment his disciples engaged in. The refrain from one of the popular Catholic renewal hymns that recalls Isaiah 6:8 must become a stirring and memorable heartbeat of every discipled leader: "Here I am, Lord. Is it I Lord? I have heard you calling in the night. I will go, Lord, if you lead me. I will hold your people in my heart."

CHAPTER 18: DO AND DIE

There is a well-known virtuous and chivalrous axiom: "'Do or die." Our Master changed it for his own style of leadership as "do and die." It means "Whoever wishes to come after me must deny himself, take up his cross, and follow me" (Mark 8:34). Indeed, it is the most difficult part of Jesus's teachings. He was very clearly proclaiming that if anyone wants to covet the destiny of eternal glory, they must live his own life of "do and die." And Paul reiterated in his letters, "If, then, we have died with Christ, we believe that we shall also live with him" (Rom. 6:8; 2 Tim. 2:11).

SIGNIFICANCE OF JESUS'S UNCONCEIVABLE DEMAND

Undoubtedly, his disciples, like us, found it hard first, to understand it and second, to apply it in their lives. Jesus tried his best to enlighten their darkened ignorance of this amazing "Gospel blend." And when they resisted this eternal truth with stubbornness and showed their reluctance toward his "do and die" discipleship, and even tried their best to stop thinking such weird things, he rebuked them, calling them, saying, "Get behind me, Satan! You are an obstacle to me. You are thinking not as God does, but as human beings do" (Matt. 16:23).

He too forewarned about the ugly future after their death if they didn't comply with his demand: "Whoever is ashamed of me and of my words in this faithless and sinful generation, the Son of Man will be ashamed of when he comes in his Father's glory with the holy angels" (Mark 8:38). As we hear in the Gospel of Matthew 21:41, "The owner of the vineyard will bring those wretches to a wretched end and lease the vineyard to other tenants who will deliver the produce to him when the season arrives," God's punishment would be worse than the others for those of us who have not lived up to his Son's call for "do and die" discipleship.

Humanly speaking, this audacious demand from our Master is very risky and a painful one. Nonetheless, we should know in historical reality that there were millions of Jesus's discipled leaders who led chivalrous life of "do and die." For our personal encouragement, therefore, first, we must look up to the "cloud of witnesses" sitting there around Jesus in heaven, who had followed exactly what the Master demanded from them. In the light of Jesus's desire, we hear Paul and the apostles telling us that only those of us who die with Jesus will rise with him. Only by taking up our crosses and following Jesus in self-sacrificing love can we share his resurrection. And they too lived up to what they wrote and preached.

SEEING THROUGH JESUS'S REDEMPTIVE LENSES

We should approach Jesus's hard demand in his way and light. Some of us, as martyrs, are called to suffer in the same physical way in which Jesus died. Even some of our saints, like Francis of Assisi and Padre Pio, begged Jesus to offer his stigmata in their bodies. Some others, as church history testifies, actually arranged to have themselves scourged, nails pounded in their wrists and feet, and raised on a cross. But we should recognize that not all of us are called to be so. By his painful demand of "do and die," Jesus does not expect all his discipled leaders to meet an ignominious death as he went through. He actually desires his discipled leaders to suffer and die small deaths in our daily performances of leadership duties. One series of such deaths we encounter on daily basis is the troublesome situations in human relationship. Just consider how each one of us in our leadership role psychologically, mentally, and emotionally is affected and pained daily by the arguments, oppositions, misunderstandings, and disagreements occurring in our human relationships. The grade of pain depends on each one's formation of their sensitivity. It is literally for many of us descending into hell as the Lord himself gone through.

In one parish, a lady sent me, through some of my friends, an information that until she gets a new parish priest, she wouldn't come to church. She misunderstood that by this horrible decision, she was going to hurt me. But in my personal prayer time, I was thanking her hating me and helping me get closer to Christ and carry his cross. She made me stand in front of God, humiliated and humbled. There was some inner peace that entered my heart, and I began settling on the lap of my Father. Unfortunately, after a week, I saw her in the church, and I felt sad that I have lost one of my crosses to carry for my Lord. Invariably, the Lord arranges for me such experiences wherever I have been chosen to serve him. I am sure all the priests, pastors, and preachers, if they are really worth in the eyes of God, are in the same boat like me.

When the disciples misinterpreted what Jesus said about his suffering and death, he insisted that no pain, no gain. We notice, as we mentioned earlier, a relationship situation of pain and suffering occurring between Jesus and Peter. On that occasion, Jesus ruthlessly ordered his disciples like this: "Don't cling onto your silly self-centered attitude and conviction. When you stand for truth or against injustice for the sake of God's will, there will be many deaths you have to undergo. Don't use your mere human wittiness, rather your adherence to me and my values."

DYING THROUGH SHARING WITH THE NEEDY

There are other kinds of small deaths we should undergo. While the first kind is in our relationship with equals, coworkers and sophisticated church members, the second kind happens in our relationship with those who are considered below to us, the needy, downtrodden, and neglected ones. Echoing the Master's clarion call of "selling everything, sharing them with the poor, and then follow him" (Ref. Mark 10:21), James teaches in his letter (James 2:14–18) that simply staying upholding our creed and faith is not enough to be called Jesus's disciples. We have to get out of our couches or comfort zones and say something about God's values and do something about it among people so that our Father in heaven will be glorified. "What good is it, my brothers and sisters," James asks, "if someone says he has faith but does not have works? Can that faith save him?" This is how we meet the temporary death of our self, through pains and sufferings our charitable deeds bring in our daily life. Because of our commitment to Jesus's command of neighborly love and help the needy as best as we can, we lose our money, talent, and time, which perhaps would have been used for our self-gratification and self-entertainment. It pinches our undisciplined self; it makes us many times feel we have lost a lot. This is our daily cross. This is the straight result of our efforts to alleviate the sufferings of others.

BRINGING DEATH TO OUR SELF-CENTERED LEADERSHIP

There is one more set of deaths happening in the life of discipled leaders very much related to their ministries. Once we, the discipled leaders, decide to do Jesus's salvific ministry, he expects us not to quit, whatever be its cost. We should never quit for the sake of our whimsical view of our duties. We notice in parishes that many leaders desire every bit of their undertakings should entertain them or at least be pleasant and fertile, reaping lots of money and popularity.

That was how my past life story runs: I personally felt from the moment I was conceived—I imagine—I decided everything I perform in life should be like a play or a game of offering me happiness and pleasure. I was acting always on that "pleasure principle" throughout my youth and middle life. In my middle age (sixties), when I began reviewing my past life, I realized how much such principle had spoiled my true joy and fulfillment in life. Acting on that way gave me only greater sufferings, disappointments, dejection, and depression. So I said to myself, "The policy I had regarding my life's undertakings is totally false, farcical, and unreal. Every human task, for its success, is combined with hardship, sweating, bleeding, and burdensome." I realized also that to perform every duty, which my social roles and positions demand from me in a balanced and realistic way, begets tremendous "soul-satisfaction."

Surely ministerial duties the church assigned for us, both religious and laypersons, are not sweet gums to be chewed as long as we want. For instance, priests, like me, have many public duties as celebrating Mass. I always prefer to perform those masses in front of "mass gatherings," in Basilicas, and in some prestigious shrines and holy places. As a main celebrant, though many times being criticized by the attendees, I love to become a focal point of the crowd. At that moment, humanly speaking, I turn out to be the center-forward hero on the stage, wearing all beautiful and colorful costumes.

And so the same is true with other leaders, lay and religious as well, as they are assigned for conducting and participating in public functions in spotlights and cameras. Though our Guru does not discourage such occasional glamorous, high-profile, and enchanting performances, knowing our inner self-gratifying tendency and consequently going against his norm, "do and die," he compels us to kill first our self-centered engagements and then to accomplish them with purity of intention only for "the greater glory of the Lord." If not, he dumps them into bad-smelling trash bag.

PARADIGM SHIFT CAN BE A CLOSE CALL TO TINY DEATH

Leaders who have continuous taste of such self-gratification in their job never like to be moved or transferred from those high-level positions or fields. If their superiors or so-called commandos compel them to accept the ministerial shifts, they are totally upset, hurt, and start living a depressed and dejected life. Some of those even quit the religious leadership Jesus had entrusted to them. But Jesus expects his discipled leaders not simply to go with the flow of their puffed-up mind setup, rather to swim against the current of earthly life, which surely means a daredevil effort in accordance with Master's wish of "do and die."

Moreover, most of the discipled leaders' duties are performed in the life situations of one to one, groups, and in private, such as visiting the sick, offering spiritual counseling to one or two confidentially, and conducting adult catechism classes to a group of adults or adolescents, which most of the time dwindles as the days go on. At those occasions, we should quickly wake up to remind ourselves of our Master's demand "do and die" and accept willingly such chances of "dry" ministries and do the best we can. In those moments, I have practiced to tap on my shoulders, saying to myself, "Bloom where you are planted."

Undeniably, there are some occasions when we need to make a paradigm shift, if need be, to take a U-turn in our performances of roles and move (I won't say "quit") from a person, a congregation, a job, a city, and even a country to another comfortable and peaceful state. I won't also say we should search and look for some new "comfort zone." However, before we do such a move, first, we should struggle with God as Abraham, Jacob, and Jesus did and also try the best we can in mending or in enhancing the place, person, congregation, and other life's issues we face in present milieu and then make an unflinching decision to move away according to the legitimate and valid instructions of the social system such as by divorce, by retirement, or by leave of absence, but never withdraw totally and grudgingly from the remarkable discipled leadership entrusted to us.

BECOMING MATURED IN A CHRISTIC STATURE IS ALSO A DEATH

As a child, a person keeps others such as parents and elders as proxy to profess one's faith, to say together with them "Amen, Amen" to everything that is handed down to him/her. But a grown-up person is entirely free and independent to say "amen" or to say no. An adult always takes his/her religion in his/her hand and goes forward to find intimate relationship with God: "When I was a child, I used to talk as a child, think as a child, reason as a child; when I became a man, I put aside childish things" (1 Cor. 13:11).

Unfortunately, there are among us who are physically grown-up but still behave like children in their relationship with God. They act or react as if their entire faith and relationship with God is in the hands of other people. So as children, they find their religion so good if the fellow parishioners and the priests or preachers are good, or they react toward their religion, either quit or deny or hate it, according to the moods and reactions of other people. They hold on to a childish religion rather than an adult religion. If they are truly grown-up, they will never care for other people's reactions in the church and continue to hold on to their faith strongly and would never quit or absent themselves from the church worship. They would rather slowly and gradually change the attitudes of other people whom they consider the worst devils and more sinful than themselves through their kindness, prayer, and other means.

DIE TO LIVE AND LIVE TO DIE

As most of my fellow Christians in this postmodern age, at my adolescent period, I always felt very much tensed at reading and listening to Jesus, specifically some of his hard sayings. That might have been one of the many reasons why I had been reluctant in following him faithfully. But in later years, during my middle age, I began deeply reflecting over those same hard words of Jesus. I had also a mentor, spiritual father, whom I met very often and discuss with him my feelings on this matter. In one visit, that good Jesuit priest told me, "Vima, our Master Jesus is very practical in his instructions to us about how to conduct our life in an uninterrupted, joyful way."

He too reminded me of Jesus's promise before he left to his heavenly Father as we heard in today's Gospel: "I have told you this so that my joy may be in you and your joy might be complete" (John 15:11). My mentor clarified his statement, saying, "My son, all the sayings of Jesus, especially those of his hard words, can be summed up in two principles of joy-filled life: 'die to live and live to die.' I know it would be sounding to you very philosophical. I want you to go back to your room, reflect over this, and gather all the hard sayings of Jesus. You will surely agree with me what I stated is totally true." Thus, my spiritual father enlightened me and opened my inner eyes to see the genuineness and reality of our Master's words.

DISCIPLED LEADERSHIP LIFE IS PARADOXICAL

Indeed, many utterances of Jesus challenge all believers to authentic discipleship and total commitment to himself through self-renunciation and acceptance of the cross of suffering, even to the sacrifice of life itself. For instance, "Whoever finds his life will lose it, and whoever loses his life for my sake will find it" (Matt. 10:37–39). It is simply an expression of the ambivalence of life and its contrasting destiny. Life that is seen as mere self-centered earthly existence and lived in denial of Christ ends in destruction, but when lived in loyalty to Christ, despite earthly death, it arrives at fullness of life. The disciple's family must take second place to the absolute dedication involved in following Jesus. Christian life is nothing but a paradoxical blend of both life and death.

Jesus advises us we have to first die to live. Namely, we must deny our "fake self," restrict our unhealthy and unnecessary earthly ambitions and dreams, restrain from physical pleasures, and be ready even bleeding to die, losing our parts of the body for the sake of maintaining our inherited divine self life. We should remember what he said about our avoiding of sinful situations in life: "If your hand or foot causes you to sin, cut it off and throw it away. It is better for you to enter into life maimed or crippled than with two hands or two feet to be thrown into eternal fire. And if your eye causes you to sin, tear it out and throw it away. It is better for you to enter into life with one eye than with two eyes to be thrown into fiery Gehenna" (Matt. 18:8–9).

Paul, being inspired by the Spirit of Jesus, labels our discipled leadership life as glorious death: "We . . . always carrying about in the body the dying of Jesus, so that the life of Jesus may also be manifested in our body. For we who live are constantly being given up to death for the sake of Jesus, so that the life of Jesus may be manifested in our mortal flesh" (1 Cor. 4:7–18). History tells us, as Paul indicated, all disciples committed to Jesus's way of life lived a life of death but finally died a victorious death that led them to eternal joy and bliss. The more they died in life to sin and other imbalanced ways of humanness, they were the happiest people in the midst of sufferings, trials, and persecutions.

THE SWEET AGONY OF SURRENDERING TO THE DIVINE

In the OT scriptural passages, prophets like Jeremiah, Isaiah, and Ezekiel proclaimed the one and only message from God and led their people to obey him, who lovingly ordered them, "Return to Yahweh." Before they began sharing this God's message with people, they personally listened from the same God who compelled them to obey his message first and then to preach about it. Like any other prophets, Jeremiah (Jer. 20:7–9) truly returned to his God but seemingly and surprisingly, the Person whom he returned to didn't offer him a lot of hope and consolation. Being duped by God, as the prophet confesses, he was compelled to preach about the "reform" at the time of the destruction of Jerusalem and subsequent exile. Sadly, obedience to God's call brought him great misery and abuse. Showing his negative reaction, he tried to evade from performing this onerous duty, but as he indicates, it became like fire burning in his heart, imprisoned in by bones. He grew weary holding it in; he couldn't endure it.

Jeremiah also adds that his relationship with God seemed destroying his youthful life. Not only did it force him to remain unmarried, but it also created situations in which his fellow Jews regarded him as a traitor to them and their country. In truth, more than any other prophets, Jeremiah suffered the worst, and this is why biblical scholars name him as "a man of constant sorrow." Delivering God's Word brought to the prophet tremendous pain and woe; worst still, not delivering it brought him even greater pain and woe. This is why he felt as if he was trapped by God. We can call this as a "sweet agony" or a "bittersweet." However, we too know Jeremiah survived many ordeals to compose the majestic verses of both lamentation and consolation that encompass Israel's exile and restoration. His fidelity through trial to triumph made him one of the great voices in the Bible.

This sort of being seduced and overpowered by Almighty God is not an experience only of Jeremiah or any other OT prophets. Anyone who was and is fully committed to God the Supreme has been undergoing such ordeals in their spiritual and social lives. As David, they constantly have been crying aloud, "My soul is thirsting for you, O Lord my God!" (Ps. 63).

Jesus, our Master, was the embodiment of that costly and bleeding encounter with God in his life. God created within him a certain insatiable hunger and unquenchable thirst for fulfilling God's will. Throughout his life, he was fully aware of what God wanted him to accomplish, even though sometimes he could spell out his inability to carry on. We can remember what he experienced while he was in prayer at the Garden of Gethsemane: "Father, if you are willing, take this cup away from me; still, not my will but yours be done." He was in such agony, and he prayed so fervently that his sweat became like drops of blood falling on the ground (Luke 22:42–44). During the time of his crucifixion, he had the same agonizing moment: "My God! My God! Why have you forsaken me?" Jesus esteemed God's possessive and compulsive deal with him as the most burdensome cross in his life. But knowing the benefits thereof, he carried it willingly and freely because that is the only way for attaining the "ultimate destiny." Indeed, he considered it as sweet agony.

Hence, he advised his disciples to follow him strenuously in taking up our crosses. Before he underwent his final agony of that "cross," he advised them not to be afraid of this "cross" of life and resurrection, even it would demand from them denial of one's self, relatives, and even their very life (Matt. 16:21–27). True discipleship happens only after we hear and accept this challenge. Jesus's statement helps us understand that carrying one's cross originally didn't refer to patiently enduring some dramatic moment of suffering. It described an ongoing, generous, open, and honest relationship with God, a daily quest to discover what God wishes of us during this specific day. Such a quest involves a real death to self and real sacrifice.

We should uphold a mysterious truth that every cross is an altar where, as Paul points out (Rom. 12:1–2) in his revelatory style, we need to die with the Master to sin so that we would rise, resurrected to eternal life. This death is not once but lifelong. We should "not to conform ourselves to this age; rather, we should offer our bodies as a living sacrifice, holy and pleasing to God, our spiritual worship" (Rom. 12:1). In other words, every cross is an altar where we should offer our entire breakable and vulnerable earthly life as a living sacrifice to God. In this meaning, I always love to assert that the cross is, after all, the "crisscrossing of God's seducing vertically and humans' surrendering horizontally."

GO WITH THE FLOW IS A GREATER CROSS THAN GO AGAINST CURRENT

I love to categorize the crosses in discipled leadership into two groups: crosses of going against the current and crosses of floating over the current. Life is a river that never becomes dry. It brings a lot of challenges. We have to take them willingly and swim against the unfairness of life. We have millions of people as our role models for such audacious efforts. We also must go against our own self, which is the number 1 enemy to our positive growth. We have to override this monstrous self-love that often demands too many pleasures, too many possessions, and too many slaves that can worship us, obey us, and do what our selfishness demands. To be a disciple of Jesus means to follow his Kingdom principles, the Ten Commandments. Many times, observance of them hurts against our self-love. They become crosses to us.

The other group of crosses that burden us are the most burdensome for postmodern people, and they emerge from our acts of floating over the current. God wants us to go with the flow. This means to accept our inability to know the mind of God and to obey his will in our life. This is the most painful cross a modern man and woman should face. Even after breathing the air of enlightenment, technical, scientific discoveries, the Lord wants us to humbly acknowledge our creatureliness.

While some call our human sufferings as misfortunes, unfair deal of life, curses, and so on, Jesus alone called them as crosses. No Jew in the time of the Lord dared to use this term because it was a sign and symbol of degradation, death, crucifixion, criminal punishment, curse, and suffering. Jesus used it in his prophetic references to his death. His disciples took the same term more seriously and used it profusely in their writings and preaching. It referred to Jesus's death, to their own persecution, to their cost of discipleship, and mainly to Jesus's redemptive work.

Jesus, in a very positive way, accepted his crosses, embraced them with full freedom, and carried them from his conception till his death (Ref. Phil. 2:6–8). But always, he used them for the greater good of the world. He made his own crosses as the wooden platform to gather people together, as the wooden ladder to take them up to greater vision and mission, and as the wooden weapon to fight against the enemies who live and enjoy in injustice, in war, in hatred, in lies. He wanted his followers to follow his footsteps in carrying our crosses with the same attitude he held. Consequently, as he promised, our yoke would be easy and our burden light.

A GREAT LEADER IS ALWAYS A TRIUMPHANT SUFFERER

Being part of the baptized human community, inevitably, all leaders suffer just like any other disciples and even many times more than others. Nonetheless, the difference consists in how the discipled leaders suffer with grace and even with gratitude. They stay focused on their heavenly call, try to be functional during times of suffering, and do not lose sight of their principles. Discipled leaders avoid focusing only on their own suffering, even in times of intense pain.

People admire the heroism of such men and women who can suffer without losing their trust in God or their commitment to others. If they discover their weakness in this mind setup, they make over for it by attempting many spiritual means to attain that ability for themselves. As an expected result, those who walk in the company of this kind of leaders become willing to follow the leaders more joyfully. Otherwise, leaders who lose their poise in sufferings too often usually be deprived of influencing those they lead.

It is said that St. Teresa of Avila was blessed by the Lord with continued mystical encounter with him and with his sufferings of "sweet agony" uninterruptedly. This remarkable mystical experience has inspired and motivated her with lifelong desire to identify with the sufferings of Jesus. She expressed that amazing desire in her frequent prayer: "Lord, either let me suffer or let me die." Doesn't it sound like the demand of Jesus we have discussed in this chapter, "Do and Die"?

CHAPTER 19: BE A SACRAMENTAL ADMINISTRATOR

I n the previous chapters, we talked about the fact that all disciples or followers of Jesus are called to be discipled leaders in God's Kingdom, as Jesus who is King, Prophet, and Priest. Addressing the identity of the church as the mystical body of Christ and all baptized Christians are its members, Paul underscores that as we differ from one another in talents, gifts, and abilities, so are the discipled roles we take also vary according to the human institution of the church as designed by the Creator. He writes, "Some people God has designated in the church to be, first, apostles; second, prophets; third, teachers; then, mighty deeds; then, gifts of healing, assistance, administration, and varieties of tongues" (1 Cor. 12:28).

CALL TO SACRAMENTAL LEADERS

To me, religion, as I discussed in my book *My Religion—Reel or Real*, is simply an environment to put into practice the twofold command or will of God for humans: "Love your Lord God with your whole heart, whole mind, whole soul, whole body, and whole strength. And love your neighbor as yourself." The Christian religion, the church, is a situation conducive to fulfill such will of God. By nature, human person is inclined to one's own self. It is very difficult to go out of oneself; to withdraw from ego; to love a Being who is beyond all beings, a Life beyond all lives; and to love others as oneself. Religion offers an environment to perform certain exercises, practices, rituals, and duties to enhance the observance of those commands of God. Hence, all institutions, in the qualified name of religions, are simply human systems, with strategies to manage and maintain God and human interactions securely "in [earthly] situations." That is why I uphold Christianity as a social "institution" (in-situation).

This means, first of all we should be very clear about the Triune God, with whom we interact in this in-situations, who is a Supreme Spiritual Being. We deal with things pertaining to spiritual realm. Therefore, the Spirit of the Lord must individually inspire us to do certain things in the name of God and for the name of God. We must be ready to listen to his promptings and also try to discern its credibility and genuineness because we should remember we have our own human spirit that has been already tarnished by sin and that possesses its own trickery and deceptiveness. This truth, needless to say, pertains to any kind of leadership works performed in this spiritual Kingdom. As the church identity is nothing but a "sacrament of Christ," every one joining into this sacramental institution is also called to be a "sacramental person," and any portfolio he/she handles takes the same qualification.

ALL DISCIPLED LEADERS ARE SACRAMENTAL ADMINISTRATORS

In this chapter, let us deal with only the ministry of administration to be performed by discipled leaders. What is the meaning of the term "administration"? In secular dictionary, it refers to the process or activity of running a business organization, and so on. It includes the tasks connected with the institution's vision, mission, and objectives. Those functions may be managing, maintaining, directing, conducting, leading, controlling, governing, exhorting, counseling, and so on.

The Greek word for administration is *Kubernesis*, which is alternatively translated in the Bible as leadership, administration, or governance. The actual root meaning comes from a nautical term for "steersman" or "helmsman," the one who handles the tiller, who provides the direction for all. Most of its English versions translate it as "ad-min-is-tra-shun," taking seriously its root meaning "minister," "ministration," denoting *service*: to supply, to conduct, or to attend to anything. In other words, administration is the performance of official duty, the conduct of affairs, the various forms of spiritual or social service. In apostolic thought and ideal, it is very well used as "ministering" either of an act or of an office in the church.

According to this definition, all discipled leaders are eligible to be administrators ministering to people in various ways in accordance with different needs. Besides, generally speaking, every move, role, and duty of humans calls for proper management. For example, individually, every one of us cannot be an efficient leader unless we personally manage well our body, our mind, our time, our crisis, and our daily problems connected to the roles we take in family, in community, and surely in church.

In the same vein, we can ascertain that every leader in the church, being a minister of salvific services for the people, must handle one's pastoral task as a "sacramental administration." As all baptized people participate in the common priesthood of Jesus, they are called to be sacraments of God's love as our Master and his church are identified. Therefore, all the tasks the discipled leaders perform in church environment—be it private, group, or public—must be qualified and beautified as "sacramental administration."

EXCLUSIVELY CHOSEN FOR SACRAMENTAL ADMINISTRATION

However, as Paul writes, one group of discipled leaders in the church perform the ministry of administration as their main role. They can be either pastors; parish priests who are solely formed, qualified, and ordained by the church;

or administrators who are deacons or qualified laypeople, who are specifically chosen and appointed by the local church authorities. These discipled leaders involve in church affairs—be it establishing or pastoring or any other services like monetary, social, educational transactions—are not just disciples or even disciple-makers. Rather, they are to be identified as discipleship system builders.

Hence, these specially chosen disciples to lead and administer in the Lord's vineyard must never forget their primary duty is to supervise and manage the spiritual ministering of God's salvific gifts promised and bestowed to the congregation through the church. Besides being a "minister" or "server," according to its root meaning as we saw earlier, an administrator is a shipmaster or a captain. The literal meaning is "to steer" or "to rule or govern." It carries the idea of someone who guides and directs a group of people toward a goal or destination. This role therefore is closely related to the discipled leadership but is more goal- or task-oriented and is also more concerned with details and organization such as to organize, direct, and implement plans to lead others in the various ministries of the church.

TWOFOLD TASKS OF SACRAMENTAL ADMINISTRATORS

Being the proxy captain of Jesus for his congregation, all administrators are specially chosen out of the chosen race, royal priesthood, and people set apart to comply with the Master's demands of witnessing as his sacrament of love, truth, and justice to the congregation, plus of supplying God's gifts and graces to people through his Words and sacraments.

Let me emphasize repeatedly. All discipled leaders should in no way erase from our mind the unique and pivotal sacramentality of their administrative role in all their undertakings, be it social, physical, educational, financial, and various community actions. Our religion we are employed in is "human spiritual life-management in-situations." What I mean by this is that every religion is not just a "social institution" as any secular systems but also mainly a personal spiritual life-management strategy "in-situations." It is in this "in-situations" we, the discipled administrators, are invited to serve and supervise.

More than any other disciples or discipled leaders, the sacramental administrators are expected by our Master to be shaped, molded, and filled by his Spirit so that we work strenuously and sincerely with a single mind and heart, always intimately connected to the Lord, both morally and spiritually. This is the advice Paul offers to Titus, who was appointed by the apostle to recruit sacramental administrators in the churches he had established. He enlists the requirements for this august role of administration: they should be blameless, not arrogant, not irritable, not a drunkard, not aggressive, not greedy for sordid gain but hospitable, lovers of goodness, temperate, just, holy, self-controlled, and so on (Titus 1:6–8).

AN INCARNATIONAL ADMINISTRATION

We are accustomed to hear politicians claim that the concept of democracy means it is a government "of the people, by the people, and for the people." However, administration in the church is not only democratic but also theocratic. The church holds fast this twofold dynamics of leadership, especially in her administration. This view is learned from Jesus, who emphasized it in his life and teaching. He said once regarding our obedience to both political leader and God, "Give to Caesar what belongs to Caesar and to God what is God's" (Matt. 21:23–33). What he meant was we should behave incarnational until we die. We are both spiritual and physical, we are social as well as individual, and we are political as well as religious. We cannot separate one from the other. We cannot divide and rule them. We have to give all that we have to God as our only and one Master and give to the political and religious leaders what we are supposed to give to them. We are both citizens of this world and of God.

The same incarnational principle holds good in handling our administrative leadership in the church. The main reason for such a unique style of administration is that the church in which we minister is principally spiritual. As we read in a homily written in the second century, "At first the Church was purely spiritual, even as our Jesus was spiritual, but it appeared in the last days to save us. The spiritual Church was made manifest in the body of Christ, in order to show us that if we uphold its honor in the outward, visible form, and do not defile it, we shall, through the Holy Spirit be made its members in the true, spiritual sense. For the body of the Church is a copy of the Spirit, and no one, who defaces the copy, can have any part in what the copy represents." If we fail to do the will of the Lord who expects his discipled administrators not to deviate their authoritative role into mere secular and worldly, we shall be among those with whom Jesus got angry and said, "It is written: 'My house shall be a house of prayer', but you are making it a den of thieves" (Matt. 21:13). "Stop making my Father's house a marketplace" (John 2:16).

Accordingly, church administration is nothing but spiritual service to the body of Christ, which involves the wise stewardship of God's resources for the accomplishment of the work of ministry. Many cling on to the role of administration as an end in itself, but rather, it is a means for serving people effectively while making efficient use of resources in a manner that glorifies God.

While the enemies of Jesus wanted him to succeed in his leadership by dividing the spiritual dimension from the political one, he never yielded to their advice, and he too exhorted his disciples to combine the two leaderships, divine and secular, but always recognize each one's territory. Whenever we exercise our administrative leadership, we should always look up to how Jesus esteemed and exercised it. His caregiving leadership was holistic, namely, whenever he did something physically good to the humans, he never missed to bestow to them a spiritual healing, liberation from their sins. His leadership always stood as number 1 to appreciate anything he found good in the people. Jesus's leadership never lost sight of his Father in heaven and his sole authority; plus, in all his undertakings as a leader, he made sure people who witnessed them would encounter God and praise the Almighty. While the public praised him in different styles and appreciative words, he preferred their silence not to publicize until his death, and also as we read in Mark, he loved their glorifying his Father: "They were all astounded and glorified God, saying, 'We have never seen anything like this'" (Mark 2:12b).

Jesus never let us becoming sweet talkers and liars in the mask of diplomacy like the some worldly leaders or shepherds or kings who are puffed up and take pride in being the sole champion of protection and caring. Many of those leaders wrongly consider their promotion to administrative leadership is exclusively their own effort and choice. Jesus admonishes us not to think so. As the Book of Proverbs instructs us, our Creator God holds all power on all his creations, and he can do anything he wants with them: "A king's heart is channeled water in the hand of the Lord; God directs it where he pleases" (Prov. 21:1). All the powers on the earth and under the earth are in God's hands. Humans, whether they are leaders or lovers, elders, or friends, and any helpers who come in between God and humans, are only his candidates, his appointees, his choices, and his stewards. This means anybody who climbs the ladder of administrative leadership both in the world and in the church is ultimately the choice of God.

Another blunder the church administrators make is to utilize the tricks of survival to save our skin from troubles:

We make sure our words do not correspond to our actions. We say one thing in the public and do another in private. And the funny thing is we legitimize and justify such double-dealing and call it cunningly a sort of diplomacy. This is what Jesus hated as we hear him in the Gospels. He called those persons hypocrites. "Hypocrites" in Greek means "actors." It is like our kids who, with their Halloween costumes, play trick or treat. On the contrary, God expects everyone whom he chooses to be his leaders, teachers, and elders and priests to do our part in building up his world but not merely acting. As Jesus observed, there was no integrity between the preaching and life of the scribes and Pharisees of his time. He exhorted his followers, "Do and observe all things whatsoever they tell you, but do not follow their example. For they preach but they do not practice."

The Sovereign Proprietor continuously would be warning them at every night, as I experienced in my tenure of administering, not to follow a policy of divide and rule-dividing God from their power and their territory and, consequently, destroy the belief, fear, and trust the ordinary people, whom they serve, possess toward the merciful and just Father. If they didn't pay heed to them, history proves, the Almighty would not only throw those fake leaders to the dustbin but also would choose leaders from the humans, anybody who is according to his design. God, anointing them in his own style, chooses men and women to lead his people toward a peaceful, safe, and secure life. That has been the historical fact in the world and especially in our church circle.

As Paul exhorts the early churches, we should build our institutional churches on the power of the Gospel, in the Holy Spirit, and with much conviction. Thus, whenever our parishes or our cities face any problems regarding governing, finance, management, institution, and so on, they must be tackled not only by mere human politics but also above all, by the power and wisdom of the Holy Spirit as true and faithful citizens of the city of God.

TEAM-ORIENTED ADMINISTRATION

As discipled leaders of the church, our job is to create a local community-based system in which Jesus's followers who voluntarily join can be involved in relational environments for the purpose of discipleship. This was the highest expectation of our Master when he commissioned his disciples to go to the entire world and preach, teach, and baptize the humans. "Disciple all humans. Build them up as communities exclusively for me." Disciples obeyed him, and we hear from the Acts how they implemented the Master's dream. The people who welcomed their invitation started practicing "communal life" in the Lord (Acts 2:42–47).

As the disciples of the early church, today's church entrusts to us, specially recruited, the same role of being overseers of disciple-making communities. To realize fully the heaven-given community bond, Jesus's Spirit inspires us to build teams of discipled leaders in parishes who work together to fill in the gaps. Those who are ordained, selected, or appointed as administrators must not act like overseers or chieftains, rather, in humility and honesty, work together with the teams of other ministers in planning and implementing pastoral programs. For which, certainly, either the administrators themselves or any other well-experienced and skilled in church management from outside make the team trained, inspired, encouraged, challenged, and fully developed.

In this regard, we, the discipled administrators, should be spiritually mature and able to work well with others. More than any other secular organizations or business firms, where the democratic style of management is well observed in this postmodern age, church administrative style must be totally democratic—working as a team bonded in love; being transparent and trustworthy in any undertakings, especially money-handling; and totally theocratic-accomplishing with the Lord, in the Lord, for the Lord, and surely like the Lord all the organizational tasks, such as planning, organizing, delegating, overseeing, and evaluating ministries wisely according to the biblical and church principles and goals.

Our team-based administration should not be a leadership strategically incoherent, predictably unpredictable, and wrongly assuming ourselves as private sector lords who run our family business by doing what we want, when he want, and with limited consideration for consequences stretching beyond our own immediate interests and gratification. I know, I am sure, many of you would have already encountered such administrators in many parishes and churches. Gone are the days of such disconcerting, dictatorial, intemperance-possessed leaders in the church. The Holy Spirit has been washing clean of those erotic, toxic leaders from our midst.

ADMINISTRATION IN THE WORLD, NOT OF THE WORLD

One journalist beautifully writes about the situation of administrative leadership in today's church: "The Church is in this world but not of the world. Christian leaders, I say majority, who intensively seek to be 'of the world', cannot even be purged by social strategies. That we have seen for two thousand years. The main reason is, the Church, established by Christ as the Way, has become in the long run a typical human and earthly society against which so many saints like Francis of Assisi combated."

In the Bible, we read a Proverb: "Where there is no vision, the people perish" (Prov. 29:18, KJV). As John Maxwell, an American author, speaker, and pastor, often says, "Everything rises and falls on leadership." We, the discipled leaders of Christ, who are entrusted with Jesus's power and authority to serve and to oversee and bring our people to their destiny, must never lose sight of the fact that our parish or local church is a reflection of our leadership. If we don't lead our people with vision and intimacy with the Master, they would certainly lose their salvation and heavenly bliss.

As our first parents foolishly deceived by Satan and lost their joyful life in the Garden of Eden, most of us, as we grow older, developed and qualified in education and skills of life and finally climbing the ladder of life to the high peak of life, all certainly with the providence of God, we sideline God, and our puffed-up self takes our priority. We create our own petty kingdom and form our own laws for which we become strongly opinionated. Our unaccounted supremacy replaces God's own, and we use even God's authority, his money, his podium, and his words for our vain glory. We forget God is only one Father, one Source, one Parent, one Master, and one Superior. Many times, we abuse our titles and recognitions to delete God's power and glory.

When many church leaders thus turn aside from God's path and cause many to stumble, corrupt their covenant, and show partiality even in their teachings, the Lord notices it. Noticing their callousness, as we read in the Bible, he would threaten these leaders with curses, saying, "I, therefore, have made you contemptible and base before all the people." Mary, Mother of Jesus, points out in her Magnificat hymn this reaction and proaction of God over the centuries: "The Lord has shown might with his arm, dispersed the arrogant of mind and heart. He has thrown down the rulers from their thrones but lifted up the lowly."

It is pride that breaks the bond we have with God and the bond he has been building with his people. It is pride that keeps us stonyhearted. It is pride that leads us to exploit and cheat others, especially those who are ignorant and weak. Sometimes this pride takes a different ugly shape of patronizing others and bring them under our control. If we have humility, truth, and obedience to God, we will respect others' rights.

To be always getting blessing from the Lord and walk as a blessing in the midst of our friends and relatives, we, the specially elected to act as his administrators, need to be obedient to God, truthful to our words, and humble servants to others only for the sake of God. Let us remember this in season and out of season: "Puffed-up self will always pull us down to the pit!"

CHAPTER 20: BE A MEEK AND HUMBLE LEADER

BASICS OF CHRISTIAN LEADERSHIP

In this book, I try to expound in detail the what, the why, and the how of discipled leadership in the church. As a summary of those descriptions, let me share here some of Paul's thoughts.

In his "pastoral letters" (cf. first and second letters to Timothy and letter to Titus) sent to his disciples Timothy and Titus, the apostle Paul offers us a detailed description of the portfolios every Christian holds in the church. Beginning from bishops, presbyters, and deacons, he shares his thoughts about the leadership roles of all the faithful, of the elderly, and of youth. He underlines all the prerogatives, as well as responsibilities, of those who are chosen and invested with the church leadership ministries. Interestingly, while he stresses the faith-filled and Spirit-anointed life as a core and basis for any leadership in the church, he includes as such life's outward symbols and signs some exquisitely human qualities such as hospitality, sobriety, patience, meekness, reliability, and goodness of heart. In his other letters, Paul summaries them as "love," which is supposed to be the alphabet, the basic grammar of any Christian ministry. The virtue of love should be the underlying attitude of any disciples, especially of the discipled leaders of Jesus.

This has been the mind of our Master when he called people to be his disciples and his leaders in the past, at present, and surely in the future. One is not a bishop, priest, deacon, elder, or any leader in the church because one is more intelligent, good, and better than others but only because of a gratuitous gift freely given by the merciful God, in the power of the Holy Spirit, and for the good of his people. Such a humble and sincere mind setup would never make a Christian leader adopt an authoritarian attitude as if all the sheep in their jurisdiction were at their feet and the community were their property and their personal petty kingdom.

Paul's insistence of the awareness that everything we are endowed with is gift, and everything is grace, helps all pastoral and social leaders of the church not to fall into the temptation to put themselves at the center of attention and to be confident only in themselves. Such self-focused leadership is simply the upshot of vanity, of pride, of sufficiency, of arrogance.

CHRISTIAN LEADERSHIP IS "SERVANTSHIP"

The NT books profusely exhort all discipled leaders to uphold the Spirit-filled attitude of Jesus (Phil. 2:5), namely, an attitude of serviceability about which Paul explains, "Serve one another" (Gal. 5:13), "Submit to one another out of reverence for Christ" (Eph. 5:21), and "Carry each other's burdens, and in this way you will fulfill the law of Christ" (Gal. 6:2). Plus, the apostle ascertains that he became the servant of the church when God made him responsible for delivering God's message to the church members (Ref. Col. 1:25). Peter stresses the same point: "Each one should use whatever gift he has received to serve others" (1 Pet. 4:10).

In the Christian realm, all leadership should be servant leadership. That is how Jesus defined his leadership as well as that of all his discipled leaders. Our Master knew well what our human feeble hearts are aching for. John refers to it when he writes, "Jesus would not trust himself to them because he knew them all, and did not need anyone to testify about human nature. He himself understood it well" (John 2:24–25).

By experiences, we too know a bit how our human nature misconstrues of leadership as something coming with glory, power, and positions of honor. Hence, human hearts yearn for being singularly selected, elected, and promoted as unique of one kind. To this rapacious hunger for worldly greatness, so many self-made teachers provided plentiful food of schemes blended with intelligence, cunning, and hypocrisy. In contrast, Jesus Christ expressed his unique style of coveting leadership greatness. He plainly stated, "I came to serve and not to be served; serve as humble servants as I told and did." He, being the "Wisdom" coming from God as his Word, emphasized what his Father pronounced in the OT books about what kind of leadership should be in his Kingdom: "If you are chosen to preside at a dinner, do not be puffed up, but with the guests be as one of them; take care of them first and then sit down; see to their needs, and then take your place, to share in their joy and receive a wreath for a job well done" (Sir. 32:1–2).

In addition, he firmly advised his discipled leaders, "No disciple is above his teacher, no slave above his master. It is enough for the disciple that he become like his teacher, for the slave that he become like his master" (Matt. 10:24–25a). We should note here, for Matthew, servant means slave. Not every servant was a slave, but every slave was a servant. Hence, Paul goes further to remind all the discipled leaders about the how of performing their leadership duties in the church: "Whatever you do, do from the heart, as for the Lord and not for others, knowing that you will receive from the Lord the due payment of the inheritance; be slaves of the Lord Christ" (Col. 3:23–24).

As an American proverb says, "Too many chiefs and not enough Indians," it is sad to notice in today's church, we have many celebrities but very few servants. As Pope

Francis bluntly repeats, one of the greatest evils distorting and disrupting God's Kingdom today is "the clericalism." He is totally correct, our church institutional structure is grim because of the traditional view of considering leadership in the church as an exclusive possession of "ordained" leaders. This wrong view marred the teachings of Christ as well as his apostles and Church Fathers. Pope exhorted the ordained clergy repeatedly to outgrow their feudalistic attitude, which, though it has been sacked out of the secular political world, still survives within the church. Returning from his visit to Fatima on May 12 to 13, 2017, Pope held his traditional inflight "press conference" with journalists onboard. Answering to a Portuguese journalist's question about one of the church impending issues in his country, Pope advised all priests and deacons "to flee from clericalism because clericalism distances people." He too added, "Clericalism a plague in the Church."

Paul, observing even in his time the tarnished approach among his church members, underscored the genuine origin and reason of church leadership: "Jesus gave some [ministerial gifts] as apostles, others as prophets, others as evangelists, others as pastors and teachers, to equip the holy ones for the work of ministry, for building up the body of Christ, until we all attain to the unity of faith and knowledge of the Son of God, to mature manhood, to the extent of the full stature of Christ" (Eph. 4:11–13).

This means with Jesus Christ being the head of the church, the entire church body is served in the act of providing leadership. It's not just the ordained leaders but all those within the body of Christ. All his disciples are called to mutually submit ourselves to Jesus just as he was in submission to the Father. Forgetting such remarkable identity of church leadership, a certain elite group chosen publicly as the role models of such excellent Christian leadership have been abusing and misusing their leadership according to the proud instigation of the devil.

Humble servant leaders of Jesus must seek to invest themselves in the lives of his people so that they may grow to be more like Christ. This motivation is testified in the discipled leaders by their willingness to serve in God's vineyard to meet the needs, but not inevitably the wants, of his people. That is the dream of our Master about us. When many of us don't smell "sheep," as Pope Francis commented, the people whom we lead are apprehensive of our leadership. When we put on airs and seem to feel ourselves too important to do ordinary and modest works, we will be deprived of influence spiritually over them.

BE A CHILDLIKE SERVANT

Anything Paul preached about Christian leadership is simply taken from the spirit, life, and teachings of the Master Jesus Christ who dreamed of his discipled leaders as "childlike servants." Every human possesses in the heart and mind certain indelible thirst and hunger for power, prestige, and promotion. As avariciously craving for daily food, everyone ambitiously longs for subduing and subjecting at least a few of others. Sadly, in his public life, Jesus witnessed such ferocious attitude dominating his chosen disciples.

Gospel writers vividly expose this, underlining frequently that disciples were quarreling and debating about it: Who is the greatest in Jesus's campus? (Ref. Matt. 18:1–5; Mark 9:33–37; Luke 22:24–27). Sometimes they within themselves are arguing about it; other times, they straightaway came to Jesus and put the question, "Who do you think is the greatest in the kingdom of heaven?" Surprisingly, every time such occasions arose, Jesus brought in the midst of them a child and answered their question: "Amen, I say to you, unless you turn and become like children, you will not enter the kingdom of heaven." Plus, he insisted the eternal parameter for being the "greatest" in his Kingdom, saying, "Whoever humbles himself like this child is the greatest in the kingdom of heaven."

Once, he also emphasized that the total difference between the paganistic attitude and that of Christians regarding earthly power, position, status, promotion, and prestige is nothing but living a leadership life of childlike, humble serviceability. Not only is he quoted saying, "The kings of the Gentiles lord it over them and those in authority over them are addressed as 'Benefactors'; but among you it shall not be so. Rather, let the greatest among you be as the youngest, and the leader as the servant," but he also offered his own mindset and performance of his leadership as an example to it: "For who is greater: the one seated at table or the one who serves? Is it not the one seated at table? I am among you as the one who serves"; "I came to serve and not to be served."

When I deeply meditate on Jesus's words quoted above, I get into the greatest truth implicated to my leadership: If my greatness flows out of how I measure up to one another, such greatness hinders each one's ability to be great. Rather, if I pursue my greatness by serving others, my "being great" makes it easier for my neighbors also to become great. I realize therefore the comparisons I nurture within me against others' promotional, professional, and influential greatness never assist me in my climbing the greatness ladder; rather, it only obstructs it. Only by humbling myself and becoming childlike would certainly raise me to the true and valid greatness.

BE SIMPLEHEARTED BUT NOT SMALL-HEARTED

Recently, I came across in social media a news about one of the large denominations convening its annual meeting of its delegates to do their soul-searching exercise regarding their religious holdings. One among them was to acknowledge and confess the past history of their male church leaders and members about their treatment of church women. The "Me Too movement" listed out four injustices done against women: wronged women, abused women, silenced women, and objectified women. My only thought was this is not anything new; it is a perennial and scandalous problem existing in all the churches, such kind of nasty power play, unchristian infights for climbing as well as maintaining the leadership position by degrading, belittling, and rejecting certain groups of disciples in the name of gender, caste, race, richness, and intelligence.

The Bible confirms that all these and more social and national evils dominate and prevail for centuries. Scholars and writers try to fathom out the right reason and cause for such power struggles seen among the disciples of Jesus. In the light of God's words, they underline two reasons: ignorance and arrogance. We read in human history and even in our own time we experience that every country, every religion, every business, and every family has been terribly damaged and destroyed only by human ignorance and arrogance. Our destructive and damaging ability first starts with ignorance and proceeds with arrogance, and finally, it ends in destroying ourselves and others.

Jesus's Spirit, through his humble starting and his simple public life, has been exhorting us who are ambitiously joining in his team of leaders not to be ignorant of our humble beginning. In his parable of the mustard seed, he stresses this truth (Matt. 13:31–32). First, through the metaphor of the mustard seed, Jesus reminds us of our life's tiny little beginning: As in nature, biologically from one single tiny, little seed, like a mustard seed, almost all living creatures, including inanimate beings like plants and trees, are born. Interestingly, every human being, like you and me, is conceived from semen of a man, a single one chosen out of five hundred million male sperms. Second, our reading of

God's words and our own daily experiences of participating in other humans' death advise us to be aware of our humiliating end. Human death is the most unbearable insult and the worst deficit. Despite all the struggles, hardships, and laboring we do for survival and success, what is our end? We would be either buried in the grave or cremated in fire. We become dust unto dust.

The psalmist portrays candidly our human inevitable plight: "For he knows how we are formed, remembers that we are dust. As for man, his days are like the grass; he blossoms like a flower in the field. A wind sweeps over it and it is gone; its place knows it no more" (Ps. 103:14–16). And Peter (1 Pet. 1:24) confirms it, quoting Isaiah: "All flesh is grass, and all their loyalty like the flower of the field. The grass withers, the flower wilts, when the breath of the Lord blows upon it. Yes, the people is grass!" (Isa. 40:6–8).

Simultaneously, our Master desires we should never forget our dignity and glory. Though our beginning is very small, the amazing intervention of the Creator in our life is he has established his Kingdom within us as his image and likeness. However, be it a tiny start like the mustard seed, our Creator does mind-blowing miracles every day of our life from our mother's womb to make his image and likeness together with our physical stature grow and flourish as we notice in the earthly ground of Mother Nature. Jesus underscores this factual truth in his parable of the mustard seed: "Once it is sown, it springs up and becomes the largest of plants and puts forth large branches, so that the birds of the sky can dwell in its shade."

Prophet Ezekiel, confirming the statement of Jesus, points out that all this natural conception, growth, and bearing fruits of every creature is the marvelous deed of our Creator God. Through the prophet, God compares the seed to the people of Israel whom he lovingly planted on a high and lofty mountain called Zion. He made them grow as a majestic cedar and arranged in such a way that under that tree, every kind of humans like the birds take shelter of safety and security. God also exhorts us to be mindful of our glorious "end death" becoming a passage to eternal bliss. With Paul, our Christian belief affirms it: "We would rather leave the body and go home to the Lord" (2 Cor. 5:8).

Whenever we gather together in front of Jesus's altar, Jesus proclaims these monumental creative and redemptive deeds of his Father among us. Sadly, this eternal wish of God is not well recognized, and most of us, especially the so-called leaders of Jesus, live and move in a kingdom of our own as ignorant and blindfolded people. It is this grim ignorance leads us to become the cruel, arrogant persons highlighting we are the masters, we are the sole gardeners, we produce, we make it grow, and we can survive and successful by living like an island, not permitting anybody to take shelter under our wings or the kingdoms we build.

It is high time for all of us who are designated to lead others, to listen to God's curses pronounced against these ignorant and arrogant leaders. We are told that the same benevolent Creator can be the destroyer of those whom he planted if they are not fulfilling the purpose for which they have been planted. God underlines his valiant and mighty power: "I, the Lord, bring low the high tree, lift high the lowly tree, wither up the green tree, and make the withered tree bloom" (Ezra 17:24). Being fully aware of such horrible curses of the Creator, Paul, our role model in church leadership, reminds us in his letter about our final judgment day: "We must all appear before the judgment seat of Christ, so that each may receive recompense, according to what he did in the body, whether good or evil" (2 Cor. 5:10).

BE HARDHEADED BUT NOT HARDHEARTED

Unquestionably, a discipled leader should be a person of integrity. Being humble and meek doesn't mean we should be delinquent, wishy-washy, or wavering in our decision-making as well as in implementing our visions. Most of the times, we experience in our leadership ministry being tattered by situations, by devil, and our people. During those occasions when either bucks stop with us or members of church committees or councils eagerly wait for our final "veto" verdict, we had to demonstrate our leadership, showing our strength of character, but always with composure, balance, and commitment to the discipleship to Christ.

Our yes or no that any decision committee wants to take should come only out of our pursuit of right visions, goals to live, and serve for the glory of God even if no one else cares about it. However, every discipled leader must make sure he/she never disowns his friends who behave as strayed sheep in Jesus's Kingdom; rather, as the Good Shepherd claimed, we should be with them, go after them, and continue still our ministries together with them in patience, tolerance, and love.

Humble and meek leaders are wrongly judged by the public that their leaders are unstable and sometimes unpredictable in their application, as well as in their implementation, of programs of renewal. It is also possible a group of people who love to call themselves as protectors of traditions and fundamental values of the church may criticize the humble discipled leaders betray the traditional holdings in the name of bringing renewal to the church. Politically, they may sound correct, but if the renewal efforts are generated from the truly discipled leaders of Jesus, and if such plans and deeds are the heartbeats of the Master, I don't think any humble and meek discipled leaders should be battered by such criticisms, but they again should show their "hard levelheadedness" in their pursuit of renewal.

In times of crisis occurring in and out of the church, ordinary people may tend to fall apart and panic, and in that edgy mood, they often propose destructive radical solutions to the impending problems. The discipled leaders, even their hearts being melted and broken, must stand firm under crisis and cannot be moved from the foundation of truth. Such kind of stability and reliability of the leadership spirit certainly would attract people. Rightly reckoning that sort of immovable attitude is the result of clear vision for God's way.

POSTMODERN WORLD NEEDS A HUMBLE SERVANT CHURCH

A religious preacher, explaining the words of our Master: "I am in your midst as one who serves you" (Luke 22:27), boldly states in one of his online articles that there exists a fourth vow for a religious who is sincerely committed to Jesus, and that is "humility." He means "it is a mind setup that is not seeking any ecclesiastical dignity or honor within or outside the order." Expounding this vow further, he adds that like other three vows, it is related very much with uprooting pride, which otherwise shapes itself as a plague, destroying the goodness of any disciple of Jesus.

The fact is, in these modern days, after the Age of Enlightenment, not many followers of Christ desire to become ecclesiastical dignitaries. However, what we refer here is more than the titles. Pride is something deep-seated in our human aspiration "to be great or to be someone rather than no one to say the least." Power hunger, dignity search, and honor hunt among ourselves seem a crude violation of the first commandment of Go: "I am the only God among you." Sadly, what many of us do in our leadership life is that we create our personalities, our titles, our jurisdictions, and so on as some sort of petty idols among and for our people to worship, to salute, to pay homage, and to obey ourselves, and thus, they satisfy themselves thinking such human idolatry, obeisance, would take care of their spiritual duty to the Creator.

I don't deny the necessity of the hierarchical positions for the church in the world. However, as one of our vows given to our Master who selected us to be leaders on his behalf, those positions should never be desired or aspired by us in a political way and with secular mind setup. Worse than any other promises given to Jesus, most of our leaders in the church have coveted such glamorous positions through their cunning maneuvering tactics of secular politicians do in the world. Because of this sort of secularly handled election, selection, and promotion, everything these leaders handle in their leadership ministry has become corrupted, contaminated, and poisonous to their discipleship as well as other disciples who "obey" their orders. Plus, it breeds a ripple effect of the same bad behavior among church members.

This is why Jesus expects all his leaders to embrace their leadership in humble and childlike way: The one and only ecclesiastical authority is God in Jesus. Any such portfolio must be esteemed as an act of service and not as an opportunity for one's own glory, and the sole intention of the one who has been promoted to high rank and file of the church must not be for oneself but for others as our Master "took the form of a slave."

We profess in our creed: "I believe in one, holy, catholic and apostolic Church." I desire to add "humble" as one more characteristic of the church in the modern world. This is the dire need of today's church as an effective sacrament of Christ in this postmodern world. The entire humanity longs to get an authentic statement for Jesus and his truthful values from his two-thousand-year-old agent, the church, whose leadership has tarnished, disowned, and betrayed her greatness, and because of such miserable failure in humble serviceability, her leaders scandalized millions of God's children who have been drifted away from the greatest gift God in Jesus has bestowed to the world.

So many Christian leaders are consumer-minded; most of them seek what they can get and not what they can offer. Consequently, their so-called ministry has become about themselves. In short, we can say we don't find any difference between church leadership and the leadership that governs and leads the secular world politically.

Any leadership without the close spiritual connection with Christ can commonly fall into two lowest "nadirs": either those leaders become prey very easily to the evil temptations of devil who devours them with allurement of money, lust, and hypocrisy, or they turn out to be devil's agents using their power to make their people, especially the young ones, prey to their own self-gratification, immoral libido, and illegal behavior.

Humble leaders committed to Jesus as servants always work toward the interests and needs of God's people before their own (Ref. Phil. 2:4). They would be ready to perform willingly even menial or unpopular assignments. Accordingly, they would be appreciated and rewarded by their Master at his Coming for their loyalty in a few things (Ref. Matt. 25:23). They would not accomplish their jobs overtly to be a showoff; rather, they would keep a low profile in any undertakings and serve the community with no publicity and applause because they are certain that their Father in heaven who sees what is done in secret will reward them (Ref. Matt. 6:3–4).

With this "servant mind setup," all humble leaders of Jesus in God's Kingdom care so much all about pleasing their Master in everything they perform as services to their people that at the end of fulfilling their duties, they would loudly tell their Master, as Jesus instructed them, "We are unworthy servants; we have only done our duty" (Luke 17:10).

CHAPTER 21: BE A WOUNDED HEALER

We observe our Master in his leadership life very often exhibiting through his daily chores and valuable teachings an ever-glowing and unquenched fire burning in him. He once stated, "I have come to set the earth on fire, and how I wish it were already blazing! There is a baptism with which I must be baptized, and how great is my anguish until it is accomplished" (Luke 12:49–51). This fire was nothing but bestowing holistic healing to the wounded humanity. He desired all his discipled leaders should retain in their inner spirit.

DISCIPLED LEADERSHIP AND ITS POST EFFECTS

Some years back, I got a letter from one of my priest friends in India. He mentioned that he was leaving the Catholic priesthood soon; he too explained the events that led him to take such hard decision. The summary of it is this: He was on fire with the ambitions and ideals of Jesus as he learned from the Gospels and saints. With other pastoral responsibilities of administering the sacraments and assisting the needy, he wanted to go little further to encourage youngsters to get the fire of Jesus. He started an organization called the Catholic Christians on Fire. Many youngsters came and joined the organization. They began learning more about Scriptures, gathered very often to get baptized in the Holy Spirit, prayed together, and sang together as often as they could. They tried their best to bring down the fire of peace among the families and communities, the fire of prayer, the fire of joy, and much more, the fire of love among the parishioners. All the members of that organization were fully convinced that the fire Jesus brought to this earth was the fire of nonviolence, the fire that would lead us to uphold "do or die" faith, namely, be active in following and observing the truth of Jesus, whatever be the results to our own lives.

Sadly, all his superiors, including his parents and many other senior priests, criticized him, advised him to stop this "nonsense" as they named. He was moved to a parish in a very interior, rural place where he couldn't do anything more than being a rural pastor. It was actually a punishment imposed by his bishop. When I read his letter, I shed tears. Isn't it true as we grow older, our blood has turned to be very cold except for some earthly pleasures? Our past experiences of fingers burned and other bitter encounters in life have groomed us to be neither cold nor hot. We think we possess age-old wisdom to handle life with prudence and diplomacy. In other words, we do not want to lose life or good name or conveniences because of some "do or die" faith attitude. We want to keep our comfort zone intact.

However, God, through his Son and messengers, wants his children to be burning with the heavenly fire. God is Fire in himself. That is what the NT describes the descent of God's Spirit like fire. In continuation of all God's prophets obliging such wish of God, we know how Jesus handled his life in fire. He was isolated, cornered, criticized, blamed, stoned, driven out, scourged, crucified, killed, and buried; all these happened because he began setting the earth on fire. His disciples followed his way, were glad they were beaten, punished, and killed for the sake of Jesus's fire.

We adults know also those who accepted this death wish of Jesus as their own became troublemakers. Most of our saints were troublemakers. St. Francis of Assisi, St. Theresa of Child Jesus, and Mother Teresa are a few among them. There were many such troublemakers found even among last century politicians. Take for example George Washington who fought a revolutionary war to free the colonies from foreign rule. Abraham Lincoln waged a civil war to save the union of the north and south. Susan B. Anthony launched the women's rights movement that is still a bone of contention in our society. Martin Luther King united the country in his crusade against racial segregation. Even in our recent times, the church canonized two such "dangerous saints in desperate time": Archbishop Óscar Romero and Pope Paul VI.

HEALERS OF ILLNESS OF COLD AND COMPLACENT HUMAN SPIRIT

Now you see why we adults do not get our fingers burned. However, I am sure as I feel certain emptiness in my life, and so you adults would feel the same. We too from years of experience learned to hide this emptiness or vacuum in our life. That is surely the result of our coldness toward the fire Jesus ignited. We should, for a while, reflect over this coldness or indifference to our Christian call of upholding "do or die" faith and take some steps to rejoin with Jesus on fire.

With this heavenly fire, we, the discipled leaders, carrying our own wounds and scars, should comfort our flock in the footsteps of Good Samaritan, binding up their wounds and applying the balm of compassion and love. In essence, we are accomplishing the eternal promise of God that he will "bind up the injured and strengthen the weak" (Ezra 34:16). Millions of Christians in the world today suffer many injuries to their spirits, and they need compassionate leaders who will bear their burdens with them, sympathize with their critical circumstances, exhibit patience toward them, encourage them in the Word, and bring their concerns every day before the Father's throne.

As we discussed previously in detail about our Master's goal of sending us to the world, we are sent to proclaim and perform his "Gospel of healing." It is for this reason each one of us has been elected, selected, promoted, and ordained in different ways, styles, and processes and for different roles. Quoting Pope Pius XI, Pope Francis pointed out in one of his audiences to the participants in the General Chapter of the Missionary Oblates of Mary Immaculate that all the discipled leaders are "the specialists of difficult missions." According to him, every land, every neighborhood, every village in the globe is indeed a mission land. Pope also affirmed that "today the mission field seems to widen every day, always embracing new poor, men and women of the face of Christ who ask for help, consolation, hope in the most desperate situations of life. Therefore, there is need of you, of your missionary daring, of your readiness to take to all the Good News that frees and consoles."

WE ARE HEALERS WITH AND THROUGH OUR WOUNDS

At this juncture, let us remember the admonition of St. Augustine to the discipled leaders who throw overboard the duty of healing: "You have failed to strengthen what was weak, to heal what was sick, and to bind up what was injured, that is, what was broken. You did not call back the straying sheep, nor seek out the lost" (from his sermon On Pastors). The healing ministry of discipled leaders is very much expected by our Master at the times our people are drastically wounded by their own mistakes, messing up of their life decisions, and by their disobedience to the Holy Spirit's promptings and admonitions. Having had the experiences of such darkened moments and of the miraculous escapes out of sin-brought crisis, we should approach our friends who undergo such sufferings and testify to them boldly but lovingly the merciful deeds of God in history and in our own stories. We can quote Job in this agonizing moments: "Happy indeed the man whom God corrects! So do not refuse this lesson from the Omnipotent: for he who wounds is he who soothes the sore, and the hand that hurts is the hand that heals" (Job 5:17–18).

Thus, we would be lifting our friends from the muddy ground and put them on the rock. Also, we would help them to center their attention on Christ and his sufferings through which he has paid ransom for our failures and sins. We would encourage not to glorify human sufferings but to underline how effective sufferings would be for human liberation and resurrection if they are endured patiently. We should proclaim to them that all of us are children of the good and loving God, and therefore, whatever he does to us is for our better life: "Whom the Lord loves, he disciplines; he scourges every son he acknowledges" (Heb. 12:6; Prov. 3:14).

In explaining Jesus's miraculous curing of a blind man and restoring his eyesight with "mud paste" (John 9:1–7), David Knight, in his book *Living God's Word*, writes that we, the baptized Christians, the disciples of Jesus, are the mud paste, which Christ has made with the dirt of this earth and his own saliva. According to Mr. Knight, "Mud-paste means that we are people molded by Christ's truth, transformed by his words. It is we who with our daily physical contact with the world heal the blindness of others, fill others' emptiness, heal others' physical and emotional sickness, and fulfill the needs of others."

The author is correct in his explanation of "mud paste" for the fact that the unique mission of our Master was to turn his followers, especially those whom he predestined to be his leaders, as the healing sources in the world. He wanted us to be not just his instruments but also and much more to be another Christ. When one of our people suffers out of want, poverty, ignorance, sickness, and other human maladies, God presents himself visible, audible, and tangible to that person in the form of his Son's discipled leaders, who extend our helping and healing hands to that sufferer. The persons who are healed by our loving services start glorifying God.

For the past two millennia, there were thousands and thousands of Jesus's discipled leaders all over the world who have opened a new door to the darkened lives of millions of people. Through the ministry of education, information, medication, and arts and sharing of their possessions, talents, and even their own lives, they have helped heal the physical, emotional, intellectual, and spiritual darkness, illness, and other maladies of people. I am positive those who read this book would be continuing their healing ministries as committed discipled leaders. Undoubtedly, it is because we all know not only "we are the 'mud paste' of Jesus but much more so, 'we are ointments and not just pipelines'" that carries godly healing into the inner spirit of our flock.

OUR WOUNDS ARE CHANNELS OF SANCTIFICATION

Jesus is correct in his wisest statement: "Blind cannot lead the blind." "Can a blind person guide a blind person? Will not both fall into a pit?" (Luke 6:39). But he too pronounced splendidly that his followers can become the source of light as he is: "You are the light of the world. A city set on a mountain cannot be hidden. Nor do they light a lamp and then put it under a bushel basket; it is set on a lampstand, where it gives light to all in the house. Just so, your light must shine before others, that they may see your good deeds and glorify your heavenly Father" (Matt. 5:14–16). With no hesitance, we dare say when we are cured our own blindness and liberated from our inner darkness though the redemptive wounds of Jesus, with the same wounds and scars, we are granted an ability to sanctify others who are moving in darkness.

Nonetheless, one thing is to be remembered. All the enlightening and enlivening deeds we perform as healers and sanctifiers cannot be resourceful and truthful if we ourselves are genuinely disciples of the Crucified Master. As he reminds us every moment of our leadership ministries, "No disciple is superior to the teacher; but when fully trained, every disciple will be like his teacher" (Luke 6:40). Namely, where the Master is, hanging on the Cross with bleeding wounds, there his disciples should be, and what he taught, taking up our own crosses and carrying our own body dead to sin, that we should accomplish. This is the one and only way to become channels of sanctification for our fellow humans.

CHAPTER 22: BE A PEACEMAKER

In his Sermon on the Mount, Jesus included one of the beatitudes (Matt. 5:9) to be bestowed to his discipled leaders is "You will be called children of God." The One who taught us to call God as "our Father (Abba)" and explained how the heavenly Father is so anxious to embrace us as his children offered us in the same sermon a clue to be worthy of that remarkable title and get blessed by his Father. He added as the prerequisite of such privilege, saying, "Blessed are the peacemakers." As we are discussing in this book about the ministries of every discipled leader in God's Kingdom according to the demands and examples of our Master Jesus, let us discuss here what sort of demand our Master places before us regarding our role of peacemakers and how he sketched out for our fulfilling this role.

WHAT IS PEACE?

In the Bible, the term "peace" has several different meanings. The Hebrew word "shalom" for peace is often used in reference to an appearance of calm and tranquility of individuals, groups, and nations. The Greek word "eirene" is what Paul uses for peace to describe the feeling of harmony or tranquility to be found in his New Testament churches. But the deeper, more foundational meaning of peace is the spiritual harmony, as the unique gift from God brought about by every human's reconciliation with God. From the days of the Old Testament, we discover the Israelites came to realize very clearly this spiritual and social aspect of peace.

There's a great story in chapter 6 of the Book of Judges that illustrates this realization: When the Israelites were being terrorized by the people of Midian, God chose Gideon, the youngest and most insignificant member of his family, to save Israelites from their enemies. After much protest, Gideon listened to God, for God promised that he would be with Gideon and would give him strength, saying, "Be calm, do not fear. You shall not die." Accepting God's call, Gideon built an altar to God and called it Yahweh-shalom, which means "the Lord is peace." Consequently, Gideon, uniting Israelites in harmony and trust in God, enabled them to come out of their fear and limitations, went on with them to save them from the cruel hands of Midians, and brought peace to the land.

This biblical story brings home to us not only how the Israelites came to realize that God is the Peace lover, Peacemaker, Peace giver, and the only source of genuine peace but also that God empowers those who recognize such eternal truth of peace and obey his commands and advices of love to be bearers of true peace. That is why we hear Isaiah praying confidently to the Lord: "With firm purpose you maintain peace; in peace, because of our trust in you . . . Lord, you will decree peace for us, for you have accomplished all we have done" (Isa. 26:3–12).

WHO IS A PEACEMAKER?

Generally, the term "peacemaker" refers to a person who brings about peace, especially by reconciling adversaries. He/she can be an arbiter, mediator, negotiator, pacifier, appeaser, peace lover, and so on. Scripturally, a peacemaker is one who first enjoys the peace of God within oneself (Phil. 4:7), one who is at peace with the God of peace and his Son, the Prince of Peace (Rom. 5:1; Phil. 4:9). Consequently, such a peace-filled person turns out to be a peace lover in all his interactions with neighbors (Rom. 12:18), becomes a proclaimer of the Gospel of true peace (Eph. 6:15) with the strong intention and belief that one day those who listen and observe the Gospel of peace will enjoy the same peace, which is not as the world thinks and pursues.

A few verses after stating the beatitude of "peacemaking," Jesus instructs the worshippers to leave their gifts at the altar to make peace with those who have something against them (Matt. 5:21–26); plus, some more verses later, he tells us we should love our enemies and pray for those persecute us, that we might be like our father in heaven who provides the righteous and the unrighteous with sunshine and rain (Matt. 5:43–45).

Interpreting the abovementioned Jesus's words on peacemakers, James, who is writing to a church fractured with partiality, encourages Jesus's disciples to take the role of peacemakers; he too lists out nine characteristics of an effective peacemaker (James 3:13–18): "Moral purity, meekness, gentleness, open-mindedness, fullness of mercy and good fruits, impartiality and sincerity, enduring patience, willingness to go the extra mile, and all the above-listed traits must evolve from the growth of Gospel seed sown already in every discipled leader."

In sum, a genuine peacemaker is one who, being blessed and enlightened by the God of Peace, walks in every moment of life as a peace breather, peace lover, peace seeker, and peace giver.

UNIQUENESS OF THE MINISTRY OF PEACE

At the Last Supper, Jesus had told us, "Peace I leave with you; my peace I give to you; not as the world gives do I give it to you" (John 14:27). The Scriptures esteem Jesus the Prince of Peace. Plus, we fully believe with Paul who, quoting from Isaiah (9:5), underlines in his letter to the Ephesians (2:14) that "Jesus is our peace, who made both Jews and Gentiles as one family of God by breaking down the dividing wall of enmity." There is no doubt about our Master's command, demand, and longing about our intense and active role of managing, maintaining, and repairing, if needed, the true peace he brought to this world.

However, we are wonderstruck by one of the sayings Luke quotes in his Gospel: "Do you think that I have come to establish peace on the earth? No, I tell you, but rather division" (Luke 12:51). This is a statement that critics of religion would cynically agree with, especially as they notice through the history the social divisions among human beings and, especially, the religious infights, civil wars, mushroomed inside God's Kingdom sadly because of religious upholdings. In our own times, we have only to look at the Middle East (Jews and Muslims), the Eastern Europe (Catholics, Orthodox, and Muslims), India (Hindus, Muslims, and Christians), Northern Ireland (Catholics and Protestants), and the past and present history of America (Catholicism and anti-Catholic fundamentalism).

First and foremost, we should be clear about the eternal attitude and dream of Jesus regarding genuine peace for his people. Second, with the light given by the biblical scholars, we should analyze the above-quoted verse from Luke. Jesus, by his striking statement, should mean something other than what we understand at its surface level. It is about the true peace he has been concerned about. As Jesus had stated little earlier to his saying about "division," he brought from his Father a Gospel, which is a refining and purifying fire. According to his presumption and certainly a prediction, his fiery message would meet with acceptance or rejection and, consequently, would be a source of conflict and dissension even within families (Luke 12:49–53).

The most important role of his Gospel message is nothing but to bring and stabilize a "genuine" peace and not a fake one. We hear him emphasizing this factual factor as his aim: "Peace I leave with you; my peace I give to you. Not as the world gives do I give it to you" (John 14:27). As we are told by the biblical scholars, the term "peace" Jesus used here is not a mere traditional Hebrew salutation, but he used the word "shalom" referring to a gift of salvation, the bountiful messianic blessing. It is in this view of "peace" Jesus breached out of all other peace promisers or peacemakers.

We should know no human being can survive even a single moment without some sort of inner peace. Physically, emotionally, and mentally, a person should be in balance. This is called tranquility. Every bit of our human system within us must be at its balanced level. When this is lost, all kinds of problems start in the body, mind, and soul. Hence, the genuine and real peace is some equilibrium or balance in our mind and heart that keeps us "cool." When it is diminished or disappeared, we become peaceless and get a hurt feeling within us, and we become so low, down in the dumps. So we make recourse to many wrong strategies to bring back that mental and emotional balance such as alcohol, drugs, perverted sex, even unlimited food and parties, being moneymangers, workaholics, and above all, by our compromises and complacency. Sure, we will establish peace by the above-mentioned worldly endeavors, but that peace is always temporary and fake.

Jesus came to proclaim not only about true peace but also how to achieve this. He wanted us to be burned with his fire of truth, justice, and love. He says, "I have come to set the earth on fire, and how I wish it were already blazing!" Once this fire is burning within us, surely there will be lots of things and even persons our near and dear ones have to be knocked out. Division starts there. He wants us to meet such chances as challenges of faith in him, stand in the battle, and never to quit. He demands the Gospel fire he ignited should never be extinguished in our leadership ministry.

ACT LIKE BRIDGE BUILDERS WITH HOPE

While so many descriptions on this prerequisite are mushrooming around the globe and for ages, Pope Francis explained it in simple a phrase: "Be bridge builders." Rightly and succinctly, he has said it. As we recite in opening prayer of every Mass for Peace Day, "Our God is God of peace, who are peace itself and whom a spirit of discord cannot grasp, nor a violent mind receive." Only the devil is the person of discord, violence, and war. Whoever meditates or plans and performs such hideous actions is totally the servant of that Satan, the archenemy of God. Fixing a sixty-five-foot photo of "toddler peering over U.S.-Mexico Border Wall, JR, a French photographer and artist, witnesses to the Gospel Value of Love and Unity: While 'satan-ians' erect walls of fear and hatred in relationships, 'Christ-ians' build only bridges" (Ref. Pic Border Wall). Unfortunately and sadly, there are thousands of people, especially many leaders of nations and religions, are overpowered by God's archenemy and bring divisions, infights, dissension, discord, civil wars, and world wars.

When we are called to be Jesus's discipled leaders and when he willingly sends us into the world to develop the Kingdom of peace he has already established, he is fully aware of the hurdles and hardships we would be facing: "Go on your way; behold, I am sending you like lambs among wolves" (Luke 10:3). Indeed, our Master was cautioning us about the evil-rigged life situations we would be facing in our leadership enterprises. But much more than that, Jesus's heart-throbbing longing was to instruct us how we should be engaged in bringing peace to his people among whom there exists too many wolflike personalities who try to rip off the unity, harmony, and peace to be existed in God's Kingdom.

Normally, the saddest thing every sincere "bridge builder" encounters as he/she tries to bring the true peace among the divided people of God is that the so-called wolves and Satan's agents of disunity and hatred, hidden in sheep's clothing, do their best to relate the peacemakers of Jesus to any one of their artificial bases of disunity such as the caste, creed, race, language, and even their subgroup connections. That is the cunning way of the powerful spiritual being, the fallen angel devil. In this situation, the discipled leaders of true peace should act prudently and never yield to the devil's promptings of one-siding.

Jesus's bridge builders must act out tirelessly their role of peacekeeping with relentless hope. God the Creator never intended his creation being blown to pieces by rifts, wars, hatred, and violence. Let us look at the nature he designed. Every inanimate and material being is created in an orderly fashion, and they still beautifully preserve its unity with no discard whatsoever. In Sirach, we hear the great teacher describing this awesome unity among creations and gratefully glorifying the Creator: "When at the first God created his works and, as he made them, assigned their tasks, He arranged for all time what they were to do, their domains from generation to generation. They were not to go hungry or grow weary, or ever cease from their tasks. Never does a single one crowd its neighbor, or do any ever disobey his word. Then the Lord looked upon the earth, and filled it with his blessings" (Sir. 16:26–30). Such amazing blessing of being and moving in harmony came to exist because, as the Bible underlines, God the Creator did all this only in, through, and for his beloved Son, the Blueprint of God (Ref. Col. 1:15–18).

Indeed, we observe in today's universe there is no harmony at all, especially among humans and more specifically among and within families, communities, and churches. They thrive mostly by being divided and move miserably well with discord and divergence. This had been a perennial problem for humanity. Most of us consider that the foremost cause of the distortion and deterioration of Good God's plan of unity and peace in many regions and ages of the church has been his own leaders who were careless of their discipled pledge given to their Master. This reckoning may be perhaps in certain cases. But any bad leader is not the problem for disunity in the church. He/she is only a symptom, not a cause of divide. We must be very clear about an eternal truth about peace on the earth: godly peace is possible only in the offing of its blossoming. With Christ, we continue to hope for its fulfillment. The Creator knew it and, finally, in his time, sent his own Son as the Messiah to restore again the creative harmony existed from the time of creation.

Prophesying about the coming Messiah, Isaiah wrote (9:5), "For a child will be born to us, a son will be given to us; and the government will rest on His shoulders." He too praised the Messiah's name with many glorious titles of which one is very relevant to our discussion here. He named Jesus of Nazareth as Prince of Peace. In accordance with that prophecy, we now have Jesus, the Prince of Peace, among us as Emmanuel. Paul, in his revelatory exposition, uncovered this mysterious truth: "For in him all the fullness was pleased to dwell, and through him to reconcile all things for him, making peace by the blood of his cross through him, whether those on earth or those in heaven" (Col. 1:19–20).

The church, which Jesus established, has been seen as "a people made one with the unity of the Father, the Son and the Holy Spirit" (Lumen Gentium, para. 4). It is this truth, as the base and as the goal of every peacekeeping effort we make, that must be in our blood and flesh. It is to this noble task of restoring the original peace and unity of humanity all discipled leaders are chosen. Our dreams are often petty, perverted, unreal, and earthly. But God's promises are real and truthful. Among them, the most benevolent and desirable is his promise of establishing his Kingdom of peace and harmony. Seemingly and surprisingly, as many of God's promises have not been realized fully till this day, the promise of peaceful life too is one that has not been totally fulfilled.

AN EFFICIENT PEACEMAKER IS A SLAVE TO GOSPEL VALUES

We come across the exhortation of God's Spirit that no humans, by their own natural IQ or diplomacy, can bring or maintain the true peace among people. It all needs the human hearts, which are beating with the values of the "Prince of Peace." The true peace the Lord offers comes out of the heart that is filled with love, truth, and justice: "Observe the person of integrity and mark the upright; because there is a future for a man of peace" (Ps. 37:37). Also, the prophecy, which the Psalmist sings about Jesus, holds good for every discipled leader of peace today: "I will listen for what God, the Lord, has to say; surely he will speak of peace to his people and to his faithful . . . Love and truth will meet; justice and peace will kiss. Truth will spring from the earth; justice will look down from heaven" (Ps. 85:9–12).

The archenemy, Satan, dreams he is going to win and defeat God in Jesus. Over the centuries, he proves himself a fool because he couldn't and cannot defeat God's omnipotent power of his holy and peaceful reign. He sent to this war-stricken world his beloved Son Jesus Christ to bring not only true peace but also an unfailing scheme or strategy to defeat the devil's efforts to destroy peace. We follow this Jesus, who is the Prince of Peace.

According to his Father's peace strategy, first, he offers peace in our hearts, not as the world perceives or gives, but the true peace as we heard him in today's Gospel. His true peace is based and generated by thinking and doing, as Paul says in his letter, "Whatever is true, whatever is honorable, whatever is just, whatever is pure, whatever is lovely, whatever is gracious, if there is any excellence and if there is anything worthy of praise." Thus, we become peace lovers. And the second phase of God's peace strategy is to empower us to become peacemakers. This is what the church of Jesus Christ has been doing as God's peacemakers, bringing peace to the world. And this is why every time the devil starts his evil deeds of destroying peace with the help of his servants, history testifies, popes decried against wars and inspired church members to take action to defeat the devil.

THE UNIFIED SPIRIT OF UNIVERSAL SALVATION

Historically, as any other deviations occurred in discipleship attitudes and observances, in a notorious way, the disciples expressed their deep concern in becoming more and more exclusive by cruelly differentiating themselves from other nondisciples and went to the worst kind of groupism, avoiding, hating, and even murdering other groups of religions and denominations.

On the contrary, our Master Jesus behaved differently but the same as his Father. While his "exclusively appointed" disciples were bestowed power to cast out demons in his name, they discovered someone who didn't belong to their group did the same powerful act. They complained about it to the Master, who immediately retorted, "Do not prevent him. There is no one who performs a mighty deed in my name who can at the same time speak ill of me" (Mark 9:38–48). Jesus taught his followers to recognize the work of God from with and from outside the immediate community. He expects us to treat all those outside our religious campus with deep respect because we recognize that God can and does speak through them as he can and does through our church. The Second Vatican Council said that "the Holy Spirit offers everyone the possibility, in a way known only to God, to be associated with this paschal mystery of Christ and, therefore, to be saved" (*Gaudium et Spes*, no. 22, Editor's note).

Such attitude never mutilates the outstanding privilege of the disciples' recruited, set apart, and appointed status as long as we continue to believe two things: First, that Jesus is, objectively and in fact, the only mediator and savior of the whole human race and that also those who do not know him, if they are saved, are saved, thanks to him and his redeeming death. Second, that also those who still not belonging to the visible church are objectively "oriented" toward her, form part of that larger church, and known only to God. Maturing in the holiness of God, with Paul, we should unhesitantly proclaim that "salvation from God is for all." Our human puny hearts may be beating for exclusiveness and inclusiveness for our church existence.

We may think in our church there is no room for tyrants and despots, for atheists or agnostics. Our hardheadedness may shout out that God did not intend for the chosen ones to rub shoulders with the disreputable and the depraved. And therefore, some of us may work or support others for "constructing walls" among families, communities, parishes, denominations, and nations. But God categorically cracks down all our provincial attitudes and our ever-narrowing ideas of who belongs to the people of God and proclaims that, without any discrimination whatsoever, God wants all to be included in the loving and gracious embrace of salvation. The same is true with the Master's demand and dream. This is what his eternal prayer in heaven that all his disciples should be united not only among themselves but also with those outside their campuses as the union existing between him and his Father: "I pray not only for them, but also for those who will believe in me through their word, so that they may all be one, as you, Father, are in me and I in you, that they also may be in us, that the world may believe that you sent me" (John 17:20–21).

BRING UNITY FIRST WITHIN YOUR MINISTRY

Our Master said, "My sheep hear my voice; I know them, and they follow me" (John 10:27). Interpreting these words of Jesus, St. Augustine emphasizes the incredible unity to be demonstrated among the leaders: "All shepherds should therefore be one in the one good shepherd. All should speak with the one voice of the one shepherd, so that the sheep may hear and follow their shepherd; not this or that shepherd, but the one shepherd. All should speak with one voice in Christ, not with different voices. Saint also begs the leaders: Have no dissensions among you. Our flock of Christ should hear His one voice; a voice purified from all schism, and freed from all heresy."

Strong leaders are effective at bringing others together in a team. Before we start building the bridges in our communities, we should first engage ourselves in "team building." This is often the difference between discipled leaders and others, who also get good ideas but never have much impact on the body of Christ. Bringing people together and helping them overcome barriers to understanding, personal resentments, jealousies, and prejudice is typical work for discipled leaders. They often engage in conflict management with peaceful results. Those who try to manage conflict between others but end up fanning the flames or consistently repudiating one or the other party in conflict usually cannot lead for long or at least must have a small following. Team building also means that the leader is a consensus former. She is able to get more than one person to agree about key values or directions of movement. Thus, we first should live and witness the unity of Jesus within our groups or subgroups and then proclaim it to the outside world.

Whenever we come together in many events and occasions, we express our unity in various dimensions— politically, nationally, racially, gender-wise, or class basis. But when we gather together in the church religiously, we not only express our unity as Catholic Christians but also much more so experience and being strengthened in genuine unity based and centered on Christ's love. When we touch base with our Master Jesus together as his team of lovers, we are purified, nourished, and enlightened to broaden our idea of unity from its fake, crooked, narrow, and self-centered approach to God-oriented relationship among ourselves as the one and only family of God.

We too discover our diversity in right sense: Diversity, when inspired by God, is a manifestation of the many gifts, talents, ways of life, and charisms that God chooses to use to fulfill his plans and promises. But more importantly, we plan out more effective ways of working together—to discover the complementarity of our diversities. Unity, when inspired by God, is a manifestation of how the many gifts, talents, ways of life, and charisms can work together toward a single goal and mission to witness the variety of ways people are living lives of service to strengthen our church and the entire world.

BUILD UP A EUCHARISTIC COMMUNITY IN THE PARISH

Almost all the discipled leaders in a parish community not only participate in the Eucharistic celebrations either weekly or daily but also have ample chances to serve as ministers in many ways. More than ordinary people, we should possess a clear understanding of the fact that the Eucharist is the greatest resource for our peace-making ministries in the community. The assertions of Paul in this matter must be ringing in our minds throughout the celebration: "The bread that we break, is it not a participation in the body of Christ? Because the loaf of bread is one, we, though many, are one body, for we all partake of the one loaf" (1 Cor. 10:16b–17).

Unquestionably, we fully believe in our church teaching that says, "Mass is an act of both God and man in and through Jesus to offer sacrifice, to celebrate our communion in a sacred meal, plus adoration of God in Jesus by handling in a holiest way the precious Body and Blood of Jesus." And we too know that when someone forgets or omits even one dimension of the three factors of the Eucharist, he/she will be dishonoring the Lord's goodness and will. We should never forget that during every Eucharistic celebration, a mind-blowing miracle is occurring, namely, all those worthily and actively participating and are involved in it are transferred into Jesus's body and blood. As our honorable Church Fathers had underlined, in that miraculous happening, "not as natural bread and wine changing into our physical system, but we turn into Jesus' spiritual system." Participation in the sacrament of the Eucharist draws one into the very life of Jesus, his very life, both his body and spirit, bestowed upon anyone who abides in his words and values.

LET US TAKE THE EUCHARISTIC UNITY WHEREVER WE GO

The Eucharist, which is fondly called the sacrament of love and unity, strengthens us to be unifying. Jesus gave himself up for us to unify and reconcile humanity with God. Our participation in the Eucharist, which is a sacrament of forgiving love, unity, and reconciliation, should make us long for and work for reconciliation peace and harmony in our own families, communities, and the world at large.

By participating in the Eucharistic Mass, we would possess an amazing ability to see dualities—the pros and cons of situations as change approaches—and to quickly and efficiently think them through before making any decisions. We would dare to look deeply into our desires, regenerate self-awareness, and recognize psychological ambiguities. This will bring balance into our home and family life. We would pay attention to the details as we bring our inner and outer life into unity and harmony. Surely we will enjoy the changes occurring within us. As we come to terms with ourselves, we would be able to see a more fulfilling purpose in life, and our field of experience broadens. We would focus on matters that affect us most deeply, and like magic, our life will become easier and things will seem to take care of themselves. We will have all the necessary resources and motivation to make tangible changes and achieve results in all our endeavors. We will become unique persons of self-giving, life-giving, and surely unifying. In every step of our lives, we will develop into a peacemaker and peace lover. We will be energized to live like a true champion of the Eucharistic unity at home, in the community, and around the nation.

This means as Jesus, we are endowed with the longing for loving others, helping others, and serving others, even sacrificing our lives for others. We are full of enthusiasm to become one body, unifying source as he is. We become fully conscious of our oneness and unity. Paul advised his Corinthian readers that their sharing in the blood of Christ and the body of Christ forged a unity among them like no other sharing. Jews and Greeks, men and women, slaves and free—all become one in Christ, whose presence in bread and cup sublimated all their differences. Centuries ago, St. John Chrysostom asked, "What is the bread actually? The body of Christ. What do communicants become? The body of Christ. Just as bread is the result of many grains and although remaining themselves are not distinguished from one another because they are united, so we too are mutually united with Christ." Whatever words we use—"the church," "the people of God," or "the community of believers"—as we celebrate the gift of the body of Christ, we also celebrate the gift of one another in Christ.

As it is mentioned earlier, such unthinkable bond among us can happen only when we consciously and with deep faith and devotion and longing participate in the Mass. Therefore, every discipled leader, who intends to be blessed as God's peacemakers, must make the best and most of this unique resource of unity. Unfortunately, our individual misinterpretation and misgiving obstructs such fruitful participation in Mass. Besides our wrong attitudes, there are so many other factors that distract us to do so. For example, the uncontrolled mannerism or habit of the main celebrant; the shabby and slovenly behaviors of altar servers and co-ministers such as readers, ushers, and other ministers serving at the Eucharistic table; the unbalanced and nonliturgical ornaments, decorations, music, and environmental climate; and many other obstacles distort the holiness of the environment.

As a final comment, I would like to remind all discipled leaders how for two thousand years our church has been demonstrating in the Eucharistic celebration her earnest feeling of realizing the dream of Jesus about her unity and peace. During her Eucharistic Prayer II, besides many of her petitions, she says, "Humbly we pray that, partaking of the Body and Blood of Christ, we may be gathered into one by the Holy Spirit." And in the Communion rite, being reminded of the risen Lord's breathtaking promise of peace, she prays to him, "Lord Jesus Christ, who said to your Apostles, 'Peace I leave you, my peace I give you,' look not on our sins; but on the faith of your Church, and graciously grant her peace and unity in accordance with your will." Becoming the full-fledged ministers of peace and unity in the Kingdom of God, let us fervently make the best use of these prayers in our celebration of the Eucharist.

CHAPTER 23: BE A WARRIOR

THE LEADER AS A FIGHTER

Any adults who enter into the arena of leadership quickly perceives that they often have to fight negative trends or false beliefs that develop within groups. They are strangled by certain conspiracy theories floating around them. Because of such unjust misunderstanding and biased attitudes, they have to face untold pains and sufferings that are generated by rejection, hatred, and discrimination. Those leaders who are not discipled under the grace of the Master frequently take a wrong and very negative reactions against such deplorable condition or even become sick with Down syndrome.

On the contrary, the discipled leaders carefully figure out before God what factors are leading to the negative trends or views among their friends and devise positive countermeasures. They take seriously the statement of St. Cyril of Jerusalem on this issue: "Certainly in times of tranquility the cross should give you joy. But maintain the same faith in times of persecution. Otherwise you will be a friend of Jesus in times of peace and his enemy during war. Now you receive the forgiveness of your sins and the generous gift of grace from your king. When war comes, fight courageously for him."

In addition to the war the discipled leaders have to wage regarding the above-said personal problem, they have to wage the same "good" war in many of their public ministries, especially of peacemaking and peacekeeping we have discussed in the previous chapter. When we focus always the salvation Jesus brought to the people and perform our peace-filled services in the light of the demands of Jesus, we get into trouble. This well-balanced role of peacemaking sometimes bring division in our churches or religious campuses between two groups: people who attentively listen to God's salvific demands and faithfully observing them and people who oppose or being careless to their Creator and Redeemer. These two groups do not live in two different parts of the world; they live side by side in the same neighborhood, and they live together under the same roof. At this juncture, what should be our approach, our attitude, and our proactions? Let us discuss here and get some answers from the Spirit and the Bible.

GOD INDEED IS A WARRIOR

Almost all the OT books authors underscore that our God is a mighty Warrior. They too prove it with many powerful deeds he did for his people. In the Book of Isaiah, we read that every person committed to the Lord is esteemed as his vineyard. And if anyone outside tries to destroy it, God assures he would fight against him/her and punish him/her: "On that day, the Lord will punish with his sword that is cruel, great, and strong. On that day, the pleasant vineyard, sing about it! I, the Lord, am its keeper, I water it every moment; lest anyone harm it, night and day I guard it" (Isa. 27:1–3). At the same time, the Lord too asserts through the prophet that even though he won't be angry at the one whom God loves to sing as his beloved vineyard, if he sees certain flaws crowded and maroon the beauty and holiness of it, he would again march on against it with his cruel sword: "I am not angry. But if I were to find briers and thorns, in battle I would march against it; I would burn it all. But if it holds fast to my refuge, it shall have peace with me; it shall have peace with me" (Isa. 27:4–5).

In Psalms, we find God's merciful and just but powerful war engagement on behalf of his chosen one and all the chosen ones: "You crush Rahab with a mortal blow; with your strong arm you scatter your foes . . . You have a mighty arm. Your hand is strong; your right hand is ever exalted" (Ps. 89). "Who is this king of glory? The Lord, strong and mighty, the Lord, mighty in war" (Ps. 24). Moses, in his writing about the creation events, asserts that God the eternal Warrior began his war against Satan already at the time of creation. Explaining the bitter but sweet words of God to both Adam and Eve: "I will put enmity between you and the woman, and between your offspring and hers; they will strike at your head, while you strike at their heel" (Gen. 3:15), St. Irenaeus wrote, "God declared war against our enemy, crushed him who at the beginning had taken us captive in Adam, and trampled on his head, in accordance with God's words to the serpent in Genesis."

THE PARADOXICAL WARRIORISM OF GOD

In the light of God's promising word about his uninterrupted waging war, we should understand his war is against the evil archenemy, the Devil. Therefore, we should be convinced that, according to the Scriptures, though our earthly life is predestined to be made of peace, joy, and love, it is nothing but a warzone. Sadly, God's enemy, the evil, continues to give us monstrous trouble in our journey with and for God. This bloodshedding battle already started at the beginning of humanity. It continues and will end only at the second coming of Jesus.

There is one striking thing we should observe in the warriorism of our God. While he used in his battle with evil all his intrinsic virtues of justice, power, and holiness, he never threw out his perennial virtue of mercy and peace. Prophet Isaiah underwrites this revelatory truth. Describing God as he enters into the warzone, Isaiah says, "Justice shall be the band around his waist, and faithfulness a belt upon his hips" (Isa. 11:5). "He put on justice as his breastplate, victory as a helmet on his head; He clothed himself with garments of vengeance, wrapped himself in a mantle of zeal" (Isa. 59:17). At the same time, God insists through Isaiah that "[t]hough the mountains fall away and the hills be shaken, my love shall never fall away from you nor my covenant of peace be shaken" (Isa. 54:10).

In the same vein, we hear God himself, a Supreme Being of peace giver, acting as the Warrior, wrestling perennially against the evil, not only speaking out war against evil but also inviting us to join in this battle: "Declare this among the nations: proclaim a war, rouse the warriors to arm! . . . Let the weak man say, 'I am a warrior'!" (Joel 4:9–10). The eternal peace God promised is not as what the world or our mere humanness look for or give. It is a real but rare blend of battling and winning-battling against evil and winning the heavenly blissful peace.

Over the centuries before the time of Jesus, God's prophets and sages like Jeremiah (Jer. 38:4–13) had been joining with the Almighty in fighting the holy war against the false prophets, teachers, and leaders who were worldly and spoke and did only what the ungodly kings, queens, and their officials wanted to hear and liked to be done. But we can notice almost all those sincere soldiers on the side of God, as Jeremiah, stuck to the truth. And they enjoyed God's protection and liberation that was arranged by the Creator even through people living outside his campus.

JESUS AS WARRIOR AGAINST EVIL

At the arrival of Jesus of Nazareth, the entire world saw the total embodiment of the prophetic and sacred chivalrous leadership in the frontline of God's warzone. Through Isaiah, God the Father already prophesized about Jesus, the Warrior: "A shoot shall sprout from the stump of Jesse, and from his roots a bud shall blossom . . . He shall strike the ruthless with the rod of his mouth, and with the breath of his lips he shall slay the wicked. Justice shall be the band around his waist, and faithfulness a belt upon his hips" (Isa. 11:1–5). And in the Book of Revelation, the Lord who identifies himself as "the Alpha and the Omega, the one who is and who was and who is to come, the almighty" (Rev. 1:8), asks John to write these words and send to the churches: "Therefore, repent. Otherwise, I will come to you quickly and wage war against them with the sword of my mouth" (Rev. 2:16).

Jesus, who has been glorified as Prince of Peace and from the start of his life in this world greeted everyone he met with "shalom" and proclaimed, "On earth peace to those on whom his favor rest," contended that he was interested in waging war against the archenemy Satan. Though he emptied himself by his detachment from all glory and honor entitled to him, he did not come empty-handed. He brought with him valiant attitudes and ammunitions for his battling. He also shared them with his soldiers who are called his discipled leaders. It was nothing but "love," a magnificent gift, which, as history substantiated, not only enriched them but also made them unconquerable in battle.

Millions of individuals, starting from Deacon Stephen through the apostles and all the martyrs, up to this day, have never been tired of battling in the warzone of Jesus versus wickedness till their last breath. It is the "ammunition of love" that kept them intimately connected first with the God in Jesus and second with their neighbors. Their obedience to Jesus's love command and demand enabled them to receive all the strength needed for coping with the fiery battleground. Jesus made his promise realized fully in their life: "If you remain in me and my words remain in you, ask for whatever you want and it will be done for you" (John 15:7). As the Master guaranteed, they accomplished so much their Master did and even more: "Amen, amen, I say to you, whoever believes in me will do the works that I do, and will do greater ones than these, because I am going to the Father. And whatever you ask in my name, I will do, so that the Father may be glorified in the Son. If you ask anything of me in my name, I will do it" (John 14:12–14).

What we notice in their victorious battles against archenemy is they fought the good and right fight with one and only ammunition—love consisting of forgiveness, service, humility, mercy, truth, and surely sacrifice. Though such surrender to love command would have been en route to physical death—cruel, ignominious, shameful as that of their Master—they, at the end of the day, won their crown of victory over all the evils generated by archenemy, especially death itself. They defeated the sharp spear of death, as Jesus did. As the anticlimax of their embattlement, they kept their head erect, eyes gazing toward heaven, and underwent their final sufferings smilingly, boldly, and contently, crying out with Paul, "Where, O death, is your victory? Where, O death, is your sting?" (1 Cor. 15:55)

EVERY DISCIPLE IS A FIGHTER

Gladiators fought and earned the olive leaves crown. Boxers fight and attain their hero title. Soldiers in wars fight and covet their medals. Jesus the great Warrior asked us to fight and die for his Gospel principles. He expected us to join him in the war that had been already started off by his Father, the God of Abraham, the God of Moses, the God of Prophets, and the God of Lazarus.

As we stated earlier, the God of Israel whom Jesus brought to our attention has been the eternal Warrior, fighting from the day of creation against the wickedness of certain rich, haughty, complacent, rebellious, and malicious people. God's perennial fight is to secure justice for the oppressed, to give food to the hungry, to set captives free, to give sight to the blind, to raise those who were bowed, and to protect the widows, the orphans, and the strangers (Ps. 146). He too made his people of goodwill who joined his battle to arm themselves with "righteousness, devotion, faith, love, patience, and gentleness." The God of Jesus has been always the winner yesterday, today, and tomorrow. It is this kind of war Jesus came to this world to continue. And surprisingly, it is in this war he invited all humans to join with him, saying, "Follow me; I will make you fishers of humans." He too named them as his disciples. He also chose among them certain disciples to go in the frontline of this war to act as the forerunners of his disciples. We now call them the discipled leaders.

The two millennia human history portrays that millions of discipled leaders, joining with their Master and his disciples, fought for reestablishment of justice, love, and peace. For them, death has not been a big deal. They may seem like the terrorists we observe these days who have the guts to kill themselves as self-immolation. However, we should know the difference between the discipled warriors and the terrorists: While the terrorists use themselves as the self-immolating bombs for the sake of murdering thousands of innocent people, the discipled warriors do not fight and die for evil causes; rather, they fight and even die in this holy war for life, for freedom, for eternity, for justice, for safeguarding others' lives, and above all, for God's truth.

GOD TRAINED US TO BE WARRIORS

In the footsteps of our Master and his committed discipled leaders as well, we are chosen, formed, groomed, and trained to join the army of God to combat against the evil. I am sure most of today's discipled leaders would have gone through sacred military training either long term of seven to ten years or short term of one year or a few months. Whatever be the initial training days, it is not at all sufficient to do the right and valid life-term combat. Spiritual warfare demands an uninterrupted grooming on daily basis, which St. Ignatius Loyola listed out as the "spiritual exercises."

Every day we are obligated to perform those spiritual exercises to equip ourselves to march on to the frontline of warzone. Certainly, we need to fill ourselves with gratitude to the Great Warrior who has been from the day of our conception training us mysteriously as David sings, "Truly, who is God except the Lord? Who but our God is the rock? This God who girded me with might, kept my way unerring, who made my feet like a deer's, and set me on the heights, who trained my hands for war, my arms to string a bow of bronze. You have given me your saving shield; your right hand has upheld me; your favor made me great. You made room for my steps beneath me; my ankles never twisted" (Ps. 18:33–37; Ps. 144:1–2).

WARRIORS AGAINST WICKEDNESS

Having accepted and vowed to join and fight with our Master and his holy men and women against God's archenemy, the Satan, who is the embodiment of wickedness, we should first humbly and sincerely recognize one important factor of this "holy war": It is against the universal wickedness and unholiness pervading the entire humanity. Indeed, humans behave blindfolded in this regard. It is based on their coldness, indifference, callousness, and ignorance.

Jesus came to reveal this bitter fact of sickening children of this world, including the true sons and daughters of God who listen anxiously to God's word. Because of such grim situation, they go on opposing God's will. This divides all humankind into two camps, the camp of the godly and the camp of the ungodly. There is perpetual conflict, a state of war, between these two groups as one group strives to raise the world to God and the other to pull it down to hell. These two groups do not live in two different parts of the world; they live side by side under the same roof, in the same neighborhood. Surprisingly and shockingly, the forces of good and evil often exist together in every individual. The holy war to which Christ calls us therefore is not a war against people of certain nationalities or cultures, creeds or ideologies, but a war in which we first have to identify the forces for evil in our own self and then declare an uncompromising war against the evil forces tormenting in the hearts and minds of people around us.

Paul, branding those wicked forces we would be fighting with as the "works of the flesh," gives us their long list of fifteen and more: "Immorality, impurity, lust, idolatry, sorcery, hatreds, rivalry, jealousy, outbursts of fury, acts of selfishness, dissensions, factions, occasions of envy, drinking bouts, orgies, and the like" (Gal. 5:19b–21a). And summarizing them all, the church enlists them into "seven deadly sins": pride (superiority complex), covetousness (greed, seeking material prosperity at the expense of one's soul), lust (sexual abuse of minors, pornography, treating women as objects of pleasure), anger (bitterness, hate, bearing grudges), gluttony (excessive eating and drinking), envy (spite, rivalry), and sloth (seeking success without working for it). To these, we also can add the mother of all evils, injustice. If we declare war against these, then we are fighting a holy war. If we are at war, then we should be prepared for some roughness. The enemy is also fighting against us, and we may have to suffer some harm or hardship.

In the war combated against Satan, the most subtle enemy, the discipled leaders must perform their battles in a prudent way. In this regard, St. Gregory the Great excellently exhorts us in his writings on Pastoral Guide: "A spiritual guide [spiritual leader] should be silent when discretion requires and speak when words are of service. Indiscreet speech may lead men into error and an imprudent silence may leave in error those who could have been taught. As the voice of truth tells us, such leaders are not zealous pastors who protect their flocks, rather they are like mercenaries who flee by taking refuge in silence when the wolf appears. The Lord reproaches them through the prophet: 'They are dumb dogs that cannot bark.'" Quoting again the assertions of OT prophets, St. Gregory emphasizes his golden advice: "You might stand fast in battle on the day of the Lord. To advance against the foe involves a bold resistance to the powers of this world in defense of the flock. To stand fast in battle on the day of the Lord means to oppose the wicked enemy out of love for what is right."

THE CONTINUOUS AND CONTENTIOUS COMBAT WITHIN US

As warriors in God's Kingdom, the first dimension of the strenuous fight we should combat against evil is within ourselves. In this battle, the number 1 standup role model is Apostle Paul, who has repeatedly underlined the scheme and strategies of this war tactics; especially, he visualizes in his letter to the Romans (Rom. 7:13–25) the exact nature of his personal contest he encountered between goodness and wickedness. According to his version of personal conflict, he says that there are two sides of his self, which is made of soul and body, spirit. Once he began committing himself to God in Jesus, he experienced a tremendous skirmish within him between the Spirit who anointed him and the flesh he inherited from birth.

As the Psalmist faced (Ps. 42), on the one hand, Paul's grace-filled self was feeling the most excruciating basic need, longing and thirsting for the living God, as the deer longs for streams of water; on the other hand, his fleshly and earthly self was twitting within him, questioning, "Are you there, God? When can I enter and see your face?" At the same juncture, his "good" part of the spirit always retorted to the first whining portion: "Why are you downcast, my soul; why do you groan within me? Wait for God, for I shall again praise him, my savior and my God."

Unfortunately, the evil dimension of the spirit daunted Paul uninterruptedly and got him into deeper downcast. He was overwhelmed with the disparaging analysis about his dark side: "I am carnal, sold into slavery to sin. What I do, I do not understand. For I do not do what I want, but I do what I hate . . . For I know that good does not dwell in me, that is, in my flesh . . . For I do not do the good I want, but I do the evil I do not want." He too is convinced about his spiritual transformation ushered by the risen Lord: "I take delight in the law of God, in my inner self."

At the same time, he regrets about the critical situation that dominated him: "I see in my members another principle at war with the law of my mind, taking me captive to the law of sin that dwells in my members. Miserable one that I am! Who will deliver me from this mortal body?" At the end of all his groaning about his tense-filled life, the Spirit resurrects him to the highest level of discipleship. He contends: "Thanks be to God through Jesus Christ our Lord. Therefore, I myself, with my mind, serve the law of God but, with my flesh, the law of sin." In other words, he encourages himself with consoling words: "The one and only thing I am able to win this horrible fight is to repeat myself: Stop groaning. Wait for God. In addition I kneel, raise my hands above and start praising my Lord." This is the revelatory story of Paul's daily spiritual combat life.

The primary battle the discipled leaders should wage against is our own natural self, which has been corroded, shrunk, or blown out of proportion; twisted; and damaged by our earlier formation, friendship, and life situations. We forget such a feeble and grassy self can turn out to be monstrous evil to ourselves and to others as well. With such enormous, dirty, and tricky enemy, we have to fight to reach the final destination of true peace and joy.

Unless we win in this battle, we certainly be failing in the large battle we lead for attaining peace, joy, and unity.

If we don't fill our personal cup of interiority with the same blessings of peace, joy, truth, love, and justice, we cannot lend them to the needy macro family members. "What you have you share; if you don't have anything you share nothing."

WE ARE SELFIERS AND SELF-BREAKERS

Human life is an embodiment of relationships, which is nothing but a technique for their self-survival. Hence, every human can be named as "selfier." But there are too many humans around us who are essentially adviser-less, friendless. Some make team of their own relations, but it is made up of cold mercenaries. Many are subdued by germophobia through most of their life and cut off contact with others. Consequentially, they experience feelings of deep sadness and pity. As they go through a single day without sharing kind little moments with strangers and friends and endure a single week in a hate-filled world, crowded with enemies of their own making, the object of disgust and derision, they would be so twisted and tortured inwardly that they would lash out and try to take cruel revenge on the universe. Not able to know themselves, to prove their own existence, they hunger for endless attention from outside. Lacking internal measures of their own worth, they rely on external but insecure criteria like wealth, beauty, fame, and others' submission.

While most of us derive a warm satisfaction when we feel our lives are aligned with "ultimate values," these self-twisted people, paranoid even by strangers' inhaling, live in an alternative, amoral territory where they cannot enjoy the sweetness that altruism and community service can occasionally bring. Such bullies experience peace only when they are cruel. Their blood pressure drops the moment they beat the kid on the playground. Their rest comes only when they are insulting somebody, when they are threatening to throw their opponent in burning hell. Their emotional makeup means they can hit only a few notes: fury and aggression. In some ways, their leadership performances look like primate dominance displays, filled with chest beating and looming growls.

In contrast, the selfiers turned into discipled leaders despite facing serious health ailments hastening their last breath, who are living lives of love, faith, devotion, and service. They uphold an ultimate confidence in the goodness of the Creator and their grace-filled place in his Kingdom. They continuously lead an "attached" life emotionally, spiritually, morally, and communally. It is true that while the first group of "selfiers," living in the howling wilderness of his own solitude, look superficially successful and profoundly miserable leaders, the second group of the "discipled leaders" fight the good fight, run the race victoriously, but always leave behind them memories of building our earthly homes on solid rock foundation.

FIT OUT FOR WINNING THE BATTLE

From our earlier discussion, we are fully aware of the malevolent nature of the enemy against whom we are waging this holy war. Peter writes superbly about our enemy: "Your opponent the devil is prowling around like a roaring lion looking for someone to devour" (1 Pet. 5:8). Besides "Satan" and "devil," we find in the Bible some other names referring to the nature, character, and work of our opponent in the holy war: Lucifer, the light bringer before the fallout from heaven to hell; the accuser of humans and of God in Jesus; Beelzebub, the lord of princes; the wicked one where the sin comes from; the prince/god of this world; the tempter; the liar and father of lies; and so on. From the biblical authors, we come to understand Satan and company have been once angels living in God's abode with heavenly brightness, subtlety, beauty, plus immense spiritual power. But unfortunately, because of their pride and disobedience, God dragged them out into the pit of hell. From then on, they began taking revenge against the Creator and Redeemer and trying their best to destroy all the salvific plan of God among his beloved human creatures. It is with such kind of powerful enemies the discipled leaders have to battle with.

We have good many exhortations in the Scriptures regarding the right way of fighting with the spiritual wicked ones. Peter adds his advice along with his description of the opponent's cruel behavior. First, he wants us to be sober and vigilant, and then he writes, "Resist him, steadfast in faith, knowing that your fellow believers throughout the world undergo the same sufferings" (1 Pet. 5:9). Paul explains candidly and experientially how to arm ourselves for the holy war. He knew fully well that "our struggle is not with flesh and blood but with the principalities, with the powers, with the world rulers of this present darkness, with the evil spirits in the heavens."

Being an experienced warrior, he exhorts us first and foremost to rely and lean on God and his power, which means we should frequently be on our knees in front of God and spend as much quality time as possible before we engage everyday "war." "Draw your strength from the Lord and from his mighty power." For this, Paul recommends strongly his precious holding about "constant prayer." With all prayer and supplication, pray at every opportunity in the Spirit. To that end, be watchful with all perseverance and supplication for all the holy ones." (Eph. 6: 18)

Paul has been so enamored by the idea of being called by God to be a warrior in his Kingdom, and continued his fight victoriously with the enemy till his last breath, he advocates all of us who intend to be warriors of Jesus to put on the unique armor he had been using and won in his battle against the "opponent": "Therefore, put on the armor of God that you may be able to resist on the evil day and, having done everything, to hold your ground. So stand fast with your loins girded in truth, clothed with righteousness as a breastplate, and your feet shod in readiness for the gospel of peace. In all circumstances, hold faith as a shield, to quench all the flaming arrows of the evil one. And take the helmet of salvation and the sword of the Spirit, which is the word of God" (Eph. 6:13–17). In his figurative perception about the armor of God, he lists out the ammunitions and armor fittings the discipled leaders should wear and use in their perennial war against evil as truth, righteousness, Gospel of peace, faith, and Word of God.

Our "holy war" against Satan may be pursued either within ourselves, or within our micro family—the church, or outside between one nation to another, one malicious group and the good-willed group. We should be aware of the one and only fact, and that is, if it is conducted in accordance with the norms and policies the Master has prescribed and proclaimed as his "Gospel manifesto" through the life and teachings of his discipled leaders in the past, it is then endorsed by the Triune God, who will join us in forefront of the army as he did in the past.

ENDURANCE AND PATIENCE IN WAGING A HOLY WAR

In our warzone techniques, we should also include the most enlivening mind setup within us: it is the enduring patience filled with hope. We should never fight against God's time but with God's time. We have a wrong interpretation of "time" as our fate, our luck, and our nature course. There is little truth about this interpretation but not the whole truth. Our belief is that though the chronology of artificially coined element of time as seconds, minutes, days, weeks, months, and years is man-made, we, as God's children, live and move our being in the "timeless time" of the Creator. As he declared himself as "the Alpha and Omega, the first and the last, the beginning and the end" (Rev. 22:13), every bit of our move, every timely step of ours and of the universe, is in

God's Hand. Hence, the "holy war" he started and continues to wage against the evil is in his "timeless time." We simply join in his battling process and perform our warriors' duties but always with the positive hope of ultimate victory belonging to God.

We learn this "timeless time mind setup" from our Master Jesus whose only preoccupation was to accomplish everything his Father has entrusted to him within the time limit stipulated by the Father. He was prayerfully moving every step of his thirty-three years life in Palestine according to his Father's time. He moved as God moved. Despite his inner self drove him faster in his battlement, he was resilient when God was passive to his speediness. So he even denied his Mother's request, saying, "My time has not arrived yet" (John 2:4–5). When his brothers compelled him to perform great things to be known publicly, he retorted, "My time is not yet here" (John 7: 6).

This sort of living with God's "timeless time" offered Jesus to be bold to face any negative realities of opposition from his archenemy and company. He was certain his death would come only in God's time. John confirms such mindset of Jesus: "But no one arrested him because his hour has not yet come" (John 8:20b). He too surrendered to his Father's bid whenever he was asked by the inner call of his Father, though it might have been wounding his chivalrousness. The Gospels narrate incidents that when Jesus's enemies tried either to hurt him or to arrest him, he escaped, hid from their evil moves (Ref. Luke 4:28–30; John 10:39).

However, when he had the premonition from his Father about the "time" to be arrested, crucified, and buried, he vehemently marched on to the den of evil predators. Jesus knew well every bit of incidents occurring in his life was well designed by his Father. He called them his appointed times (Ref. Matt. 26:17–18). The time designed for him by his Father might have been destructive and despicable. But he took it positively and welcomed it as his crowning time. "The hour has come for the Son of Man to be glorified . . . it was for this purpose that I came to this hour. Father, glorify your name" (John 12:23–27). Though his disciples coerced him not to go to such cruel environment, he ruthlessly rebuked them, saying, "Get behind me, Satan! You are an obstacle to me. You are thinking not as God does, but as human beings do" (Matt. 16:23).

It is to this perpetual "timeless-time" warfare our Master has called and chosen all his discipled leaders to join as the forefront warriors. He encourages us to intensely fight against the evil patiently, enduring all that come along with the warzone filled with bloodshed and body-broken and even carrying the battle scars to our last breath.

THE VIOLENCE IN GOD'S KINGDOM

Commonly, the concept of war brings to our mind the horrible visualization of violence, cruelty, bloodshed, persecution, and so many other menacing deeds. Does that consideration hold good regarding our war against wickedness and its devilish perpetrators? In the light of the Bible, especially of the Christ's Gospel, all those bullying scenarios of war the world encounters are unholy and ungodly. Doing evil against evil is not the norm of the Master who proclaimed only the Gospel of nonviolence, forgiveness, justice, and peace. However, those of us who are impatient with the pervading evils try to use certain biblical actions and phrases and thrive in the attitude and action of evil for evil. Two of those verses, on which those people depend in this regard, are of Jesus when he described the unique identity and ministry of John the Baptist as his forerunner: "The law and the prophets lasted until John; but from then on the kingdom of God is proclaimed, and everyone who enters does so with violence" (Luke 16:16), and "From the days of

John the Baptist until now, the kingdom of heaven suffers violence, and the violent are taking it by force" (Matt. 11:12).

But in the light of the Spirit and of the church tradition, the disciples, committed to Jesus's Gospel of love, never accept that Jesus was exonerating "violence" being used in his Kingdom, especially in the holy war against the prince of darkness. Rather, we interpret those sayings of Jesus with sincere biblical scholars, who offer us two explanations: One, "the meaning of this difficult saying of Jesus is probably that the opponents of Jesus are trying to prevent people from accepting the kingdom and to snatch it away from those who have received it." It may be correct as we notice how much the Kingdom had been suffering untold violence through the malevolent atrocities done by the enemies of that Kingdom against God's messengers and prophets, especially John the Baptizer and Jesus. Another most splendid interpretation is also to be seriously considered, namely, from the onset of Jesus's public ministry, we discover how he was anxious about the reestablishment and renewal of God's Kingdom in this world. In his Sermon on the Mount, he is quoted saying, "Seek [look for, search for, try to obtain, and desire to possess] first the kingdom of God and his righteousness, and all these things will be given you besides" (Matt. 6:33). In the middle of his journey toward Jerusalem for his climatic enforcement of the goal he was obsessed with, he told his disciples, crying out, "I have come to set the earth on fire, and how I wish it were already blazing!" (Luke 12:49)

He too added an astonishing statement referring to the war he and his disciples would be engaged in. In quoting this surprising saying of Jesus, Matthew uses the metaphor of sword: "Do not think that I have come to bring peace upon the earth. I have come to bring not peace but the sword" (Matt. 10:34), whereas Luke portrays it as baptism and establishment of division: "There is a baptism with which I must be baptized, and how great is my anguish until it is accomplished! Do you think that I have come to establish peace on the earth? No, I tell you, but rather division" (Luke 12:50–53). Jesus's reckoning of the violence in God's Kingdom clearly spelled out through those sayings, that anyone who wants to be engaged in establishing and renovating God's Kingdom, both within them and around them, must like himself actively, aggressively, forcibly not only seeking entrance into the Kingdom but also committing oneself intensely to the Gospel values. Refer to a few of his sayings besides those already mentioned: "Being born again" (John 3:3, 7), "Cutting off your hand, plucking out your eye that causes you to sin" (Mark 9:47), "Hating one's family" (Luke 14:26), "Giving up everything for the treasure hidden in the field and for the pearl of great price" (Matt. 13:44–46), "Selling everything you possess" (Mark 10:21), and "Counting the cost of building a tower or waging war" (Luke 14:28–33).

Undoubtedly, Jesus preferred and performed also in his life's battle against Satan to make the best use of Gospel ammunitions of love, justice, nonviolence, forgiveness, and surely peace. These ammunitions are entirely the gracious gifts of God's Spirit, who alone can fortify us invincibly against the wiles of the devil and the assaults of evil men and women. If we browse the histories and stories about our forbearers who had been waging war in frontline of the warzone against evils as discipled leaders, we can observe all the valor and power they had possessed came out of their intimate relationship with the Spirit who not only empowered them but also altered the whole pattern of their lives to become entirely otherworldly in outlook and emboldened with courage in their chivalrous battlement.

AT THE END OF PERENNIAL WAR

Our God is immensely faithful and loving toward all humans, especially those of us who do the maximum to be faithful to him and to his salvific plan of combating against evil. The process of "holy war" against evil may seem a failure, may look like a setback. But we observe in the history of humanity that God never abandoned his warriors. Jesus, our Master, for example, who did not escape in his holy war the suffering and death on the Cross and went to hell in a way and looked as if having been annihilated, on the third day appeared to his disciples resurrected. God had raised him to life victorious, as Jesus had been firmly convinced. As God has proven his fidelity in the past, particularly in Jesus's case, we can be assured that he will not abandon us if we fight his holy war, the war against evil in ourselves and in the world. This is what the author of the letter to the Hebrews testifies: "Consider how he endured such opposition from sinners, in order that you may not grow weary and lose heart. In your struggle against sin you have not yet resisted to the point of shedding blood" (Heb. 12:3–4).

WARRIOR OF GOD WINS WITH THE LORD

While we fight against Satan, besides trusting in the fidelity of God, we should never lose our hope of ultimate victory. That has been the chivalrous and sportive attitude of every champion and soldier upheld in the holy wars. Let us remember David's starting troubles as he volunteered to go against the evil person Goliath (Ref. 1 Sam. 17:32–51). The troubles were generated first from his own leaders like King Saul. But David never lost heart. His only heartbeat was proclaiming to himself and to others: "I come against you in the name of the Lord of hosts." And story ends with his amazing victory.

We notice in Jesus this same victorious view about the holy war against prince of evil. In his own life, he was fully confident about it (John 12:32–33). This is because he steadfastly believed God was fighting with him. His heart was ceaselessly beating the words of Wisdom: "God will shelter them with his right hand, and protect them with his arm" (Wis. 5:16). He too would have repeated with King David: "Had not the Lord been with us, let Israel say, had not the Lord been with us, when people rose against us, then they would have swallowed us alive, for their fury blazed against us. Then the waters would have engulfed us, the torrent overwhelmed us; then seething water would have drowned us. Blessed is the Lord, who did not leave us to be torn by their teeth. We escaped with our lives like a bird from the fowler's snare; the snare was broken, and we escaped. Our help is in the name of the Lord, the maker of heaven and earth" (Ps. 124:1–8).

Jesus also never forgot the victorious reward God had promised and bestowed to the holy warriors. Therefore, he ascertained, "When I am lifted up from the earth, I will draw everyone to myself." And John interprets Jesus's saying as "He said this indicating the kind of death he would die" (John 12:32–33). Plus, not only Jesus cautioned his disciples and his community of believers (church) about the atrocious battle they would be encountering in their ministries: "Go on your way; behold, I am sending you like lambs among wolves" (Luke 10:3), but he also made them be convinced of their ultimate victory in holy war: "Upon this rock [Peter] I will build my church, and the gates of the netherworld shall not prevail against it" (Matt. 16:18).

THE FINAL REWARD TO THE WARRIORS

Whenever we look up to the crucified Lord on the Cross, as Paul had in his first vision of conversion and kept it intact in his soul, we observe in it the significant sign of the victory of Jesus, the one individual human being reminding us that we too in our own individuality can be victorious as he was. Jesus, through his Cross, reveals the ultimate portrait of the threatening power of love so we can be an energizing and uplifting others through our love wastefully poured out.

In one of the parish churches where I had been pastoring, I frequently looked up there above the sanctuary a remarkable "Calvary portrait," under which a verse in Latin is written: "In hoc signo Vinces." This means "By this sign you conquer." This should be our life's mission statement: By this sign, we will win. By the vision it projects, we will be victorious as Jesus. Unquestionably, as the Book of Wisdom spells out, all the righteous warriors "will live forever, and in the Lord is their recompense; and the thought of them is with the Most High. They shall receive the splendid crown, the beautiful diadem, from the hand of the Lord" (Wis. 5:15–16).

Undebatably, this incredible crown promised by God can be possessed only by those who fight against one's own habits and behavior with discipline and die to self, fight against the injustice done by others and to liberate oneself or the others, fight against anyone who hates others and inflicts harm or death to others and die to save or bring life back to others, and fight to eradicate any kind of evils that is in opposition to God's Kingdom of justice, peace, and love.

A war can't be called a holy war of God if it's to fight for our own rights, to fight for our own gratification, and to fight for competing with each other in procuring or hoarding wealth and prosperity. God in Jesus never dreamed of it, or endorsed it, or promised the noble crown in eternity because he underlined, "They have received their reward already."

In my own leadership/warrior life as a priest, I have come across hundreds of evil persons encircling me, and exactly, they began ruining my inner courage, peace, and joy. I was gradually losing not only the war but also myself as the powerful fallen angel infected certain antiwar sentiments and discouraged me to the maximum. I started quitting my frontline position in the "war" and going backward; at one time, I was even tempted to quit my priestly leadership ministry my Master entrusted to me. However, my God never lost his parental hope in me. A day came when I was asked by one of the retreat preachers to go back to my past life with the Master joining him in "Galilee trip," I found out while I was faithful in daily praying the Psalms, I had been energized by Jesus's Spirit to cope with the devilish resistance, but when I stopped that ceaseless praying, the enemy prevailed me, thus happened my terrible downfall. I was fully convinced on that day, if I had persevered in praying, I would have been strengthened to fight against any sort of wickedness from outside as well as from my own inside.

Hence, as a total revert, I started praying in Psalms: "The Lord is with me; I am not afraid; what can mortals do against me? The Lord is with me as my helper; I shall look in triumph on my foes. Better to take refuge in the Lord" (Ps. 118:6–8). I began believing more intensely what I heard from a preacher saying, "I myself cannot resist temptation and trials the archenemy set before me. Hence, when I get into trouble, I hide myself behind the cross."

Let me end this chapter with one of the Morning Prayers of the church the discipled leaders have been praying as Psalm prayer: "Lord God of strength, you gave your Son victory over death. Direct your Church's fight against evil in the world. Clothe us with the weapons of light and unite us under the one banner of love, that we may receive our eternal reward after the battle of earthly life."

CHAPTER 24: LEAD A LIFE OF POVERTY

We hear Solomon in the OT esteeming and longing for the spirit of wisdom as an "unfailing treasure," as a package of priceless and countless riches of which wisdom is the leader and mother (Ref. Wis. 7:7–14). When we come to the NT, we find among the authors an unmistakable view of the spirit of wisdom is none other than our Master Jesus Christ. And they too claim that this heavenly Wisdom that came down from God has proclaimed a unique Gospel for humanity to attain eternal life of justice, love, peace, and joy in this world and the world to come. Astonishingly, his Gospel was "the Gospel of poverty." Jesus proclaimed this Gospel by life, actions, and words. As he started his earthly life in the form of a poor baby, wrapped in swaddling clothes and being laid in a manger, he began his preaching ministry with the first blessing: "Blessed are the poor in spirit for theirs is the kingdom of heaven" (Matt. 5:3).

MASTER'S GOSPEL OF POVERTY

Whenever our Jesus called humans to be his discipled leaders and whenever he sent them out to proclaim his Gospel, he ordered them to obey his "Gospel of poverty." Offering a clarification of the demand of the Master Jesus, Pope Francis told the group of religious, "Poverty, which teaches solidarity, sharing, and charity and which is also expressed in a soberness and joy of the essential, to put us on guard against the material idols that obscure the true meaning of life. Poverty, which is learned with the humble, the poor, the sick, and all those who are at the existential margins of life. Theoretical poverty doesn't do anything. Poverty is learned by touching the flesh of the poor Christ in the humble, the poor, the sick, and in children."

It is not easy being poor. It is not easy to wake up in the morning and not having anything on the table. It is even harder when we see our children staring at us with sad and gloomy eyes with nothing to eat. When in my youth days that I personally witnessed children begging in the streets for money and food to survive the day, I have never really understood fully why there is such a thing as poverty in the world. As I get older and older, I realized it is not God the reason for this; it is me, you, and all our friends who have been blessed with either minimum possible riches or abound with them. Everything our heavenly created and filling us is meant for nothing but sharing them with the unfortunate people who don't even get square of meal a day. I too realized such distributing my riches would hurt me, sometimes empty my bank account. But the distributive and merciful justice demand such hurting. This is how I consider the poverty my Master demands from me.

Poverty for us is rooted in the reality that we are dependent on God. We are nothing without God, and everything we have is God's. Poverty is not just simplicity of life or material deprivations. It is a spiritual attitude and culture or way of life. Some of us can be materially destitute, but our pride could be taller than the mountains; on the other hand, some others who have everything—wealth, talents, looks, and a good name—may remain to be poor in spirit. They don't boast of what they have; they remain humble and simple in other people's eyes. In addition, such a spirit of genuine poverty will make them generous to the needy.

Not forgetting how hard his demand would be, Jesus included in his expounding of that demand another synonymous definition of the Gospel of poverty as the

"Gospel of total surrender and dependency to God." He simply underlined it to his disciples as the only way to fulfill his demand of "being poor in spirit." And he too promised to those who totally depend on God: The more seriously and faithfully they observe his Gospel demand of poverty, the greater would they receive their rewards both in this world and the world to come (Ref. Mark 10:28–30). In one of the events of proclaiming his Gospel of poverty (Luke 18:18–23), Jesus included four demands: (1) Sell what you have, (2) Give it to the poor, (3) Hold firm hope that you have saved and secured a large amount of stocks and bonds in the heavenly treasury, and (4) Then follow me. When we consolidate all those four demands of Jesus, we discover the most admirable and the wisest advice for our life: "Total dependence on God."

Though such expectation of our Master seems risky and unrealistic, there subsists a holistic truth in it. He expects that our heart (in biblical sense, our inner spirit and attitude, our personality) should be as larger, bigger, and better as the rewards we would receive in future. Unquestionably, the eternal treasures of heaven promised to us cannot be contained in any ordinary, puny, tiny, little heart. If our inner spirit is like a small bowl, its capacity to contain would be only small. It needs to be enlarged with love, humility, contrition, and fidelity, plus, above all, with total dependency on God. It is this demand of "being poor in the spirit" is identified as Jesus's Gospel of poverty. It is this Gospel all discipled leaders of Christ must follow and proclaim in every action of their ministries.

TWO-DIMENSIONAL POVERTY IN GOD'S KINGDOM

Certainly, those who are literally poor, unsuccessful, losers, ranked last, and considered pauper in material goods and riches are the first group of "the blessed poor." They are like the widow in the OT (1 Kings 17:10–16) or like the widow

Jesus praises (Luke 21: 1–4). Psalmist underscores that this kind of poor is affectionately protected by God: "Father of the fatherless, defender of widows; God gives a home to the forsaken, who leads prisoners out to prosperity" (Ps. 68:6–7). There is another group of the blessed ones who are poor in spirit. Those are the leaders who possess the spirit of wholehearted and smiling sharing with the neighbors.

The widow, whom Jesus pointed out, gave her tithe to the temple and knew well it would go not to the Lord directly but through the needy and the community members who are supported by those offerings. She shared what she could maximum possible. She gave up everything she possessed. There was no any strings attached to her giving; she never calculated her giving as one percentage or ten of her income. She offered all that she had as her own. The widow, mentioned in the OT, behaved the same way too. Even though she did not have any surplus food except a little for her son and herself, she obeyed as ordered by the man of God, who said, "First make me a little cake and bring it to me. Then you can prepare something for yourself and your son." She never hesitated to take all the food she had and presented it to the prophet.

Jesus expects from his discipled leaders this two-dimensional poverty of the spirit. He was candid to his followers when he said, "Sell everything and follow me; if you want to be my disciple, leave your relations, possessions, names, riches, goodies that give you physical and emotional pleasures and follow me." A wholehearted and total giving is the norm of true discipleship of Christ.

While many among the discipled leaders contribute most of their time, talent, and treasure in Jesus's Kingdom, so many yet behave miserly and calculating. Some others share grudgingly. There are some others who are ready to offer their everything, but they make sure their names are spotlighted, bragged about, and let not only the left hand but also the whole world know what their right hand is doing so that they are esteemed great in the good book of superiors and people. Jesus's Gospel of poverty urges us to perform anything in the name of religion and charity, not for any personal agendas, except for the rewards of God who sees everything we do in secret and reward us in the future.

There are many in the world who share their riches, possessions, titles, and even their very lives. Though we are incapable of doing such weird things, still, what we share as time, talent, and treasure inside our communities is only a sign and symbol to signify our desire of total giving of our lives to the Lord. We should esteem ourselves as humble laborers of the Kingdom. And every day after all we have accomplished for the community, we should tell our Master in sincerity of heart: "We are unprofitable servants; we have done what we were obliged to do" (Luke 17:10). Let me list out little more ingredients found in Jesus's Gospel of poverty.

MAKE LIFE TRAVEL EASIER AND LIGHTER

When our Master sent leaders to perform his ministry of proclaiming his Gospel and of healing (Mark 6:7–13), "he instructed them to take nothing for the journey but a walking stick, no food, no sack, no money in their belts. They were, however, to wear sandals but not a second tunic." It sounds like one of the wise advices every airline posts to us, to "travel happily with less luggage." Airlines may have certain profit-motivated strings attached to their advice, but our Master's only intention was his leaders must first observe his Gospel of poverty and then proclaim it to people. Yes, his "light-luggage demand" was a portion of his Gospel of poverty.

Explaining it very splendidly, Pope Francis underlined (Ref. Pope's Angelus Address on July 15, 2018), "The Master wants them free and light, without supports and without favors, certain only of the love of Him who sends them, strong only from His word, which they go to proclaim." He also added that "in God's Kingdom no leader is omnipotent manager; not immovable functionary; not divas on *tour*."

AVOID UNDUE ANXIETY

Anxiety within humans is a necessary starting point to roll over our sleeves, to get up from slothful state of couch potato and begin our works or jobs to earn our livelihood and survival plus success. Our Master, through his Gospel of poverty, asks his discipled leaders to avoid overanxious mindset in everything we handle, hold, and manage.

In his Sermon on the Mount, Jesus instructed us, "Do not worry about your life, what you will eat or drink, or about your body, what you will wear. Is not life more than food and the body more than clothing?" (Matt. 6:25) Our Master is the wisest Teacher and Prophet who has said it right, we should not allow worries creeping in our mind and heart unnecessarily or excessively. As the Lord underlined, none of us by our worrying can add a single moment to our life span (Ref. Matt. 6:27).

Reasonable persons, especially those who have reached their venerable golden age, are well aware of the undebatable fact that worry is futile and that we cannot, by worrying, add anything to our lives and improve our situation. If our act of worrying could instantly make change in certain things we are worried about, making it either better or greater and even disappear, then such act of worrying would be highly recommended. Unfortunately, it seems only to be a terrific problem-solving technique.

Living through my life more than fifty years with and under the superiors, leaders, of the church, I am vexed to observe the undue anxiety by which most of them were distorted and disturbed in their ministerial election, selection, and promotion. In his address to the religious superiors general in 2013, Pope Francis deplored about the decadence of the attitudes and activities of today's laborers in today's church: "The men and women of the Church who are careerists and social climbers, who 'use' people, the Church, their brothers and sisters, whom they should be serving, as a springboard for their own personal interests and ambitions . . . are doing great harm to the Church."

In my personal life, I have learned that, besides offering nothing positive, worry actually does harm. As Leo Buscaglia once wrote, "Worry never robs tomorrow of its sorrow, it only saps today of its joy." Disproportionate worrying causes many physical ailments, such as ulcers, insomnia, and other maladies. Worries weaken all forms of goodness, generosity, and truthfulness. Rather, they promote hatred, insecurity, and foolishness. The main problem with worry is it makes us irreligious as it keeps God out of the situation and places the trust on human person.

TOTAL DEPENDENCE ON GOD FREES US FROM UNWARRANTED WORRIES

Our Master teaches us how to conduct ourselves in those critical life situations that prompt us to worry. He asserted that by recognizing humbly we are beggars before God, our entire spirit and body become energized and capacitated to bear anything, come what may. Pope Francis, in his homily during Mass for World Day of the Poor on November 19, 2017, stated, "All of us, none excluded, need this, for all of us are beggars when it comes to what is *essential:* God's love, which gives meaning to our lives and a life without end."

His main advice is to trust in God who has asserted himself possessing love for us more than our mothers: "Can a mother forget her infant, be without tenderness for the child of her womb? Even should she forget, I will never forget you" (Isa. 49:15). In addition, God, the loving Parent, announced the incredible truth that "Upon the palms of my hands I have engraved you; your walls are ever before me" (Isa. 49:16). You know why? He says it is because we are precious in his eyes and honored, and he loves us (Ref. Isa. 43:4).

Besides, our God is all-knowing and all-powerful. Therefore, he is in front to be fully aware of our needs and problems. He is also bold enough to encourage us, telling, "Don't worry and don't be afraid; nothing is impossible with me" (Luke 1:37). Revealing to us such bewildering personality of our God, Jesus recommends we have to rest in that powerful and loving Parent God who has the ability to create and destroy; who takes good care of all his creatures, tiny or big (Ref. Matt. 6:26–34); who knows all the three times; who even uses the evil for better results; and who knows well what is within us and outside us; nothing is hidden from him. Therefore, we have to place our trust in him, no matter how small and insignificant we are.

Did he not point out that "only those who become like little children can enter into the kingdom of God?" (Mark 9:30–37) Childlike trust and dependence on God is the only way to go through the Pearls Gate. As the children abandon themselves into the hands of their parents, so all the discipled leaders of Jesus must surrender completely to the will of the Father. He has a beautiful design of life for each one of us. He brought us down to the earth. He will take us up to heaven one day. I am so indebted to the sage who coined the saying "Go with the flow."

Totally, it is correct in our life with God. Our journey of faith calls us to float calmly and consciously in the current of living water in God's stream. I, for one, has been formed and groomed by the modern, trendy teachers who brainwashed me that the only way to develop ourselves and to realize as many ambitious dreams as possible is nothing but "to play the game of swimming against the current odds of life." And I listened to religious critics who exhorted me to swim against even God's will. But days later, I experienced the whole mess has backfired my personal life. I came to know fully: After all, God is God. The only way to win the race, to fight the good fight, and to covet the genuine fruits of life is purely a simple and unassuming childlike abandonment to God, the Creator. I began to fully believe the words of my Master: "If anyone wishes to be first, he shall be the last of all and the servant of all" (Mark 9:35).

Jesus's God has a wonderful plan for our lives, and part of that plan includes taking care of us. Even in difficult times, when it seems that God doesn't care, we should put our trust in the Lord and focus our attention on his Kingdom. Through Peter, Jesus invites us to "cast all our worries upon God, for He cares for us" (1 Pet. 5:7). Great and holy leaders of choice in his Kingdom heard every moment of their life his voice instructing them: "Depend on God, and on Him alone! Left alone you are nothing! You can do nothing! He is everything!" Our master confirmed this truth in his earthly life, and he made sure his leaders should hold it also firmly: I am weak, so I should depend fully on heavenly Father. And in his name, I have all authority and power in my leadership ministry.

BE GOD-CONFIDENT AND NOT SELF-CONFIDENT

In the Gospels, we read that Jesus called his disciples together and gave them power and authority over all demons and to cure diseases. Because of human ignorance and pride, the disciples are evidently assuming that because of their inherent talents and past success, they could do it all again. Sadly, they were self-confident rather than God-confident. They lacked continued dependence on God. They preferred to exalt themselves rather than to die to self. Many times, the Master corrected them, exposing how fickle-hearted they were. Sometimes they showed them their "worthless worth."

In Matthew 17:14–20, we read these disciples were trying by themselves, with the same conceited attitude, to cast out demon from a man but failed in it. When Jesus observed it, he chided them: "O faithless and perverse generation, how long will I be with you and endure you?" And he healed that demon-possessed man. The disciples were cut to the quick and asked Jesus why they were unable to do this miracle. Jesus took that occasion once again and admonished them: "Because of your little faith. Amen, I say to you, if you have faith the size of a mustard seed, you will say to this mountain, 'Move from here to there,' and it will move. Nothing will be impossible for you."

There, the Master underscores a needed norm for discipled leadership in exercising power and authority effectively in his Kingdom. That is, we have to depend on God and his power of grace and love. Everything is possible with us. This is why, in his Sermon on the Mountain, Jesus repeatedly emphasized one single tip for leaders' successful and fruitful ministry: "Seek first the kingdom of God and his righteousness, and all these things will be given you besides."

LET'S NOT CHEAT OURSELVES

Today God's only clarion call to all his Son's discipled leaders is, as Pope Francis decries, "Constant conversion. Every day conversion." What is that conversion? It is a change of heart to move our entire identity and ministry toward Jesus's Gospel of poverty. This indicates to let willfully the Word, the two-edged sword of God into our spirit so that it would shake of our complacency, our fear of this world, our petty compromises with the ways of the world, as Pope defines, our "spiritual worldliness." It is a need of the day for the church to move on to her ultimate destiny of holiness that the life of all her leaders manifests the Gospel of poverty. Unquestionably, it is only by becoming ourselves first more and more poor in spirit our blindfolded inner eyes would be opened to see around the little ones of Jesus. It is a pity that what the world is gratified with exclusiveness, division, and horrible inequality, the discipled leaders also swallow and are feeling comfortable and complacent with such worldly stupidity.

As a personal note, I am not that rich as the rich man mentioned in the Gospel (Luke 18:23). However, my Master dictates to me, "Don't deceive yourself, boy. I personally have bestowed to you riches such as good health, somewhat good brain and intelligence, chances of being well-qualified for the profession you are holding, plus good many accomplishments and achievements." He also warned me, "Giving some money and gifts to the poor and needy may be easy for you; but not all your self-possessions within your spirit. Sell everything for the sake of salvation of the entire humanity and follow me. As the widows my Spirit pointed out, offer me anything you possess as your own, even the little of your money or the large bundle of many talents and qualifications." The Lord is absolutely correct. I was wrong in making a cover-up of my inner complacency and in cheating myself and never my God.

Let me end this chapter with an anecdote I read some years back in a magazine. It was about St. Mother Teresa. When Mother visited a school in Hong Kong, journalists took many pictures of her. She was seen wearing over her habit an old gray cardigan and on her feet an aging pair of leather sandals. A couple of weeks later, our Mother was back in India, receiving the Templeton Award from Queen Elizabeth of England. Photographs showed her shaking hands with the queen and wearing the same cardigan and the same sandals. The queen did not seem to mind or probably even notice.

Can we imagine the tizzy that many persons, especially the so-called discipled leaders, would be in on such an occasion? What will I wear? How will it look on TV? Maybe so many would have thought Mother Teresa behaved rustic and uncouth. But her inner spirit should have directed her that way, dictating to her, a servant for the poor must be also poor in all its essence and sense.

CHAPTER 25: SHARE WITH AND CARE FOR THE POOR

In the previous chapter, we had a lengthy discussion of Jesus's Gospel of poverty and of how discipled leaders in the church should live and testify to it. The same Master has categorically slated out this poverty in spirit must be held to enrich the needy, the poor, and the least.

BE POOR IN GOD BUT BE RICH TO THE POOR

Our Master's hard-core demand to the rich man who wanted to gain eternal life was "Sell what you have, and give to the poor" (Mark 10:21b). In a way, we can say it in a different version: "Sell all your possessions to be poor in God and share them to the poor as an enriching person." This is the central focus of the church from the day of its inception. This "care and share ministry" of the church is clearly detailed in Acts starting from the cure of crippled beggar (chapter 3), proceeding with amazing community sharing (narrated in the following chapters) by which "there was no needy person among them, for those who owned property or houses would sell them, bring the proceeds of the sale, and put them at the feet of the apostles, and they were distributed to each according to need" and developed into an organized system (chapter 6) through which regular care and share ministry has been continued.

There is no escape for any committed disciples from the core ministry of Jesus and his church. Emphasizing this truth, Pope Francis is quoted saying in one of the homilies in his visit to Manila, "The poor. The poor are at the center of the Gospel. At the heart of the Gospel. If we take away the poor from the Gospel, we cannot understand the whole message of Jesus Christ."

On the basis of such long history of "church's care and share ministry," when Pope Francis was criticized by certain modern-day thinkers about his frequent audacious proclamation of Jesus's Gospel of poverty, he skillfully trolled them, saying, "I can only say that the communists have stolen our flag. The flag of the poor is Christian. Poverty is at the center of the Gospel," citing biblical passages about the need to help the poor, the sick, and the needy. "Communists say that all this is communism. Sure, twenty centuries later. So when they speak, one can say to them: 'but then you are Christian'" (Pope Francis via Reuters). In other words, as Elizabeth Stoker Bruenig on July 4, 2014 *The Week* online expounded, "Since his concern for the poor causes critics to accuse him of Marxism, Pope Francis reversed their accusations: Rather than Christianity looking suspiciously communist over its concern for the poor, perhaps communism looks suspiciously Christian. After all, justice for the poor is hardly a communist invention; as Pope Francis points out, a focus on helping the poor was native to Christianity long before the 19th century."

POOR ARE ALWAYS AMONG US

When an unhappy Judas found fault with the Master's acceptance of thankful gesture of Mary, Lazarus's sister, with a costly anointing, Jesus said, "You always have the poor with you" (John 12:1–8). The synoptic Gospels, especially Luke's, have developed a broader notion of "the poor." In their calculation, they include not just the poor and hungry but also those who cry, left out, marginalized, neglected, excluded, exploited, desperate, and so on. Thus, the number of poor who need support multiplies many times over, support, in particular, from every disciple of Jesus, particularly and more from church leaders through their office, their institution. Their ministry of "share and care" is more than just comforting and encouraging words; it means deeds of mercy and charity.

Both from the Scriptures and from our own life experiences, we can ascertain there exists around our life three different kinds of poor people: spiritually poor, materially poor, and psychologically poor. We may be included in any one of those categories: "Look upon me, have pity on me, for I am alone and afflicted. Relieve the troubles of my heart; bring me out of my distress. Look upon my affliction and suffering; take away all my sins" (Ps. 25:16–18). These kinds of words frequently we hear from the Psalmist, begging the Lord to rescue him from all those three poverties. He mentions all three poverties any humans are afflicted with: being alone, being afflicted, being burden with the troubles of one's heart, being distressed, and being tormented by the burden of sins. And in the translation of these verses by the Confraternity of Christian Doctrine, Washington DC, we read the right term "poor" is used: "Turn to me and have mercy on me, O Lord, for I am alone and poor."

Among these different kinds of poor people, many are poor from their birth and, even sadly, continue to be so till their death; some are poor for a while as their age and community imposes; many others are poor until they are graced with God's mercy and liberated from certain kinds of poverties for the sake of fulfilling God's plan of salvation in the world. The mother church upholds a firm conviction that she is the sacrament of God's love on the earth, especially through all her charitable deeds, as she is proud to be the dispenser of "fuller life" to the poor and the needy in all dimensions. She confirms this conviction in her Vat. II constitution: "The Church reflects the light of the divine life over the whole world, especially through her work of restoring and enhancing the dignity of the human person, of strengthening the fabric of human society, and of enriching the daily activity of men with a deeper meaning and importance. The Church believes that in this way she can make a great contribution, through individual members and the community as a whole, toward bringing a greater humanity to the family of man and to its history" (*Gaudium et Spes*, no. 40).

THE MAIN REASON FOR SHARING WITH AND CARING FOR THE POOR

We hear in the Gospels, that our Master would be telling us at our final judgement-moment: 'Amen, I say to you, whatever you did for one of these least brothers of mine, you did for me." (Matt. 25: 31-46) He also portrays his list of the least: The hungry and the sick, the stranger and the prisoner, the poor and the abandoned, the suffering who receive no help, and the needy who are cast aside. The inconceivable reason he offers for assisting these 'least' is 'You do it for me'! Namely, 'this is my Body'. He wants us to see through those poor faces 'His Own'. And we, his selected leaders, who claim that we love him, must also love these 'least' whom he loves most dearly.

Secondly, when we overcome our indifference, self-centeredness and take the charitable ministry to the poor as our priority, we will be considered by him as his 'friends'. Plus, through all our charitable performances, we too will become His Father's well-pleasing children and we will be praised by the Father as His Spirit appreciates a charitable lady in the Book of Proverbs (31: 10-20): "Who can find a woman of worth? Far beyond jewels is her value…She reaches out her hands to the poor, and extends her arms to the needy."

Thirdly, our charitable ministry is the uppermost evangelical duty as our Master demanded his discipled leaders when he sent them to proclaim the Good News of Salvation.

Once in a vision he asserted to Paul who requested to liberate him from afflictions: "My grace is sufficient for you, for power is made perfect in weakness." I will rather boast most gladly of my weaknesses, in order that the power of Christ may dwell with me." (2 Cor. 12: 9) In the performance of charities two poor people meet together; two afflicted shake hands together; and two weak and fragile persons hug together. It is this time is calculated by the Lord as an occasion of 'saving power' of God present visibly, audibly and tangibly.

BEING BLESSED FOR AND BY BLESSING THE NEEDY

God is just always, may not seem distributively just, but He never fails to be just honestly, generously, prudently and faithfully. As a Creator, He filled the earth and the universe with everything that He found 'good'. "God looked at everything he had made, and found it very good" (Gen. 1: 31). Especially when He created humanity he enriched every human with His own image and likeness. After creating all the creatures, He said: "Let us make human beings in our image, after our likeness." (Gen. 1: 26) becoming aware of ourselves as the masterpieces in the hands of God, we recite daily with the Psalmist a hymn of thanks but with awe and humility: "What is man that you should care for him? You have made him little less than the angels, and crowned him with glory and honor. You have given him rule over the works of your hands, putting all things under his feet" (Ps. 8: 5-7). This admirable and undebatable truth of humans, being the center and crown of all creatures, has been for many millennia well-accepted unanimously by both believers and non-believers.

Such an incredible creative work of God, as the Bible expounds, contains a portion of Godly creative and redemptive power, Godly wisdom and intelligence, Godly managerial capacity and authority over other creatures, and above all, Godly freedom and love. This is why a newborn baby enters into the universe with a load of abilities, talents, virtues and qualities to share with other fellow-humans to make the world rolling in balance and make it a better place to serve and glorify God. Unfortunately all that we are endowed with at our birth are only potentials which need to be actualized in course of time. From the moment we start breathing a fresh air as others, such as parents, siblings and relatives, we slowly and even quickly understand we cannot survive without companionship and relationship that is to be created by intimate, interpersonal communication and in course of time by social bond with group like family and friends or with communities. This demonstrates our innermost nature of being 'social animals'. We too come to realize our survival and development of our potentials in life depends very much on how we relate to others.

Mother Church who never dare enough to split her twofold ministry of justice and love. To love the poor means to combat all forms of poverty, spiritual and material generated by injustice and indifference. Though in interim period her leaders and people were careless in this issue, God in Jesus reminded us, about this paramount responsibility in season and out of season, including through Karl Marx's 'The Communists Manifesto'. Thanks to II Vatican Council, the Church again underlined her desire of fulfilling Her Spouse's Command on Option for the Poor'. She has deplored of the current condition of the unjust world we live in: "Never has the human race enjoyed such an abundance of wealth, resources and economic power, and yet a huge proportion of the world's citizens are still tormented by hunger and poverty, while countless numbers suffer from total illiteracy. Never before has man had so keen an understanding of freedom, yet at the same time new forms of social and psychological slavery make their appearance. Although the world of today has a very vivid awareness of its unity and of how one man depends on another in needful solidarity, it is most grievously torn into opposing camps by conflicting forces" (*Gaudium et Spes*, no. 4).

In God's eyes, every human is a beloved child to him; he wants his children, with no discrimination whatsoever, should be filled with prosperity and talents fairly but in reality according to each one's capacity to contain and according to his design. We should therefore never deceive ourselves saying "We are useless" and so poor that we cannot help others who need what is lacking in them to survive, grow, and join the crowd in the race to achieve ultimate goal. When we observe in the world the atrocious situation of while 80 percent of people can have access to only 20 percent of the resources of the world, 20 percent of people enjoy 80 percent of them. This unjust disparity must be leveled only by the Jesus's Gospel of justice and love. This Gospel reiterates how injustice, inequality, and indifference can take humans at their end: "Those who store up treasures for themselves, do not grow rich in the sight of God" (Luke 12:21). Where heaven is concerned, what matters is not what we *have* but what we *give*.

The Creator has shared with us all his resources, especially earthly and physically and even intellectually, for some more than others for the only reason: the more fortunate can turn out to be more godly and more heavenly by sharing their possessions and riches with the unfortunate who, in turn, when they are filled can do the same sharing with others.

POVERTY ENRICHES OUR DREAMS OF BEING RICHER

There is a prayer in the OT that has been so many years the talk of the bestseller books and Christian communities. It is called the Prayer of Jabez (1 Chron. 4:10). It has many petitions within it, but the authors took out one of those petitions and spoke and wrote about it in millions of words, and that petition is as every human heart beats with: "Enlarge my territory."

I don't deny God ever denied and cursed against earthly possessions or properties or other riches. His Spirit does make the scriptural writers groan for such prosperities, and when they are filled with them, they thank for such benevolence of God. Jesus too did the same. Just one incident to prove it: when he saw a rich man living a righteous life in obedience to God's Law and religion, he looked at him, and he loved him (Mark 10:21). Jesus too went to rich people's homes and dined with them; he too accepted gifts from rich women for his ministry. The only thing we have to add here he loves the rich with difference.

By origin, our Master was rich. But as Paul says, "He became poor." We know this fact is true from the Gospel passages and early Church Fathers. He was born poor in a small, tiny, little family in an unpopular town with hand-to-mouth income-giving carpentry labor. Paul, in his letter to the Philippians, writes, "Jesus emptied himself." Jesus was both materially and socially was poor; he too was poor in holding his breath. I mean, he could survive only for very limited years, thirty-three. After portraying the scale and scope of Jesus's poverty, Paul adds the reason why he became such poor: "By his poverty we may become rich." When we put into practice his poverty, we become rich.

Jesus's poverty was the following: (1) He allowed himself being restrained by the needs of others around him—their ignorance, their stupidity, their hardheadedness, their deception, their double-standard living, their injustice. (2) He was very frugal and lived a simple life, possessing only necessities and not much luxurious and glamorous things. (3) He opened all the doors and windows of his life to the needy. He was not like many among us who shut our eyes and ears, our houses and even nations, thinking like a rich man who thought by shutting all his home's doors and windows to the needy neighbors and homeless, his conscience will not prick him while he was eating and drinking sumptuous food and wine. Jesus was always on the road, seeking the needy to help them. (4) Above all, he behaved like the champion of the poor and the downtrodden. Hundreds of times I have read, reread the Gospels. I come to a conclusion that his Gospel or his religion is centered only on the poor; even he has spoken a little bit about the rich and that too in reference to the rich people's attitude and action toward the poor only.

Such kind of Jesus's poverty will make the poor rich and the rich richer. We know well enough his dynamics of poverty spiritually kept the richest person ever born in this world. He longs to make us that kind of rich persons. Let us, within our limited resources, help the needy. Let us not wait for their SOS call, knocking at our door or through the church or pastors. Let us see around our family, our neighborhood, our nation, and our world.

Christ has chosen us as his spouses, the partners in his salvation project. Therefore, he expects us to be as he has done in his life to empty ourselves—our self-glory, self-pride, self-comfort-zone—to empty even our riches, properties, and so on. Every human being is filled with sores interiorly and many times exteriorly too. But the rich persons who live an independent and abundant life hide their sores under riches and sumptuous banquets and glamorous garments while the needy Lazaruses cannot hide them in any way; even dogs come and lick them. We can divide ourselves into four groups in our way of running and managing our lives: very rich but very humble, very rich but very proud, very poor but very humble, and very poor but very proud.

As one preacher puts it, death is not a level, but it is a scale. In the Gospel parable in the earthly lifetime of both heroes the rich man and Lazarus, there is no any reference of their adherence to God or religion. All spiritual and religious references come only after their death. Even the meaning of the name Lazarus, as "God helps, God provides," comes as a follow-up of what happens in the other world.

MONEY MATTERS IN GOD'S KINGDOM

All humans, rich or poor, masters or slaves, strong or weak, may differ in many value holdings except in one naked truth: no one can survive in this world without money in any form. Money is a means of bargaining for our livelihood among one another. It is only a symbol of what we give and what we get. It is a basic instrument for any human interaction. Most of the relationships, however intimate they may be, are built on this "money." It has played an important role in human life as a necessary medium of transaction and trade, especially for those living in a complex civilization. Primitive peoples were able to bargain through goods, for example, "I will give you two fish and you give me a basket of corn." In later days, when the transactions were going beyond the frontiers and boundaries of one's community and nationality, people began using small coins in gold, silver, or bronze. Then came currency bills and now those checks and magic plastic credit cards.

Therefore, money is as good as our body. It stands as a symbol of our own identity and worth. We labor, and through the wages, our labor is acknowledged. As Jesus's people, we are not asked to hate this money. When the Lord said, "You cannot serve two masters: God and Mammon" (Matt. 6:24), he never intended to put a conflict between God and the money; rather, he pointed out the war to be waged between the Supreme God and the avaricious possessors of money. We also must read very carefully how Paul interpreted Jesus's Gospel of money. He writes very clearly that money by itself is not evil; rather, the "love of money is the root of all evils" (1 Tim. 6:10).

From the Scriptures, especially from the manner Jesus treated money and money owners or moneylenders in his life and from the Gospel of money he preached to his disciples, we can conclude money, by itself, is blameless. The problem begins only when we handle it for our self-centered evil purposes. But when it is managed with spiritual care, it becomes the greatest tool of inheriting heavenly treasures.

Many times, he cautioned rich people; sometimes he cursed them for their misusing riches: "How hard it is for those who have wealth to enter the kingdom of God!" (Luke 18:24) "Owe to you who are rich, for you have received your consolation" (Luke 6:24). He too used many parables to teach us how to use our money: the parable of the dishonest steward (Luke 16:1–8), the parable of the rich man and Lazarus (Luke 16:19–30), and the parable of the rich fool (Luke 12:16–21).

At the same time, during his life at Nazareth, Jesus, being the single breadwinner for his family, earned money through his hard carpentry works, and later in public life, he accepted money provided by his own friends out of their resources (Luke 8:3). He followed the cautious advices of the OT prophets regarding the proper manner of earning money. He remembered always how the Lord forewarned about the curses his people would face in future as punishments for their unjust, deceptive ways of acquiring wealth by exploiting the innocent, the poor, and the ignorant of the society (Amos 8:4–14).

Most of Jesus's admonitions about wealth were generated out of those God's fiery words. We see how carefully he used money for different right purposes (Matt. 17:24–27). He too praised those who used their money, even be it a dime, for good causes and with a cheerful heart: "[B]ut she [widow] from her poverty, has contributed all she had, her whole livelihood" (Mark 12:41–44), and "If you wish to be perfect, go, sell what you have and give to the poor, and you will have treasure in heaven" (Matt. 19:16–30).

Jesus wants us to acquire money in a right and just way, by our sweat and blood, by our toil and talents, by our sincere efforts and smartness. At the same time, he demands from us to start using this money in his ways, as his faithful stewards, because he is the giver and owner of all our resources. He advises us to use this money to make numerous friends so that they can assist us in reaching our home sweet home—heaven. Money should help us not to buy people for our own gratification and self-glory but for the greater glory of God and for earning our dues in the life to come after our death. This is why I always love to proclaim this Jesus's "Gospel of money" to all my friends, saying, "Earn justly, spend and save wisely, share generously, and store heavenly!"

CARING THE POOR WITH THE RIGHT SENSE

In one of the discussions with some friends on the ministry of charity to be done to the needy, especially of the third-world countries, one retorted to me, "Father, after seeing what is going on in those places, violent and untruthful behavior of those people, we should just throw some coins toward them and leave from there, not performing any deeds of justice and peace." I felt really sorry for that friend because she has not grasped well Jesus's Gospel of poverty.

In fact, the poor and the needy, who are "the little ones" and "the least," may appear to us very uncouth, rough, and unrefined. But we should never judge them by their external look and from their mental abilities; rather, as Jesus teaches us, we should see them through our inner faith-filled eyes as the proxies of Jesus Christ. Our Master loved the poverty they carry within them so much that he decided to be born poor, to be treated as fool, as criminal, and as outcast by most of the public. It is with his Spirit we should care for the poor; we should offer respect and never diminish their self-image and prestige. In all our caregiving ministries toward the poor, first and foremost, we take good care of their individuality made in God's image and likeness.

We also should show our sincere affection and concern for them as God in Jesus has. When we have decided to love our neighbors as Jesus loved, we would be doing all our tasks for the welfare of the poor with the remarkable love Jesus possesses. As Job lived like a champion of the poor and needy, Jesus also was proud of being the hero for the poor: "For I rescued the poor who cried out for help, the orphans, and the unassisted . . . the heart of the widow I made joyful . . . I was eyes to the blind, and feet to the lame was I. I was a father to the poor; and the complaint of the stranger I pursued" (Job 29:12–16). Besides, whenever we step toward the poor and the needy, we listen to our Master's demand in our soul: "Whoever wishes to be great among you will be your servant; whoever wishes to be first among you will be the slave of all" (Mark 10:43–44). Surprisingly, he expects us to stand at the presence of the needy, not just as servants but as slaves to them.

The Bible testifies all proud and cold disciples, after receiving the power of Jesus's Spirit, being purified in his fire, behaved as the Master admonished. One among them is St. Paul, who has become one of the role models to all leaders of Jesus in how to fulfill Jesus's demand. He writes about his attitude and behavior in front of the needy: "Although I am free in regard to all, I have made myself a slave to all so as to win over as many as possible . . . To the weak I became weak, to win over the weak. I have become all things to all, to save at least some. All this I do for the sake of the gospel, so that I too may have a share in it" (1 Cor. 9:19–23). That should be our mantra in all our caring and sharing ministries.

WASTING TIME FOR AND WITH THE POOR COSTS FORTUNE

In the postmodern age, time is esteemed as gold. None of us prefer to waste our time on things that are not pragmatically profit for our earthly life. The time we spend for the care of the needy surely may seem unprofitable to the worldly eyes. But when we spiritually relate that of our compassionate action to the unknown truths we mentioned earlier, we would certainly conclude we are indeed using our time most profitably.

Most of our discipled leaders may resent to spending our precious hours with our charitable ministries while we feel there are too many valuable matters of leadership we need to accomplish or engaged in certain particular time, for example, assorted prayer hours, supervising the planning and executing of certain parochial impending programs, and so on. Here, I want to quote the golden words of Saint Vincent de Paul, who is the patron saint for charities in the church.

He writes, "It is our duty to prefer the service of the poor to everything else and to offer such service as quickly as possible. If a needy person requires medicine or other help during prayer time, do whatever has to be done with peace of mind. Offer the deed to God as your prayer. Do not become upset or feel guilty because you interrupted your prayer to serve the poor. God is not neglected if you leave him for such service. One of God's works is merely interrupted so that another can be carried out. So when you leave prayer to serve some poor person, remember that this very service is performed for God. Charity is certainly greater than any rule."

THE BEST AND WORST WAYS OF CHARITIES

While all discipled leaders contribute regularly most of our time, talent, and treasure in the name of God and through the Church, so many yet behave very miserly and calculating every penny that goes out of our pocket, especially when it goes to the religious and charitable causes. I mean, our contribution of our material riches to the ones to whom our riches are reach. At the same time, we never calculate in the case of spending for self-pleasures and entertainments. Some of us very grudgingly contribute to the causes beyond our self and family. There are good many who do contribute to the right causes yet look for detailed explanations of how it is spent. There are good many of us who are ready to offer our donations, but we make sure our names are spotlighted, bragged about, and let not only the left hand but also the whole world know what our right hand is doing.

Jesus wants us to perform anything in the name of religion and charity not for any personal agendas, except for the rewards of God who sees everything we do in secret and for whom we are waiting. There are many in the world who share their riches, possessions, titles, and even their very lives. Though we are incapable of doing such chivalrous things, still, what we share as time, talent, and treasure inside our communities is only a sign and symbol to signify our desire of total giving of our lives to the Lord.

Though end doesn't justify the means, most of the time, our charitable deeds must be generated with a genuine interest and focus on attaining a heavenly goal. This is our Master's intend. Once, his disciples, on their return from their apostolic ministry, explained to Jesus exuberantly how they were successful in their healing deeds, saying, "Lord, even the demons are subject to us in your name!" (Luke 10:17) As he saw their joyful excitement, Jesus advised them, "Do not rejoice in this, that the spirits are subject to you, but rejoice that your names are written in heaven" (Luke 10:20).

Yes, by our obedient and sincere deeds of love, we are guaranteed of our eternal, never-changing life of joy. Our share and care ministry, accomplishments toward the poor, certainly may build up God's Kingdom; they may perhaps elevate our earthly position and status or increase our fame or success. But we should never rejoice over those earthly results. Rather, we should rejoice and be content that God in Jesus has well-pleased and that his promise continues to echo in our inner sanctuary: "Well done, my good and faithful servant. Since you were faithful in small matters, I will give you great responsibilities. Come, share your master's joy" (Matt. 25:21).

When we plan to get into the ministry of sharing with and caring for the poor and needy in our communities, as Jesus's discipled leaders, we need to purify first our motifs. In addition to above-listed right motives, I would insist one more that many of us fail. As soon as we see the poor and needy people coming and knocking at our doors, we shouldn't esteem ourselves that we are their guardians or sponsors or superiors to these mouthless little ones. According to Jesus, we are their servants and friends. If we forget this elated relationship, we would behave as some political and even religious benefactors treat, we would begin to treat our beneficiaries as our slaves, our errand boys and girls, and the worst of them all, to exploit, to manipulate for our personal self-gratification, to abuse their sex and dignity for our fun, plus to keep them under our foot as bonded slaves, even to misuse their poverty and dependency on us as the confidential conspirers and cooperators in our wicked deeds.

ACCOUNTABILITY AND ETHICS IN DONATIONS MANAGEMENT

Although all nonprofits managed by churches and charity organizations may brag about they have a strong ethical culture, the public and the social media do not think so. Recently, I read in the *Nonprofit Quarterly* a staggering report of the National Nonprofit Ethics Survey taken by the Ethics Resource Center. According to the report, "Slightly more than half of employees in nonprofits observed misconduct in the previous year, and this is roughly on par with that observed in the other sectors." The report states, "On average, nonprofits face severe risk from a handful of behaviors: conflicts of interest, lying to employees, misreporting hours worked, abusive behavior, and Internet abuse." The value of a well-implemented ethics program is beyond question. In organizations with little to no ethics and compliance program, 68 percent of employees observed two or more types of misconduct over the course of a year. This is significantly reduced to just 22 percent in organizations with a well-implemented program.

Personally, I am fully aware of the pros and cons of fund dealings in charities. To start with, I had to learn the governments' policies of raising and using charitable funds. I had to start first a nonprofit organization according to the guidelines of the existing government; getting legal and political approval from it, I should perform all my charitable deeds under that singular umbrella. One of the things that I learn quickly when starting and operating a 501(c) (3) organization is that all its by-laws echo our Master, who has been instructing me about handling of earthly properties and possessions that includes money, most wisely as his prudent steward. I too perceived because I handle a religious organization, I cannot consider my charitable system is no different from any other business in that it must make ends meet. Otherwise, my communitarian charity will cease to exist.

There arose a few occasions when my coworkers in my deeds of love for the poor tempted me to misappropriate funds raised to keep the programs running strong. For example, during one Christmas season, there was not enough cash in the general operating fund to buy all the food and dresses for our center's beneficiaries. Some trustees advised me to divert to the food fund some of the fund money raised for constructing or repairing facilities in our charity center. But because of my timidity and discipled conscientiousness, I didn't do as per their recommendation. When I consulted with my auditor on this issue, he made me understand that there are two types of funds.

There are restricted funds that are set aside for a particular purpose either temporarily or permanently. Using such restricted funds for impending needs of the day or season, though be it good, is morally bad. The unrestricted funds, which don't have strings attached, may be used by the nonprofit for whatever purpose it deems necessary. This money typically goes toward normal operating costs. Besides, my auditor also instructed me that there are some funds donated and solicited by people with some particular causes. When they are used for causes different from the benefactors' wish, it is illegal and morally bad. But any kind of fund with unsolicited designation can be used for the charitable deeds of the center, provided they come under the purview of the organization's by-laws. I was truly happy then to abide by the government's guidelines for being accountable and ethical in the matters of charity funds.

In my tenure of serving as executive director in one of Archdiocesan Arts and Communication Center, so many social workers (NGOs) came to me for learning "communication techniques in rural development." When discussing about management of their rural charitable ministries, I never failed to offer clear thoughts about how the discipled leaders should handle the charitable funds. One of the main points I thrusted into their hearts and minds is "Make sure at least 80 percent of the raised fund must go straight to the service deeds and only 20 percent to managing your center or organization."

In our ministries of share and care toward the poor, as our Master demands, all discipled leaders should be poor in spirit and accomplish all our charities according to Jesus's way, truth, and life. Some may be satisfied with personal spirit and transactions with the poor and the needy. I say that is not enough. In an organizational world and holding a leadership role in a community, we should also testify Jesus's values of justice, truth, honesty, and purity in our organizational deeds. We need to make the best of our discipled ability in keeping our organizations responsible ones.

This means first, we are to be true to our organizations' missions. We are sad to see missions of church, nonprofits, engaged in commercial activities, for avoiding the hectic burden of fund-raising and of maintaining its accounts, paying attention to more for-profit goals than nonprofit. Second, we must act as if outcomes matter. As one preacher wrote, "Doing good deed requires doing the right thing, not just the easy thing." For instance, if we plan to feed the hungry, we should make sure, instead of dumping them with surplus foodstuffs of any kind, our beneficiaries are provided with a "balanced diet." Third, our organizations should be candid. Soul-searching must be conducted on daily basis whether our financial deeds are sincere and transparent, whether our services are unbiased, and whether our objective actions are faithfully adhering and heading to the realization of our stipulated goals.

WORTHY PRAYER FOR THE POOR

Our God is the source of all good; he lacks nothing. He is also a wise proprietor in managing all the good in his universe; with his immense compassion and justice, he is ready to provide all the necessities, basic, as well as paramount, of his human children. Simultaneously, he has a custom of providing to our needs with cautious wisdom and with his standardized justice in his time, in his way, and surely according to his will. One more very important thing in this God's provident deeds, especially toward the poor and the needy: he has deliberated again and again in his Scriptures and through his church teachers that while he performs his sharing actions sometimes directly as his special miracles, most of the time, he does them through his disciples and his children of goodwill.

In keeping with all the above-said facts as the background, we should turn to the Lord and present to him our petitions with full confidence, hope, and perseverance. We can beg him to make miracles of his providence for our needy people; with strong hope, we too can request him do the same miracles so that large businesses, the global corporates, will curb their profits so that there are fewer poor or at least that someone of them might directly help the poor.

Our second prayerful petition to our God must be that he would give strength to the needy to endure their misery. This doesn't mean the poor should be silenced in their outcry against injustice or in their shouting loudly to the Creator and to his messengers and discipled leaders. Rather, we pray that God may grant the downtrodden sufficient inner stamina to overcome their critical situation even by going against the current if need be.

Obviously, the last but not the least, we need to entreat God to grant ourselves the virtues and rich heart and wise mind to see his Son in the needy and to enable us to act as his Son Jesus to perform our share and care ministries during our leadership life.

Such ceaseless prayer for the poor and the needy will be the source of including us with the needy in solidarity of love and justice. As Pope Francis stated, "If the prayer we make for the poor does not move us to work creatively for them, we are doing something wrong."

Let me end this chapter with the amazing words of St. Francis of Assisi from a letter he wrote to all the faithful: "Let us love our neighbors as ourselves. Let us have charity and humility. Let us give alms because these cleanse our souls from the stains of sin. Men lose all the material things they leave behind them in this world, but they carry with them the reward of their charity and the alms they give. For these they will receive from the Lord the reward and recompense they deserve."

CHAPTER 26: CELEBRATE LIFE OF LEADERSHIP WITH JOY

WE ARE THE LEADERS OF THE JOYFUL MASTER

Jesus, though not portrayed or spoken in the Scriptures as a "smiling" Person, always kept his inner spirit rejoicing as his Mother Mary, who sang, "My spirit rejoices in God my savior" (Luke 1:47). This fact has been once documented by Luke in his Gospel: "At that very moment Jesus rejoiced in the Holy Spirit and said, 'I give you praise, Father, Lord of heaven and earth, for although you have hidden these things from the wise and the learned you have revealed them to the childlike. Yes, Father, such has been your gracious will'" (Luke 10:21).

Besides, Jesus prayed and wished for such heavenly gift of genuine and complete joy being bestowed to his disciples. We hear this from him at during his Last Supper: "I have told you this so that my joy may be in you and your joy may be complete" (John 15:11). He told his Father the reason why he was sharing so many mysterious things with the disciples: "Father, now I am coming to you. I speak this in the world so that they may share my joy completely" (John 17:13).

He too encouraged them offering two promises: One, if they pray for joy it will be granted: "Until now you have not asked anything in my name; ask and you will receive, so that your joy may be complete" (John 16:24). The second promise was twofold: That the result of all their sufferings will be, as the Psalmist discovered (Ps. 126:6), only the true joy: "Amen, amen, I say to you, you will weep and mourn, while the world rejoices; you will grieve, but your grief will become joy" (John 16:20), and that the inner joy they experience will not be destroyed by any earthly creatures or events: "I will see you again, and your hearts will rejoice, and no one will take your joy away from you" (John 16:22).

Prophet Zephaniah, through his prophetic words (Zeph. 3:14–18) about the remnant of Israel, portrays not only the joy and gladness filling those who are sincerely committed to God: "Shout for joy, daughter Zion! Sing joyfully, Israel! Be glad and exult with all your heart, daughter Jerusalem!" but also he underlines how the Creator God would be overwhelmed with joy by observing his chosen remnants' fidelity and happiness: "The Lord, your God, is in your midst, a mighty savior, who will rejoice over you with gladness, and renew you in his love, who will sing joyfully because of you."

WE ARE ANOINTED BY THE OIL OF GLADNESS

Given this awesome backdrop of our discipleship with the Master, every discipled leader survives by nothing but the inner joy coming down from the joyful heart of the Master. In baptism, we are initiated in this joy-filled life by Chrism, the "oil of gladness." The second time, again in the sacrament of confirmation, we are confirmed in our joyous leadership by the Holy Spirit. As a unique anointing, the third time, some of us as priests are anointed by the same "oil of gladness," not only to be filled with the true joy in their ordained life as the ministers of sacraments but also to become more resourceful channels through which others encounter the same joy. Describing about the joy of the priest as a discipled leader, Pope Francis said in one of homilies at a Holy Thursday's Chrism Mass, "Priestly joy is a priceless treasure, not only for the priest himself but for the entire faithful people of God: that faithful people from which he is called to be anointed and which he, in turn, is sent to anoint. Anointed with the oil of gladness so as to anoint others with the oil of gladness."

As Paul exhorts Timothy (2 Tim. 1:6), all discipled leaders are expected to possess such amazing joy in every moment of our ministry. It is a unique missionary joy deeply bound up with God's people. We, as a proxies of Jesus, share the heavenly gift of joy when we accomplish our services according to the roles bestowed upon by God's Spirit: in baptizing, confirming, teaching, preaching, distributing the Eucharist, healing, sanctifying, blessing, comforting, and certainly evangelizing the people whomever we meet. From the beginning, the apostolic leadership, ministries, in the Kingdom of Jesus was focused on and motivated by making the leaders' life filled with more joy. John, in his letters, underlines this truth: "We are writing this so that our joy may be complete" (1 John 1:4). "Although I have much to write to you, I do not intend to use paper and ink. Instead, I hope to visit you and to speak face to face so that our joy may be complete" (2 John 1:12).

REJOICING ESPECIALLY DURING HARDSHIPS OF LEADERSHIP

Many a time, we are tempted to ask ourselves why I should be rejoicing while I am in exile, in desert, in hell of life overwhelmed with pains and sufferings, rejections, jealousy, and discrimination. This sort of question was in the minds of those Israelites as they were sitting and weeping by the streams of Babylon: "How could we sing a song of the Lord in a foreign land?" (Ps. 137:4) At the same time, God's Spirit moves the human heart of the Psalmist to respond to the question with the admirable answer he extracted from earlier history of the Israelites, who said to themselves, "If I forget you, Jerusalem, may my right hand forget. May my tongue stick to my palate if I do not remember you!" And they go on listing out the marvelous deeds of the same God they experienced while they were saved and protected from their enemies while they were in Jerusalem.

That is how our Master wants us to cope with all the hardships we undergo in our ministries for his Kingdom. Every day, especially during those dark days, we are asked by him to remember all the merciful God has done for us through his beloved Son: "God so loved the world that he gave his only Son, so that everyone who believes in him might not perish but might have eternal life" (John 3:16). Besides, the same Son, having been massacred and buried, God brought him back to life and arranged that his Son's Spirit stay permanently among us and took away from us all the curses of sin; plus, surprisingly, he seated us with him in the heavens in Christ Jesus and transformed us to the dignity of sharing his Son's life-giving good works as his leaders in our short tenure of earthly life. Are there not enough reasons why we should rejoice?

Unfortunately, though there are too many reasons to rejoice, many of us do not want to rejoice as sadists and prefer to live and move cranky and crabby. Why? Jesus offers a valid reason for it. He says it as a verdict: "That the light came into the world, but people preferred darkness to light, because their works were evil" (John 3:19). Consequently, there are some even among Jesus's followers and leaders as well who prefer the darkness to light. They can justify their act of refusal. But according to Jesus, it is sheer human fear to be exposed to their own silliness, their guilt and sins, their disorderliness.

Once I asked one of the discipled leaders working with me to join in a charismatic group to pray intensively and to be led by the Spirit, to be on fire. But he rejected it, saying, "I am afraid I may lose some of my comfort and conveniences. The Spirit will demand from me too much for which I am not ready yet." He might have been justified as he thought. But according to our Master, my friend rather condemned himself. In other words, he has made his own hell for life. Instead of being lifted, he has made low of himself. He is going to be like a tree from which the world is going to reap only evil fruits. That means his every movement of speech and action, whether they originate out of natural love or natural talents and skills, is going to spoil himself and the entire generation.

To be lifted in a secular and earthly way and to live more conveniently and comfortably, many leaders in our midst reject the light, the God himself, from our lives. We think of the past, we perform in the present, and we plan for the future without God. We judge everything, everybody, and every event in life without God. This is how so many of us religious leaders not only lose the promised joy of the Master but also continue to maintain the evil institution of human sufferings, pains, and sorrows. They completely close their hearts to believe the perennial truth that the absence of God is surely the presence of evil and its effects.

Once we recognize our failure, like the prodigal son, we should get up from our darkened life situation and return to our Master for purification. This happens only for those uphold firmly that we are endowed with our natural worth of sinfulness and human dignity in the likeness of God and that the Christian life is after all, worth living come from the Cross of Christ, which is nothing but the symbol of our merciful God's eternal love for us and we have got ever-shining glory from Jesus crucified. Let us spare quality time in the chores of our leadership ministry to redo our inner facelift. Once we get that inner lift, then to whatever situation our leadership ministry takes us, we will keep peace and joy unfading.

THE UNFADING INNER JOY OF DISCIPLED LEADERS

The life on earth may lift us on the cross like Jesus, on the cross of terminal and chronic illnesses, on the cross of misunderstanding and rejection, on the cross of failures in planning of life, and on the cross of war and terrorism. The inner sparkling transformation will never let us down with discouragement and low spirit because we know well and it is the fact of God that only by the cross on which Jesus was lifted and on which you and me are lifted the plan of God for the entire world is being accomplished. This may sound ridiculous and weird to many in the world market. But to us who have already started to redo our inner facelift, it is the truth, nothing but the truth from God in Jesus.

Besides rewarding every discipled leader an abode of eternal joy at the end of their earthly leadership, saying, "Well done, my good and faithful servant. Since you were faithful in small matters, I will give you great responsibilities. Come, share your master's joy" (Matt. 25:21), God never denies a part of that joy to be encountered in our day today life. "When a man devotes all his thoughts to the praise and service of the Lord, he proclaims God's greatness; his observance of God's commands, moreover, shows that he has God's power and greatness always at heart; and his spirit rejoices in God his savior and delights in the mere recollection of his creator who gives him hope for eternal salvation"—these are the words of St. Bede the Venerable, which are very applicable to the daily life of every discipled leader.

Paul, the great discipled leader in God's Kingdom, has been always in joyful spirit even in the midst of his tormenting perils like imprisonment. As he advised his converted Christians to be ceaselessly praying, he ordered them to be rejoicing uninterruptedly: "Rejoice in the Lord always. I shall say it again: rejoice!" (Phil. 4:4) Plus, he added how discipled leaders should testify their inner joy outwardly in our relationship with others: "Bless those who persecute you, bless and do not curse them. Rejoice with those who rejoice, weep with those who weep. Have the same regard for one another; do not be haughty but associate with the lowly; do not be wise in your own estimation" (Rom. 12:9–16).

The discipled leaders are blessed like Mary, not only being filled with spiritual joy but also becoming the sources of true joy for whomever they serve (Ref. Luke 1:39–56). Carrying Jesus in her womb, and being filled with the genuine joy, Mary exclaimed, "My soul proclaims the greatness of the Lord; my spirit rejoices in God my Savior, for he has looked with favor on his lowly servant." And when she was prompted by the Spirit to hasten to serve another elderly woman in her pregnancy, her presence and greetings brought joy both to Elizabeth and her baby in the womb: "When Elizabeth heard Mary's greeting, the infant leaped in her womb, and Elizabeth, filled with the Holy Spirit, cried out in a loud voice and said: For at the moment the sound of your greeting reached my ears, the infant in my womb leaped for joy."

MARVELOUS RESULTS OF CHRISTIAN JOY

When we were called by Jesus to be his leaders in this world, he guaranteed that his joy would be ours and our joy would not be as the world offers; rather, our joy would be genuine and complete. Joy is the outcome of the presence of the Holy Spirit in our inner sanctuary; consequently, it is the result of our faith in our Master's words, our hope in God's promises, and our devotional love for Christ as our dearmost friend. Such joy cannot be extinguished by the circumstances of life. It is a God-given joy greater and stronger than any trouble that comes into our life. The Chilean saint Alberto Hurtado, who spent his entire life in working with the poor amidst so many trials and difficulties, including persecution, is said to have regularly uttering in his prayer to the Lord: "I'm happy, Lord, I'm happy." Yes, the joy Jesus's Spirit has generated in us cannot be extinguished by the circumstances of life. In that plenitude of Christian joy, it's hard indeed for Satan to tempt us with the empty pleasures of this world.

One online preacher is right in his statement: "Joyless Christianity is dangerous." Pope Francis, in one of his homilies on the Gospel event of rich man visiting with Jesus, recalled how the face of the rich man, not capable of receiving and welcoming Jesus's demand of selling and giving all his properties to the needy, fell, and he became very sad. He too exhorted us that "With each contribution show a cheerful countenance, and pay your tithes in a spirit of joy." He emphasized the eternal fact that "A cheerful face and eyes full of joy are the signs that we're following this path of all and nothing, of fullness emptied out." In other words, true Christians have cheerful faces and joy in their eyes.

Hopeless people psychologically cannot rise and walk in the midst of drudgeries of life; they always blame some others or some other things for their lethargy, depression, and despair. But discipled leaders have so many positive resources to be freed of their mental and even physical ailments that enslave them.

Our Christian joy testifies that we have been forgiven and liberated from sinful holding and darkness by our merciful God. The Psalmist splendidly proclaims this truth: "Happy the man whose offense is forgiven, whose sin is remitted. O happy the man to whom the Lord imputes no guilt, in whose spirit is no guile . . . Rejoice, rejoice in the Lord, exult, you just! O come, ring out your joy, all you upright of heart" (Ps. 32).

One more of the sources of our true joy is the conviction that we are assured of our life's ultimate goal of salvation. Jesus verified the importance of this resourceful gift of joy: "Blessed are you when they insult you and persecute you and utter every kind of evil against you [falsely] because of me. Rejoice and be glad, for your reward will be great in heaven. Thus they persecuted the prophets who were before you" (Matt. 5:11–12). Peter reiterated it, writing, "In this you rejoice . . . Although you have not seen him you love him;

even though you do not see him now yet believe in him, you rejoice with an indescribable and glorious joy, as you attain the goal of your faith, the salvation of your souls" (1 Pet. 1:6–9).

Remembering gratefully the amazing love deeds of God in our life through his Son, through his Spirit, and through all his angelic messengers who lived and still residing around us, such grateful thoughts surely uplift us from the dungeon and slavery of downheartedness. Especially when we hear and meditate often our Master's demands enlisted throughout this book, plus when we see we are unable to fulfill them, we are inclined to sliding downhill of discouragement and despair. If we keenly read Luke's Gospel, which is labeled as the Gospel of discipleship, after expounding Jesus's many demands to his discipled leaders, he narrates a miraculous event where the Master cures ten lepers (Luke 17:11–19). As a climax of all the discipleship requirements, Luke brings home to us the basic and intrinsic dimension of "'discipleship" through that event.

Jesus liked the ten lepers for their audacious and impudent prayerful gestures of crying loud: "Jesus, Son of David, have pity on us." However, he did not heal them immediately. As God's usual deed, he put their faith in test. He commanded them to go and show themselves to their priests. He wanted them to continue their rituals and other religious and social practices even they noticed their prayer has not been answered yet. And when the lepers hurried to fulfill the command of Jesus, on their way, they were healed. Surely they were overwhelmed with wonder, surprise, and joy. They surely headed along to the temple to show themselves to the priests. Among them, one breached out of their company and started running back to Jesus. The other nine were attentive, maybe to socialize themselves and enter into the main stream of the society, and therefore, they decided to fulfill the social and religious ritual and not to please Jesus, their healer. They would have surely forgotten the real source of their healing.

But one out of ten healed persons came back to Jesus their healer and thanked him. He was inquiring about the others who didn't return to thank him: "Where are the other nine?" In other words, Jesus exposes to us his desire and personal demand from every one of his discipled leaders who are called and healed by him to be intimately connected to him. There is no doubt he endorses all our external practices and rituals to show and increase our faith in God. It is true it is enough for appropriating salvation from God. But it is not at all sufficient to be a disciple of Jesus, much more to be chosen as his leaders.

When someone plans to become Jesus's discipled leader, he/she must go some more miles, namely, he/she must fully relate themselves to Jesus as his intimate friend and lover and connect themselves to him as branches to a vine. This personal love approach to the Master will push forward to keep Jesus as our first priority of life. This will make us to start everything, proceed in everything, and end everything in him, through him, and with him. Such intimacy with Christ should be the base and core for all that a disciple does in the name of religious and social rituals and practices. As the Samaritan leper did, before, during, and after all that we perform as rituals and other religious practices, we should express our sentiments of love and gratitude to our Master, Guru. We should first express our deep love to Christ and then perform other things our life and religion demand from us.

The disciples of Jesus must possess a grateful and mellow heart as the Samaritan leper. Let everything flow out of that heart, everything they perform and accomplish both in social and religious life, whether they are targeted to families, communities, and the entire world. For example, all that we do to our parishes—offerings, tithes, voluntary services, sexual love sharing, dreams and ambitions and plans to realize them, business, and job duties—everything must flow from the consecrated and circumcised heart that is always mellow and grateful like that of Jesus. There, surely then and there, the genuine joy takes its abode in our inner spirit, and we walk around with a smile as "sunshine" to our fellow travelers in our Christian journey.

Let us live through hectic discipled leadership life, reciting daily the hymn of Isaiah: "God indeed is my salvation; I am confident and unafraid. For the Lord is my strength and my might, and he has been my salvation. With joy you will draw water from the fountains of salvation . . . Sing praise to the Lord for he has done glorious things; let this be known throughout all the earth. Shout with exultation, City of Zion, for great in your midst is the Holy One of Israel!" (Isa. 12:2–6)

FINAL WORD

"The amazing results"

When I began writing this book and browsing the Scriptures and traditions of the church and histories and stories about saints, I was bewildered with tension and trembling as I came across the cruel final chapters of discipled leaders' lives. I even tempted to stop writing on this title. However, the good Lord showed to me in many ways and means the unthinkable results of being a discipled leader in his Kingdom.

Indeed, I have discussed about many of them in the third section of this work. Let me here reiterate and consolidate the amazing gains every discipled leader would claim to be rewarded with.

First of all, there are many references in the Bible about the future blessings we would be coveting:

Negatively speaking, we will be escaping from the eternal punishment of God: "We shall be saved from the wrath of God which is yet to come upon the world for its sins" (Rom. 5:9).

Positively, we would be granted a life unending and totally freed of trials and tribulations: "He will wipe every tear from their eyes, and there shall be no more death or mourning, wailing or pain, for the old order has passed away" (Rev. 21:1–8). I remember every day the verses the church reads in one of her Morning Prayers: "Those who are learned will be as radiant as the sky in all its beauty; those who instruct the people in goodness will shine like the stars for all eternity."

Besides the future rewards, God has promised and has been true to his oath that all discipled leader would be blessed with many unimaginable rewards even while they are in this world:

The gift of true peace: "Peace I leave with you; my peace I give to you. Not as the world gives do I give it to you" (John 14:27).

The gift of his own joy: "I have told you this so that my joy may be in you and your joy may be complete" (John 15:11).

The gift of countless possessions: As the Lord ordered us in his Sermon on the Mount (Matt. 6:31) "to seek first the kingdom of God and his righteousness" and promised "all these things will be given you besides," he offered later a detailed description of "those things": "Amen, I say to you, there is no one who has given up house or wife or brothers or parents or children for the sake of the kingdom of God who will not receive back an overabundant return in this present age" (Luke 18:28–30).

The gift of sharing of Jesus's mastership: He did say "a disciple cannot be superior to the Teacher," but he too added that when fully trained, groomed, and discipled, we will be like our teacher (Ref. Luke 6:39–40). When I think of how I would be like him as he promised, I remember the lives of many of discipled leaders whom I contacted in my short tenure of ministry. I observed in their day-to-day life the exact move in life as the Master did: Their suffering has been conquered by joy, their darkness has been conquered by light, their trials and sorrows were conquered by certain resurrected spirit and, certainly, their small daily deaths (denials of self) as well as the final death they had demonstrated inconceivable resilience and silence.

BREATHTAKING ANTINOMY OF THE END OF DISCIPLED LEADERS

In connection with sharing of Jesus's leadership, we have mentioned earlier we partake in the rare blend of his life's finale, namely, the end of our earthly life would seem a blend of both glory and disgrace, success and failure, reward and rejection. This is the fate of almost all discipled leaders starting from Moses through David to Jesus and to discipled leaders of today. We read in the Book of Deuteronomy about Moses's final days. Accepting obediently God's call to be his leader for his people, he was a very faithful messenger of God throughout his life. The Bible also ranked him as the best leader in God's Kingdom, saying about him, "No prophet has arisen in Israel like Moses, whom the Lord *knew face to face*." God also spelled out, "Throughout my house Moses is worthy of trust." Yet the same Moses who led Israel safely and securely from Egypt to Palestine as the Lord intended was denied by the Lord to enter into the Promised Land with his people, but God destined him to die over a mountain, just seeing the famous land from a distance (Ref. Deut. 32:48–52).

This may seem a repugnant end of Moses. But in the light of Christ, we find it is the rare-blend end of every God's messengers, including Jesus, whose descending into hell of sufferings and total annihilation and rejection and failure was nothing but his ascending into glory and honor. This is how every leader committed to Jesus experienced their horrible deaths, persecutions, and incredible ailments twisted them, led them to a breaking point where they began singing alleluia and praise the Lord.

CELEBRATE LEADERSHIP LIFE AS MOTHER MARY ADVISES US

God's whole life is simply a celebration. God's marvelous deeds, creative, redemptive, and providential achievements can be summed up in one phrase: "Celebration of life." He created humans breathing his very life into them so that in his place and together with him, celebration of life can be continued uninterruptedly.

In the Gospels, we read similar events happening in the disciples' life. One of the celebrating incidents was the wedding at Cana (John 2:7–10), in which three sudden twists happened: First, it was found out that there was no wine to serve the guests. The second turning point was when Mary requested Jesus her Son to do something about this unwanted happening, and everybody in that situation found out that he turned down her request. The third twist was water being changed into wine and even with better quality. We can imagine how all the characters who participate in that moment of celebration would have felt and experienced different feelings such as sad, shock, pity, murmur, and so on. Yet a few among them were there who, like Mary the Mother of Jesus, followed God's tips to maintain the balanced spirit. Thanks to them, that event again turns out to be a mega celebration.

This is what every one of discipled leaders encounter in our homes, workplaces like parishes, communities, nations, and the world. During those disparaging moments, we have to behave exactly as our Mother Mary advises: "Do whatever my Son Jesus tells you."

Wherever and whenever some horrible natural disasters occur, devastating the lives of millions, the discipled leaders of Jesus around the world pour out their love and compassion and hold on to God's greatness and goodness and bring back the celebration spirit once again in that deplorable environment. God wants us to uphold our hope, trust, and joy in the sovereignty and parental love, even in the midst of mishaps that can spoil our life's celebration. Our celebration of life then will surely take a different but very surprising turn.

A PERSONAL TESTIMONY

God's call to be a leader on his behalf and under the shadow of Christ's discipleship is not that easy. I personally know how hard it is for me to fulfill our Master's demands. My daily morning prayer time begins only in front of my restroom mirror as I stand before it to do my ablutions. Many times, I start my prayer with a big laughter telling to myself, what a funny and freaky person I am. Once at that moment, my mind induced me to laugh at God. With full-throat laughing, I told the Lord, "Lord! I wonder at you and pity you. You see, I personally find it hard to put up with the dark and weak side of mine along with a few lucid intervals at times. Besides, I find it hell to deal with the dark and weak side of people around me. If counted, they are totally up to this day a few thousands I have been dealing with. But you, Lord, have been putting up with the dark and weak side of billions and trillions of humans around the globe over the centuries. How do you manage such humongous burden eternally and intensively?"

After all my mirror-before prayer of laughter was over, I went back to my desk. As my usual custom, I took a spiritual book for reading. Interestingly, I came to a page where I found the right answer to my question to the Lord. I sincerely considered it as God was answering my laughing prayer. The author of the book writes, "God, our Creator, is not simply the Light. He possesses both light and darkness. We are aware of the fact at our every step of walking in light we find a shadow accompanying with us. The same way God's incredible light is accompanied by His own shadow. Shadow usually is the absence of light. Therefore those of us who are made in His image and likeness are filled with both light and darkness." Immediately, it struck my mind. This is why God can very easily put up with our human duality blended with both strength and weakness, light and darkness for eternity. (Though such view of God may sound far-fetched and heretical, there is some truth in it. Plus, this view strengthens us a little bit to put up with the problem of duality.)

Being a traditional cradle Catholic, I also added to the strange view of the author about God: "Our God who is holy, holy, holy, does not allow the shadow within Him to maroon and cast aside his eternal Light of holiness. This is why we read in the Bible when God found out that one of His archangels misused the shadow existed in him threw him out of heaven into hell. That archangel's name is 'Lucifer', meaning 'the bearer of light.' God deals with us the same way. He would go all the way possible to help us in our conducting life that is made of both light and darkness and that is the reason He sent His beloved Son to us to redeem us and save us from the power of darkness."

Finally, this is what I want to say to all my friends serving as discipled leaders: Yes, we are made of both light and darkness; however, we can enlarge our lucid intervals (luminous) more and more by our religious and spiritual endeavors, trying our best not to salute all the enticement of our own darkness. We may fail in conducting our lives and performing our leadership duties in a "disciple" way, but when we fail, let us believe and hope our Master is there always to empower us with his forgiveness, love, and admonition and lead us to heaven. Once we are with God, we will finally live only a total life of light. Because Lucifer has no hold in heaven; he is in hell and surely in the universe. Come, let us walk with Christ ceaselessly and trying our best to live a discipled life and to lead others into it. Let us be blessed by the Lord all the days of our lives.

Other Books of the Author

- SONDAY SONRISE: Sunday Homilies for Liturgical Years ABC.

- DAILY DOSE for Christian Survival: Daily Scriptural Meditations and Spiritual Medication.

- PRAYERFULLY YOURS: Qualityprayer for Qualitylife.

- CATHOLIC CHRISTIAN SPIRITUALITY for New Age Dummies.

- MY RELIGION: REEL OR REAL? A Postmodern Catholic's Assessment of his religion.

- MINISTRY IN TEARS: International Priests' missionary Life & Ministry (Co-authored by his brother Rev. Dasan Vima SJ).

- HILLTOP MEDITATIONS: Reflections on Scriptural readings of Sundays and Festivals-Years A & B.

- HILLTOP MEDITATIONS: Reflections on Scriptural readings of Sundays and Festivals-Years C.

- BLESSED THE MERCIFUL: Description of The CHESED-Oriented Christian Life.

- LIVING FAITH DAILY in Spirit and in Truth.

Printed in the United States
By Bookmasters